RETHINKING
MANAGEMENT EDUCATION

RETHINKING MANAGEMENT EDUCATION

Edited by

Robert French and Christopher Grey

SAGE Publications
London • Thousand Oaks • New Delhi

First published 1996

SAGE Publications Ltd
6 Bonhill Street
London EC2A 4PU

SAGE Publications Inc
2455 Teller Road
Thousand Oaks, California 91320

SAGE Publications India Pvt Ltd
32 M-Block Market
Greater Kailash – I
New Delhi 110 048

British Library Cataloguing in Publication data

A catalogue record for this book is
available from the British Library

ISBN 0 8039 7782 4
ISBN 0 8039 7783 2 (pbk)

Library of Congress catalog record available

Typeset by Mayhew Typesetting, Rhayader, Powys
Printed in Great Britain by Redwood Books, Trowbridge, Wiltshire

Contents

Preface

This book has its origins in a series of discussions between us dating back to January 1991. At that time we were both employed on the ESRC's Management Teaching Fellowship scheme and, as part of that scheme, attended a number of workshops on Management Education run by the Management Training and Development Centre at the Management School, Lancaster University. Out of the ensuing discussions a number of interesting and challenging differences between us emerged: we had different experiences of education in general and management education in particular; we worked in different types of institution; we had different intellectual and disciplinary backgrounds. And yet, despite these differences, many of our views about management education were remarkably similar. This book, then, is the outcome of what we hope is a creative tension. It is also the medium and outcome of friendship between us and, to varying degrees, with the contributors to the book.

The contributions to this volume were solicited by us and have not been published elsewhere. A number of them were subsequently presented at the *New Perspectives on Management Education* Conference in Leeds in January 1995. Taken together they provide a unique collection of scholarly and original writings on management education, and open up a series of lines of analysis which, we hope, will contribute to an on-going process of critique and renewal in the field.

In the course of preparing this volume we have accumulated a number of personal debts to individuals whose assistance and support we gratefully acknowledge. In particular we thank Nathalie Mitev, Wendy French, David French and Simon French for their patience and their message-taking. Finally, we are grateful to Sue Jones formerly of Sage for commissioning and supporting this work.

Robert French
Christopher Grey

Contributors

Peter D. Anthony BA, MSc (Wales) is Visiting Reader at Lancaster University and a contributor to the MBA course at the University of Bath. His most recent book, *Managing Culture*, was published by the Open University Press in 1994.

David M. Boje BA (Rider University, New Jersey), PhD (University of Illinois-Urbana) is Professor of Management at the College of Business Administration, Loyola Marymount University, Los Angeles. He was previously at the Graduate School of Management, UCLA. He is currently editor of the *Journal of Change Management*. His main research interests are in deconstructing organizational stories and modernist organization texts. He has published widely in academic journals and has co-edited several books, including *Managing in the Postmodern World* (with Robert Dennehy), published by Kendall-Hunt, second edition, 1994; and *Postmodern Management and Organization Theory* (with Robert Gephart and Tojo Thachankary), Sage, forthcoming.

J. Michael Cavanaugh MS (Georgetown), MBA (Rensselaer Polytechnic Institute), PhD (Massachusetts, Amherst) is Associate Professor of Management at the School of Business, Fairfield University, Connecticut. He has held numerous industrial and government posts. Currently his main interest is in developing a pedagogic agenda for critical theorizing, and he has published work on this and other subjects in a variety of academic journals.

Audrey Collin BA (London), PhD (Loughborough), Dip. An. (Oxon), MIPD is Reader in Human Resource Management at Leicester Business School, De Montfort University. She has worked in the past as a personnel manager and at Loughborough University. Her main research interest is the study of careers, and she has published widely in this area, including the edited book *Interpreting Career: Hermeneutical Studies of Lives in Context* (with R.A. Young) published by Praeger in 1992.

Robert French BA (Cambridge), PGCE (Manchester), MEd (Bristol) is Lecturer in Organizational Behaviour at Bristol Business School, the University of the West of England. Having taught for some 20 years in secondary schools, he came to work in higher education via an ESRC Management Teaching Fellowship. He also works as an independent consultant to organizations and is a Professional Associate of the Grubb

Institute, London. His main areas of interest are in individual, group and organizational learning and dynamics.

Jonathan Gosling BA (East Anglia), MBA (City) is Senior Fellow at The Management School, Lancaster University where he is jointly responsible for the MPhil course in Critical Management Studies. For several years he was the Director of the UK's first community-based conflict resolution and mediation organization. His current research is on Platonic thought in contemporary management theory and on processes of organization and community. He has published work on conflict resolution and on management education.

Christopher Grey BA (Econ) (Manchester), PhD (Manchester) is Lecturer in Organizational Behaviour at the School of Business and Economic Studies, University of Leeds. He previously worked at the School of Management, UMIST. His main research interests are in the sociology of organizations and critical studies of accounting, management and management education. He has published work in all of these areas and organized the *New Perspectives on Management Education* conference in 1995. He is Reviews Editor of Management Learning and Coordinator of the ESRC seminar programme, *Critique and Renewal in Management Education*.

Jannis Kallinikos BA (Athens), PhD (Uppsala) is Associate Professor at Stockholm University Business School. He has also worked at Uppsala University. His research draws on diverse disciplines to analyse formal organizations and he is especially interested in the decomposition and semiotic analysis of computer software. This work has given rise to several publications in academic journals.

David Knights BSc (Salford), MSc (Manchester), PhD (Manchester) is Professor of Organizational Analysis at the School of Management, UMIST. He is co-editor of the journal *Gender, Work and Organization*. Currently his main research interests are in financial services and in issues of gender and sexuality in organizations. He has published prolifically in these and many other areas of organizational analysis, and for many years has co-edited a series of books on labour process analysis. His latest book, *Managers Divided* (with Fergus Murray), was published by Wiley in 1994, and a co-edited book, *Resistance and Power in Organizations*, by Routledge in 1994.

Anshuman Prasad BA (Delhi), MBA (Xavier Institute, Jamshedur), PhD (Massachusetts, Amherst) is Visiting Professor at the Faculty of Management, University of Calgary. For several years he was an executive in the State Bank of India. Current research interests include strategic action in the global petroleum industry, epistemological issues in organizational research, organizational symbolism, and critical hermeneutics. He has published work in social science and management journals.

John Roberts BSc (Manchester) PhD (Manchester) is Lecturer in Management Studies at the Judge Institute, Cambridge University. He has previously worked at Manchester University, London Business School and St Catharine's College, Cambridge. Current research work focuses on the problems of growth in small high-technology firms, and on organizational accountability. Both areas of interest have given rise to several academic publications.

Alan B. Thomas BA (Liverpool), PhD (Open) is Lecturer in Sociology and Organizational Behaviour at Manchester Business School. He has previously held posts at Leeds University and the Open University. His main research interests are in the sociology of management education, and organizational leadership. He has published widely in academic journals and his most recent book, *Controversies in Management*, was published by Routledge in 1993.

Russ Vince BA (Sheffield), PhD (Bristol) is Principal Lecturer in Organizational Behaviour at Bristol Business School, the University of the West of England. He is also an Associate of the International Institute for Organisational Change (IOC-Ashridge) based in Geneva. He teaches about, consults to and undertakes research in organizations. He has previously worked as a community worker and as a lecturer at the School for Advanced Urban Studies, Bristol University. The focus of his research is in the fields of management learning and organizational change, and he has a particular interest in investigating both the psychology and the politics of engagement.

Hugh Willmott BSc (Manchester), PhD (Manchester) is Professor of Organizational Analysis at the School of Management, UMIST. He has previously held posts at Aston University and been Visiting Professor at Copenhagen Business School and Uppsala University. He is currently interested in a wide range of issues including the development of critical management studies, accounting regulation and new management theory. He has published extensively in management and social science journals and has written and co-edited numerous books, including *Critical Management Studies* (with Mats Alvesson) published by Sage in 1992, and *Making Quality Critical* (with Adrian Wilkinson) Routledge, 1994. His latest book, *Making Sense of Management* (with Mats Alvesson), will be published by Sage in 1996.

1

Rethinking Management Education: An Introduction

Christopher Grey and Robert French

Management education[1] is an activity of growing significance and influence, which has recently attracted extensive attention and criticism. In this volume, we present a range of different perspectives on management education and suggestions for change and renewal.

There is already a well-established debate about management education which has focused on the extent to which it contributes to the development of effective managers (Constable and McCormick, 1987; Handy, 1987; Institute of Management, 1994) or to the economic performance of particular countries (Locke, 1984, 1989). Equally, there is a burgeoning literature which aspires to provide management educators and others with techniques to improve the effectiveness of their teaching (see, for example, Gibbs, 1992; Gibbs and Jenkins, 1992). This volume is rather different in intent, since none of the authors begins with the assumption that management practice and management education are unproblematically linked and all believe that rethinking management education entails more than the elaboration of new pedagogic techniques. The contributions raise, in various ways, fundamental challenges to conventional understandings of management education: its relation to management research and knowledge more generally; its relation to management practice; its potential for critical and emancipatory thought; its connection with the lived experience of managers, academics and students.

It has become commonplace to conceive of 'management', specifically, as entering or having entered a new era, variously characterized as post-industrial, post-fordist or post-modern. This view can be found both among theorists (Clegg, 1990) and more practitioner-oriented writers (Handy, 1989, 1994; Peters, 1988, 1992). There are, however, at least two broad responses in terms of the meaning and implications of these new conditions for practising managers.

The first kind of response is to suggest that managers need new techniques and skills to deal with the problems that they face, both in their work as managers and in the management of their own careers. The most basic variety of this response has been present for several years and in a number of guises. These include ideas about creating more flexible firms through techniques such as total quality management (Crosby, 1979) and human resource management; replacing rule-bound bureaucratic structures with value-driven corporate cultures (Peters and Waterman, 1982) and, most recently, the use of information technology to implement radically re-engineered work processes (Hammer and Champy, 1993) and to create the 'virtual organization' (Scott Morton, 1991). An extension of this first response emphasizes the need not only to develop new management techniques but also to change the way in which managers think about managing. Thus, for example, Henry (1991) provides a variety of approaches to developing managerial creativity, while Peters (1988) offers us the hope of 'thriving on chaos'. What all these responses have in common is the view that, although managing may have become more difficult, it is nonetheless possible to find ways of managing. Ackoff (1981), for example, identifies the unprecedented changes in the business world, but only in order to show ways of 'creating the corporate future'.

The second kind of response is more diffuse. Its main characteristic is to argue that management is no longer a viable activity because we live in a time of irredeemable turbulence, irrationality and ambiguity. Indeed, on this view, the promises of management to be able to manage may *always* have been illusory, because of the inherently uncontrollable nature of social relations (MacIntyre, 1981). This second view is less common among practitioner-oriented management writers – unsurprisingly, since the message is hardly one of comfort to managers – and is associated with the various positions collectively identified as post-modernist (see, for example, Cooper and Burrell, 1988; Hassard 1993, 1994; Jeffcutt, 1994).

The view which underpins *this* volume is that management has become an activity of central importance in modern societies, and that the management academy has, for better or worse, a crucial role in producing and reproducing the practices of management (Huczynski, 1993). What goes on in business and management schools matters because of their enmeshment with the wider challenges and crises of the contemporary world. Thus, whether or not the pretensions of management to be able to manage the world are defensible, the consequences of the belief that they *are* remains as an irreducible social fact.[2] As Giddens (1994) argues, the current age is one of manufactured risk and uncertainty as a consequence of attempts to intervene in the social and natural worlds. In other words, the existence of a huge array of problems which need managing arises from previous attempts both to manage the world and to increase the sphere in which management is attempted.

The fact that management is socially important means that it is vital that it be exposed to critical interrogation. And since management education is such a significant arena for the reproduction of management, it follows that it is a primary site for such interrogation.

Implications for Management Education

What, then, are the implications of this for management education? If it is assumed that management education exists to provide managers with the knowledge and skills they need to operate effectively, then the first position outlined above clearly leads to the conclusion that managers need to be equipped with a very different type of education to the one traditionally offered (Raelin and Schermerhorn, 1994). Although there remains some place for learning the techniques of the 'new management', such as culture management, quality management or re-engineering methodologies, the emphasis on specific techniques must be reduced, since these become rapidly dated, whereas greater emphasis must be given to human and analytical skills, 'learning to learn' and flexibility – as in Stacey's (1993) 'extraordinary' management. The second, 'post-modern' response suggests, at the extreme, that there is little that management education can do to develop managers' abilities; although a less drastic version might suggest that managers need to be taught the limits of their influence through an appreciation of the limits of rationality (Nord and Jermier, 1992; Roberts, this volume). It should be said that this latter response is probably relatively rare and marginal within the curricula of most management education providers.

On the basis of what has been said so far, it is possible to identify two broad contemporary perspectives on management education. The first is that the content, and perhaps the methods, of management education need to be quite radically altered in order to equip managers with the ability to work effectively in a complex and rapidly changing world. The second is that management itself is an illusory activity and therefore management education must abandon its pretensions to be able to provide managers with management skills in any traditional sense. Both of these perspectives – the first now quite common, the second fairly rare – arise within the context of the assumption that management education stands in a more or less functional relationship to management practice. But this assumption can be, and has been, subjected to critical scrutiny (Willmott, 1994; Grey and Mitev, 1995a).

The idea of management education as functional to management is predicated on a model of professional training in which there exists a body of knowledge which is understood to be central to effective practice. This knowledge is produced, guarded and transmitted by, especially, universities. The archetype of this model might be that of medical training, where licence to practise is contingent on the acquisition of a defined set of knowledges and skills. For various reasons, however, management has never been strictly comparable to medicine. First, there is no occupational closure around practising as a manager: it is quite legal, and commonplace, to be a manager without receiving any training or accreditation. Nevertheless, it could be argued that increasingly management is becoming *de facto* if not *de jure* a professionalized activity, especially through such initiatives as the MBA qualification, the development of the British Academy of Management, the Management Charter Initiative in the UK, or the American Assembly of Collegiate Schools of Business in the United States (see Boje, this volume). Plainly, however, this process is not very far advanced, at least within the UK (Reed and Anthony, 1992). Second, it is by no means clear that a trained manager is more effective than an untrained one, whereas it is generally accepted that a trained doctor is more effective than an untrained one.

The second difference between management and medicine is that both the aims, and the methods of achieving those aims, are much less clear for the former than for the latter (see Burgoyne, 1995; Grey and Mitev, 1995b). Although in medicine there are certainly disputes about how the cure of illness and relief of suffering should be achieved, there is, in general, little doubt that these aims are legitimate and laudable. Moreover, there is a mass of basic, undisputed knowledge in medicine, such as anatomical structure, which is almost entirely absent in management (Whitley, 1984; Kallinikos, this volume). It is not the case in management studies that, for example, the aim of management practice is to make profits, since many organizations are not profit-making. It might be common ground to say that management is concerned with achieving organizational aims in the most efficient and effective manner. However, even this is disputed and, in any case, there is no consensus on what organizational aims are or should be, nor on what constitute effective and efficient means for their realization.

The debates in which, by implication, we are engaging at this point are extremely long-standing because they go to the heart of the meaning of education and its relation to a society. Perhaps the simplest polarity of the debate is between those (such as Cicero) who have seen knowledge as an end in itself and those (such as John Locke) who have wanted to judge knowledge in terms of utility, a means to some other end. This debate has been crucial in the development of the modern university. Cardinal Newman (1851/1960) set the tone for a conception of 'liberal education', decoupled from direct economic or professional utility, which has continued to influence educational thinking until well into the twentieth century, at least in the UK and the USA. Its influence can be plainly seen in the Robbins' expansion of British universities in the 1960s (Daiches, 1964). Management education has always been particularly, and brutally, torn between liberal and utilitarian conceptions of education (Engwall, 1992), not least because of its fragmented knowledge base and reputational structures (Whitley, 1984). In this volume, Thomas and Anthony take up many of the issues raised here in their assessment of the educational value of management education.

At present, the position of management education in relation to education more generally is complex. The political context (in the UK, the USA and elsewhere) of New Right politics has had the effect of increasingly validating a utilitarian conception of education. On the one hand, education is seen to be socially valuable to the extent to which it contributes to economic prosperity and international competitiveness. On the other, education in an individualistic, consumerist culture is seen to be personally valuable to the extent to which it enhances the economic and career positions of individuals. This ideological terrain, combined with specific institutional and financial arrangements in universities, has tended to benefit management education, which can lay claim to validity on both of these criteria. However, this claim is again contingent on the continuation of theoretically justified and empirically supported functional links between management education, the effectiveness of management practice and the performance of individual managers.

If these political developments have tended to favour utilitarianism in education in general and management education in particular, other, perhaps related, intellectual developments have made the notion of liberal education much harder to defend. Here there are several interesting and complex issues. The first relates to the way in which traditional conceptions of liberal education have become enmeshed with the controversy over political correctness (Dunant, 1994). In particular, the association of liberal education with a curriculum, especially in the humanities, devoted to the study of the 'canon' of 'dead white male' authors is one which has posed real dilemmas for those who are nevertheless opposed to the 'utilitarian' conception of education. For whatever the merits of the case, the dispute within the educational establishment on this issue has been disabling in terms of presenting a unified, undistracted and unambiguous critique of the political trend towards 'utilitarianism' in education. A related issue has been the problem of how liberal education can sustain its position in the face of questioning of the very notion of the autonomous subject, which is a key part of the post-modern intellectual terrain. Liberal education typically has recourse to concepts of humanity, which provide its ethical grounding (Hunter, 1993); yet post-modernism and allied developments render this concept increasingly problematic.

Although these concerns are genuine, it would be a mistake to allow them to prevent the attempt to articulate alternative models of management education (or education more generally). Not to proceed in the face of such difficulties would be, by default, to leave the 'utilitarians' in command of the field, riding on the political wave to which we have alluded and unhindered by an informed critique or the challenge of viable alternatives. It is possible to develop new perspectives, even if this entails a recognition of the provisionality and ambiguity of these views. Thus, in rethinking management education, a process is implied rather than a model to which we should work, an issue brought out clearly in the contribution to this volume by Grey et al. in their discussion of the nature and limits of a critical pedagogy of management, and by Cavanaugh and Prasad, also in this volume, in their analysis of the 'critical classroom'. But the development of alternative views must also be attentive to the genuine institutional constraints on oppositional thought in management education, and especially those disciplinary mechanisms outlined by Boje in this volume.

Alternative views of management education would begin from the desire to stress its 'educative' rather than its managerial aspects. Thus it becomes important to teach students how to understand management as an activity. This involves an appreciation of management as a social, political and moral practice, rather than as a set of techniques and skills to be learned and subsequently applied (Grey and Mitev, 1995a; Roberts, this volume). Students of management would not necessarily be or become managers themselves (as in the study of MBA graduates reported by Collin in this volume). The archetype for this view of management education might be political science. The relationship between politics as a discipline and politicians as practitioners is quite different from the relationship between medical education and doctors discussed earlier. There is no expectation that politicians will have undergone training in political science, and indeed this is rarely the case. Nor is there any assumption that a politics course will equip students with political skills. Instead, there is the expectation that students will learn to understand and to analyse political activity.

The de-coupling of management education and management practice implies more than a shift in the content of management education away from skills and towards analysis. It also implies a re-evaluation of the normative commitments of management education. When management education aspires to enhance managerial effectiveness it is implicitly or explicitly espousing the *desirability* of managerial effectiveness. The decoupling of management education and management entails exposing management to wholesale critical scrutiny. Several strong arguments support the belief that such scrutiny can and should be attempted. There is a long-standing, and growing, tradition in management research which seeks, from a variety of perspectives, to analyse management in ways which go beyond attempts to enhance managerial effectiveness (Alvesson and Willmott, 1992a). On this view, 'management is simply too important an activity . . . to be left to the mainstream thinking of management departments and business schools' (Alvesson and Willmott, 1992b: 3). The knowledge base thus developed might be regarded as a suitable source for rethinking traditional understandings of management education. Indeed, Collin (this volume) argues that, despite appearances, this process of rethinking already occurs in some instances.

The development, through mainstream research, of knowledge aimed at enhancing managerial effectiveness is obviously the counterpart of the view of management education as functionally related to the development of managerial competence. As such it has the same normative commitments to the desirability of effective management. This strand of management thinking, which is probably dominant within management education, may therefore be designated as *managerialist*. In contrast to this, *critical* work on management is, broadly, anti-managerial in its orientation. The intention of such work is to make critiques of management practice, or at least to call into question the claims of management in some regard.

Within this broad characterization there are several quite distinct positions. Some critical work on management is avowedly political and takes it impetus from some version of Marxism. The classic example would be labour process analysis. Although here again a great variety of positions exists, there is a fundamental assumption that the labour process in capitalist societies is exploitative and that managers have a key, albeit contradictory, role in the maintenance and enhancement of this exploitation (Braverman, 1974). Similarly, work which draws on Critical Theory (in the sense of Frankfurt School neo-Marxism) regards management primarily in a political light, although the focus will typically be wider than the labour process, encompassing the ideological, communicative and legitimatory aspects of management (for example, Lyytinen, 1992). From this tradition, too, it is possible to draw models of more emancipatory forms of management education (Nord and Jermier, 1992; Roberts, this volume).

A major development in the critical approach to management has come with the impact of post-structuralist work, and more particularly work in the Foucauldian tradition. Some of this work is a development of traditional labour process analysis, especially where the key themes are discipline and surveillance in the workplace (Sewell and Wilkinson, 1992). More radically, however, Foucauldian research draws attention to the constitution of management as a discourse and a practice (Knights, 1992), and to the construction of subjectivity within organizational contexts (Knights, 1989). The post-structuralist approach is often (although problematically) seen as a variant of post-modernism in management research (Hassard and Parker, 1993), already alluded to. Here again the focus is very much on the discursive production of those knowledges and practices known as management (Linstead, 1993). A central issue is that these knowledges and practices may be seen as centrally implicated in the definition of modernity (see Kallinikos, this volume), and hence are critically evaluated by post-modernists (Cooper and Burrell, 1988). Such approaches are critical in a rather different way to neo-Marxism. The debates here are complex (Parker, 1992), but perhaps the main issue for present purposes is that post-structuralism and post-modernism do not align with some particular set of interests and, indeed, would suggest that the very notion of interests is a construction to be problematized. More generally, these approaches have the effect of disrupting the taken-for-granted and supposedly objective representations of managerialist (and much critical) work on management. In this volume, while a number of contributors draw on post-modern and, more frequently, post-structuralist understandings of management, the main detailed exploration of the implications of these positions for management education are to be found in the contribution of Cavanaugh and Prasad and, in a very different way, in the chapter by Boje.

A third broad tradition in critical work on management is that of feminism (for example, Mills and Tancred, 1992). In fact, there are a number of overlaps with the positions already mentioned, so that some feminist analyses might be seen as located within neo-Marxist labour process theory (Pollert, 1981), while others take impetus from post-structuralism (Ferguson, 1984) and post-modernism (Calas and Smircich, 1992). Plainly, in terms of political stance the central issue is the oppression and marginalization of women within work organizations, although the theorization of this issue proceeds in a number of ways. Recently, feminist work on management has been concerned not just with the issue of gender but also with that of sexuality, particularly in relation to the constitution of organizations (Hearn et al., 1989). The implications of such work, although beginning to be explored for education in general (Luke and Gore, 1992), have not generally been considered in relation to management education. In this volume, feminist theorizations of gender and sexuality inform several of the analyses (for example Grey et al.; Vince).

There are other critical approaches to management which should be mentioned, including neo-Weberianism, environmentalism and psycho-analysis. One strand of Weberian thinking develops a moral critique of management as solely concerned with the means of action as against the ends (Ritzer, 1993). Environmental critiques are increasingly common, where management is seen as having a role in the despoilation of the eco-system (Berry, 1995). The contribution of psychoanalysis to the critique of management is to reveal, behind the thin veil of rationality, a complex set of dynamics set up by interactions between individuals, groups and organizations, as a result of the defences and possibilities that are stimulated by the emotional and political dimensions of experience (Hirschhorn and Barnett, 1993; Vince, this volume). These latter critical approaches are invoked in a number of the contributions to this volume.

Although many of these critical positions have come to the fore in recent years, and can be profitably used to rethink management education, there exist many very ancient traditions of thought which can be 'rediscovered' to the same end. We alluded earlier to the fact that debates about the relation between education and society are very long-standing. Although manage-ment education has a more recent lineage, Gosling's contribution to this volume shows how ancient thinking, in this case that of Plato, can illuminate current practice.

Finally, there is one significant approach to studying management which does not fall readily into the classification of managerialist and critical advanced above. Indeed, it is not clear if it constitutes an 'approach' in the same sense as the positions we have outlined so far. We refer to humanism. Work with a humanistic underpinning is to be found in all three of the categories identified. For example, the tradition of management thinking which dates back to human relations theory is very much concerned with identifying and accommodating the human needs of people in organizations (Mayo, 1946). Typically such work is managerial in character, in that it seeks to enhance managerial effectiveness through this recognition of human needs. However, the politics of humanism is not clear-cut, and many versions of Marxism and neo-Marxism have recourse to, for example, some notion of essential human needs as part of the rationale for the moral critique of capitalism (Freire, 1972; Geras, 1977). Similarly, neo-Weberian analysis posits that dehumanization exposes the irrationality of bureaucratic organizations (Ritzer, 1993).

Within post-structuralist and post-modern treatments of management, however, humanism takes on a rather different aspect. On this view, the humanistic notion of some essential core of Being defined in terms of attributes, needs or rights is problematic. At best it constitutes an historically specific form of rhetoric and at worst a disciplinary construct. For post-structuralists, the self is not a given but a socially and historically constituted phenomenon which, in so far as it defines and fixes us as individual subjects, is part of the process through which the self comes to be a site of knowledge (Rose, 1989). As such, it is part of the apparatus of modernity and can have only limited emancipatory significance (for a discussion, see Alvesson and Willmott, 1992c). In this volume, humanistic understandings of management education are exposed to critical scrutiny by, in particular, Vince in his treatment of conventional models of management learning.

Our purpose in outlining some of the contours of critical management research is twofold. First, as we have indicated at various points in our discussion so far, it facilitates identification of the contributions to this volume, to which we shall return shortly. Second, and of immediate relevance, it enables us to return to the issue of how management education might be rethought. The argument so far makes it plain that the knowledge base of management education, in terms of research on management, is fragmented and disputed. Although some writers (Kay, 1994) have claimed that this is merely a transient, immature, 'pre-paradigmatic' state of affairs, the enduring and, we would argue, growing plurality of management research means, at the least, that there is no immediate prospect of a resolution to the management Babel, as Collin (this volume) expresses it. There simply does not exist any agreement on what should be studied, or why, or how. This in itself suggests the need for plurality in the content of management education programmes. At present, management education is generally defined as if the knowledge base were confined to the managerial and (parts of) the humanistic research traditions. Yet the existence, and growth in size and sophistication, of critical research traditions indicates that this conception of management education is no longer viable – indeed, as Kallinikos (this volume) shows, it has never exhibited an internal consistency.

However, the significance of critical research is that, on its own, *pluralism* in management education is not enough. Critical research is not just 'another' approach; rather the positions outlined above offer a thoroughgoing critique of management studies which, if it is valid, implies that traditional conceptions of management education are no longer sustainable. For much critical research suggests that managerial knowledge is not just undesirable but inaccurate. For example, the assumption in much managerialist work of rationality in organizations or markets (an assumption which came into management from classical economics and sociology) has been widely challenged from a number of the critical perspectives outlined above. If this is true, then it suggests not that management education should comprise courses which teach that organizations and markets are rational as well as courses denying this, but that courses of the former type are invalid and should be displaced (Grey, 1995).

At this point, however, the argument reaches an impasse. The nature of rationality is a key area of dispute between different research traditions, and there is no sign of the argument being resolved or indeed 'won' in favour of one side or the other. It might, therefore, be more appropriate to suggest that management educators should always make clear to students the existence of different perspectives when problematic assumptions are drawn on. This requires managerialists to engage with critical work. It also implies the converse, but this already occurs, in that critical work typically takes as its starting point the established traditions of management thinking.

If this more 'dialectical' style of pluralism in management education were adopted, the result would almost certainly be much more akin to the 'politics' archetype than that of 'medicine', because there would no longer be the pretence of indisputable and unproblematic techniques and skills to enhance managerial effectiveness. Instead, it would be necessary for students to appreciate the complex and disputed nature of management as knowledge and as practice. We would thus have moved to a situation where management education was no longer functionally related to management, but was a reflection of prevailing debates within management research. Paradoxically, however, we would also have come full circle to the challenge facing management as an activity, where many of the old certainties have been dissolved. Thus in distancing management education from management, we would not only be doing intellectual justice to management research, but also might well be offering an education which was closer to the realities of management practice. It is within this paradoxical and challenging terrain that the contributions to the present volume aspire to rethink management education.

Overview of Contributions

The contributions to this volume are all concerned to develop an understanding of management education which more adequately deals with prevailing developments in management knowledge. There is, however, a considerable eclecticism in the contributions, and for important reasons. As we have already described, there is a fragmentation in positions on management and management education, and it is appropriate that this is reflected in the present volume. The diversity of contributions is not just an inevitable result of the fragmentation of management theory: it is also a desirable one. It is precisely the activities of questioning and representing management education which point to the limitations and sterility of the presumptions and assumptions of traditional approaches. We see a strength and a value in a pluralistic and open-ended approach to management education which invites readers to reflect on their own practices and potentialities for change.

Notwithstanding their diversity, what links the contributions to this volume is their oppositional quality. Each represents a divergence from the managerialist orthodoxy which portrays the role of management education as simply to provide the techniques and skills to enhance the effectiveness of managers and organizations, as though this notion of 'effectiveness' were an unproblematic given. The thinking and practice represented here support the view, outlined above, that the provision of more complex and theoretically informed versions of management education may, if only by default, provide managers with a more accurate account of organizational and commercial reality.

The contributions are also linked by the fact that all of the authors are actively engaged in seeking to develop for themselves, in a range of institutions, new forms of management education. By virtue of the fact that the contributors are all management educators, who have daily to work with the issues and problematics of management learning, the volume has the character of a 'report from the coal face'. Thus details of institutions, courses and degree programmes are to be found in many of the chapters, as authors seek to explain their current attempts not just to rethink management education but to enact it.

The contributions begin with Alan Thomas and Peter Anthony's broad overview of the state of management education understood *as* a form of education. In a wide-ranging critique, they take to task many of the perspectives we have identified in this introduction including, to a certain degree, our own. They draw particular attention to the fragmentation of management knowledge and conclude that there is an urgent need for the renewal – if not the abandonment – of management education.

The fragmentation of management knowledge forms the starting point for Jannis Kallinikos' analysis. However, rather than simply describing this fragmentation, Kallinikos aims to show the philosophical conditions which have constituted it, through the deployment of, in particular, Hegelian and Heideggerian categories of analysis. He goes on to offer an interpretation of the history of management education in Sweden which draws out the practical consequences of the inability of management studies to provide a unified set of basic disciplinary assumptions.

Although management may lack coherence, Kallinikos shows clearly how it is to be understood in relation to a modernist *Weltanschauung* in which the world is seen as an object to be manipulated. Recognizing the problematic nature of the form of technical rationality which such a view requires, John Roberts' chapter develops a conception of management education which transcends rather than reproduces technical rationality.

Drawing on Habermas, Giddens and MacIntyre, Roberts urges a reflexive turn in management education wherein students are encouraged to understand themselves as both the subjects and objects of management practice. He discusses the case of the Cambridge MBA programme as an example of this reflexive turn.

The dissolution of modernism also provides the background for the chapter by Michael Cavanaugh and Anshuman Prasad. They explore the implications of critical and post-modern theory for management education. They argue that, although such theory has mounted a significant challenge to management knowledge, it has yet to be widely deployed in management education. Aiming to rectify this, they explore not just the general implications of critical and post-modern theory, but also how these can be translated into strategies for reinventing pedagogical practice in the 'critical classroom'.

The reformulation of pedagogical practice is also the theme of the chapter by Chris Grey, David Knights and Hugh Willmott. They report on many years of experience running an alternative course for undergraduate students of management. They too see a need to integrate various kinds of critical theory into management education, but emphasize that institutional and intellectual constraints mean that students must be carefully introduced to ideas which often run counter to their previous educational experiences. They also point out the difficulties and ambiguities of projects of critical education.

Many of the intellectual sources, particularly the work of Paulo Freire, for Grey et al.'s course are invoked by Russ Vince in his discussion of the political and emotional dimensions of experiential learning. He recognizes that, for many years, the management learning community has developed a series of models derived from humanistic understandings of education which challenge orthodoxy in management education, but argues that, in themselves, these provide at best only a partial response to the current debates and difficulties in the management academy and to the needs created by the organizational realities of managers.

Audrey Collin is also concerned to explore the possibilities of humanistic models of education in the present context. She argues, on the basis of an interpretative study of MBA students turned management academics, that the nature of management education is a good deal more complex than conventional critiques would allow. Her study suggests that, despite the orthodoxy of much management education, it is possible to find spaces within which critical discourses can operate, sometimes by default rather than by design. It is these spaces which management educators should seek to work within and to expand.

One of the most obvious sites of more critical management education, at least within the UK, is the Critical Management Studies programme at Lancaster University. One of the architects of that programme, Jonathan Gosling, offers in his chapter a novel approach to rethinking management education. Rather than invoking modern or post-modern ideas, he returns to Ancient Greece to show how Platonic thought provides a series of insights into contemporary management education. Writing with a degree of ironic humour, he shows that many of the concerns entailed in administering the Greek city-state, including the selection and training of administrators, are as pertinent today as they were then.

The final chapter of the volume sounds a cautionary, if not pessimistic, note on the limitations to rethinking management education. David Boje's focus is on the institutional context of management education. In particular he draws attention, from a post-structuralist perspective, to the many mechanisms of surveillance and discipline which function within universities in general and, specifically, the management academy. While identifying some spaces for resistance, Boje argues that the enmeshment of management education within the wider functionings of disciplinary power means that those who would rethink management education cannot make simple assumptions about the emancipatory nature of their endeavours.

Conclusion

In this introductory chapter we have been concerned to identify the terrain within which the endeavour to 'rethink management education' is set. It has been argued that management education faces a crisis, if only because of the dramatic transformations of the late twentieth-century world within which management education is located. It has also been argued that an important element of the necessary rethinking is the very relationships between management education and the wider world, and in particular the world of practising managers. To this end it has been proposed that the existing 'medicine' archetype of management education might usefully be replaced with that of 'politics'.

This chapter has also drawn attention to the great range of perspectives which are now being brought to bear within management research. It has been suggested that these provide the basis on which management education should be reconceptualized. Finally, the various contributions to this volume have been introduced in ways which demonstrate their location within the terrain which we have mapped out.

In our view, the question facing management educators is not *whether* management education must be rethought, but *how*. The process of change is already under way. The aim of this volume is to contribute to shaping the future of management education in ways which are congruent with the developing sophistication and pluralism of management research, and which provide students with educational experiences of profundity and enduring worth.

Notes

1 By 'management education' we, and all the contributors to this volume, refer exclusively to the provision of management education in universities and comparable institutions of higher

education. Where appropriate, a distinction is drawn between undergraduate programmes and MBA and other postgraduate programmes of management education.

2 Or, to express it rather differently, while the discourses of management and manageability are not transcendentally true, they are real in their true effects.

References

Ackoff, R. (1981) *Creating the Corporate Future.* New York: John Wiley.

Alvesson, M. and Willmott, H. (eds) (1992a) *Critical Management Studies.* London: Sage.

Alvesson, M. and Willmott, H. (1992b) 'Critical theory and management studies: an introduction', in M. Alvesson and H. Willmott (eds), *Critical Management Studies.* London: Sage. pp. 1–20.

Alvesson, M. and Willmott, H. (1992c) 'On the idea of emancipation in management and organization studies', *Academy of Management Review* 17 (3): 432–64.

Berry, A. (1995) 'Approaching the millennium, transforming the MBA curriculum: education for the stewardship of the planet's resources', paper presented at the *New Perspectives on Management Education* Conference, Leeds.

Braverman, H. (1974) *Labor and Monopoly Capital: the Degradation of Work in the Twentieth Century.* New York: Monthly Review Press.

Burgoyne, J. (1995) 'Reply to Grey and Mitev', *Management Learning,* 26 (1): 91–6.

Calas, M. and Smircich, L. (1992) 'Using the "F" word: feminist theories and the social consequences of organizational research', in A. Mills and P. Tancred (eds), *Gendering Organizational Analysis.* London: Sage. pp. 222–34.

Clegg, S. (1990) *Modern Organisations in a Postmodern World.* London: Sage.

Constable, J. and McCormick, R. (1987) *The Making of British Managers.* London: CBI/BIM.

Cooper, R. and Burrell, G. (1988) 'Modernism, postmodernism and organisational analysis: an introduction', *Organisation Studies,* 9 (1): 91–112.

Crosby, P. (1979) *Quality is Free.* New York: McGraw-Hill.

Daiches, D. (ed.) (1964) *The Idea of a New University.* London: Andre Deutsch.

Dunant, S. (ed.) (1994) *The War of the Words: the Political Correctness Debate.* London: Virago.

Engwall, L. (1992) *Mercury meets Minerva.* Oxford: Pergamon.

Ferguson, K. (1984) *The Feminist Case against Bureaucracy.* Philadelphia: Temple University Press.

Freire, P. (1972) *Pedagogy of the Oppressed.* Harmondsworth: Penguin.

Geras, N. (1977) *Marx and Human Nature: the Refutation of a Legend.* London: New Left Books.

Gibbs, G. (1992) *Improving the Quality of Student Learning.* Bristol: Technical and Education Services.

Gibbs, G. and Jenkins, A. (eds) (1992) *Teaching Large Classes in Higher Education.* London: Kogan Page.

Giddens, A. (1994) *Beyond Left and Right: the Future of Radical Politics.* Cambridge: Polity Press.

Grey, C. (1995) 'The political project of critical management studies', Working Paper, University of Leeds.

Grey, C. and Mitev, N. (1995a) 'Management education: a polemic', *Management Learning,* 26 (1): 73–90.

Grey, C. and Mitev, N. (1995b) 'Neutrality, critique and quality: a reply to Burgoyne, McAuley and King', *Management Learning,* 26 (1): 103–8.

Hammer, M. and Champy, J. (1993) *Reengineering the Corporation: a Manifesto for Business Revolution.* London: Nicholas Brealey.

Handy, C. (1987) *The Making of Managers.* London: NEDO.

Handy, C. (1989) *The Age of Unreason.* London: Business Books.

Handy, C. (1994) *The Empty Raincoat: Making Sense of the Future.* London: Hutchinson.

Hassard, J. (1993) *Sociology and Organisation Theory: Positivism, Paradigms and Post-modernity*. Cambridge: Cambridge University Press.

Hassard, J. (1994) 'Postmodern organizational analysis: toward a conceptual framework', *Journal of Management Studies*, 31 (3): 303–24.

Hassard, J. and Parker, M. (eds) (1993), *Postmodernism and Organisations*. London: Sage.

Hearn, J., Sheppard, D., Tancred-Sheriff, P. and Burrell, G. (eds) (1989) *The Sexuality of Organization*. London: Sage.

Henry, J. (ed.) (1991) *Creative Management*. London: Sage/Open University.

Hirschhorn, L. and Barnett, C. (eds) (1993) *The Psychodynamics of Organizations*. Philadelphia: Temple University Press.

Huczynski, A. (1993) *Management Gurus*. London: Routledge.

Hunter, I. (1993) 'Personality as a vocation: the political rationality of the humanities', in M. Gane and T. Johnson (eds), *Foucault's New Domains*. London: Routledge. pp. 153–92.

Institute of Management (1994) *Management Development to the Millennium: the Cannon and Taylor Working Party Reports*. London: Institute of Management.

Jeffcutt, P. (1994) 'The interpretation of organization: a contemporary analysis and critique', *Journal of Management Studies*, 31 (2): 225–50.

Kay, J. (1994) Plenary Address at British Academy of Management Conference, Lancaster University.

Knights, D. (1989) 'Subjectivity, power and the labour process', in D. Knights and H. Willmott (eds), *Labour Process Theory*. London: Macmillan. pp. 297–335.

Knights, D. (1992) 'Changing spaces: the disruptive impact of a new epistemological location for the study of management', *Academy of Management Review*, 17 (3): 514–36.

Linstead, S. (1993) 'Deconstruction in the study of organisations', in J. Hassard and M. Parker (eds), *Postmodernism and Organisations*. London: Sage.

Locke, R. (1984) *The End of Practical Man: Entrepreneurship and Higher Education in Germany, France and Great Britain*. London: JAI Press.

Locke, R. (1989) *Management and Higher Education since 1940*. Cambridge: Cambridge University Press.

Luke, C. and Gore, J. (eds) (1992) *Feminisms and Critical Pedagogy*. London: Routledge.

Lyytinen, K. (1992) 'Information systems and critical theory', in M. Alvesson and H. Willmott (eds), *Critical Management Studies*. London: Sage. pp. 159–80.

MacIntyre, A. (1981) *After Virtue*. London: Duckworth.

Mayo, E. (1946) *Human Problems of an Industrial Civilisation*. New York: Macmillan.

Mills, A. and Tancred, P. (eds) (1992) *Gendering Organizational Analysis*. London: Sage.

Newman, J. (Cardinal) (1960) *The Idea of a University*. San Francisco: Rinehart (relevant essay orig. 1852).

Nord, W. and Jermier, J. (1992) 'Critical social science for managers? Promising and perverse possibilities', in M. Alvesson and H. Willmott (eds), *Critical Management Studies*. London: Sage. pp. 202–22.

Parker, M. (1992) 'Post-modern organizations or postmodern organization theory', *Organization Studies*, 13 (1): 1–17.

Peters, T. (1988) *Thriving on Chaos: Handbook for a Management Revolution*. London: Macmillan.

Peters, T. (1992) *Liberation Management: a Necessary Disorganization for the Nanosecond Nineties*. London: Macmillan.

Peters, T. and Waterman, R. (1982) *In Search of Excellence*. New York: Harper and Row.

Pollert, A. (1981) *Girls, Wives and Factory Lives*. London: Macmillan.

Raelin, J. and Schermerhorn, J. (1994) 'A new paradigm for advanced management education: how knowledge merges with experience', *Management Learning*, 25 (2): 195–200.

Reed, M. and Anthony, P. (1992) 'Professionalizing management and managing professionalization: British management in the 1980s', *Journal of Management Studies*, 29 (5): 591–613.

Ritzer, G. (1993) *The McDonaldization of Society*. London: Sage.

Rose, N. (1989) *Governing the Soul*. London: Routledge.

Scott Morton, S. (1991) *The Corporation of the 1990s: Information Technology and Organizational Transformation*. New York: Oxford University Press.

Sewell, G. and Wilkinson, B. (1992) 'Someone to watch over me: surveillance, discipline and the just-in-time labour process', *Sociology*, 26 (2): 271–89.

Stacey, R.D. (1993) *Strategic Management and Organisational Dynamics*. London: Pitman.

Whitley, R. (1984) 'The fragmented state of management studies: reasons and consequences', *Journal of Management Studies*, 21 (3): 331–48.

Willmott, H. (1994) 'Management education: provocations to a debate', *Management Learning*, 25 (1): 105–36.

2

Can Management Education be Educational?

Alan B. Thomas and Peter D. Anthony

Should the useful in life, or should virtue, or should the higher knowledge be the aim of our training? All three opinions have been entertained. No one knows on what principle we should proceed. (Aristotle, *Politics*)

'education' is a concept which is not very close to the ground. (Peters, 1967)

Dearden (1990) has noted how, from time to time, shifts can be discerned in the ways in which we are encouraged to conceive of our social arrangements. He goes on to ask 'whether we are witnessing, perhaps even assisting in, a shift in the way in which institutional learning is seen from education to [vocational] training?' (1990: 84). Since such a shift, he suggests, can indeed be discerned in primary and secondary education, we might well ask whether something similar might be taking place in the domain of management education and what implications that might have in educational terms.

It does not require much philosophical insight to realize that the mere existence of institutions which claim to be dedicated to education is not sufficient for accepting that what they do is educational. If what is done in an institution calling itself a 'school', for example, is necessarily educational, then we might have to accept that the comment made some years ago by an American visitor to a secondary modern school, that it could best be described as a 'custodial institution', implies that incarceration and the disciplinary practices associated with it are part of what we mean by education. Furthermore, if whatever those who call themselves 'educators' do is to be equated with education, this rules out the possibility of distinguishing the bogus from the genuine, the charlatan from the authentic educator. The problem of attempting to define what counts as education in this way is much the same as that which arises in attempts to define what management is by reference to what managers do. For just as without external criteria we have no way of assessing whether those who call themselves managers are actually managing, let alone managing 'effectively', so we have no way of deciding whether educators and educational institutions are actually educating. The mere existence of places called 'management schools' or 'business schools' does not then necessarily require us to believe that those schools are engaged in management education, just as the fact that organizations run 'training programmes' does not necessarily lead us to believe that training is actually taking place. One recent study of corporate training programmes, for example, suggests that in some cases such a conclusion might well be naive (Al-Maskati and Thomas, 1994).

That an institution's activities might be misrepresented, either intentionally or by default, seems all the more likely when there is considerable vagueness over how the key terms which define its primary task are to be understood. Education is, and perhaps must be, just such a term, an 'essentially contested' concept (Gallie, 1955/56) or, as Peters (1967: 1) put it, one 'which is not very close to the ground'. A bakery which manufactured nuts and bolts instead of bread would be likely to have some difficulty in making out a convincing case for its acceptance as a producer of food. But a school which turned out pupils who were versed only in the three Rs but who knew nothing else might well successfully claim to be providing an education, of sorts. Of course, it is the 'of sorts' which is the nub of the issue, for the extent to which what goes on in educational institutions can be considered educational is usually a matter of degree. To complicate matters further, management itself might also be regarded as an essentially contested concept. No wonder, then, that it is difficult to find firm ground when it comes to debating management education.

But there is a further reason why, in the case of education, we should be cautious in taking institutions' self-representations at face value. Education remains a rather special term with essentially positive connotations. To be educating or to be educated is to be engaged in or to have acquired something of value both individually and socially. It would not be surprising, then, if we were to find that those in pursuit of dubious ends were to seek to cloak their activities in the language of education. As Dearden (1990: 90), citing Illich, reminds us, 'powerful interests constantly try to define some human good in terms of what they actually provide'. We are reminded of those totalitarian regimes in which imprisonment, torture and brainwashing have been put in the service of programmes of 're-education'. While nothing so dramatic or unpleasant might be expected in management education, some of what passes for education there might nonetheless be more accurately described in other terms: perhaps as indoctrination, manipulation, persuasion, propaganda, or religious initiation. In short, what management education actually provides might not be education.

The Question in Context

Current debates about management education in Britain have arisen against the background of a broader, long-standing concern about provisions for the vocational preparation of the workforce and the role of the education system in that task (Keep, 1989). In the face of mounting international competition and faltering economic performance, the education system has been subjected to a series of radical 'reforms' and 'initiatives'. These have resulted in such developments as the introduction of a National Curriculum to schools, the founding of Training and Enterprise Councils and the construction of a rationalized system of National Vocational Qualifications. Seen in broad terms, these changes represent a drive on the part of government, backed, if not always uniformly, by business interests, to shift the emphasis of the nation's educational provisions substantially towards vocational ends.

This process of vocationalization has, however, entailed more than simply an attempt to redefine curricula along vocational lines. It has also involved an attempt to recast Britain's traditional structure of educational control. Seeing that structure as an obstacle to the implementation of its programme, government has set about dismantling it with the aim of securing 'the transfer of authority and influence over educational decision-making from the "producers" of education – among whom the teacher unions were seen as a primary target – to employers and parents' (Esland, 1990: ix). Although directed chiefly at the 'soft targets' of the schools, government aspirations extended further, to the colleges and universities, where increased business influence over funding and the fostering of internal shifts to managerialism have weakened those institutions by undermining their autonomy in favour of market relations and reducing the status and security of their staffs (Wilson, 1991). In the case of business schools, the attempt to shift control away from educators and towards the market was expressed most visibly in the Griffiths and Murray (1985) proposals for privatization. Moreover, the curricular changes imposed on schools also have direct implications for universities, both in terms of student recruitment and their influence on school curricula through the examination system.

Not surprisingly, these changes have been met with considerable resistance and hostility, most especially from the school teachers. This hostility can partly be accounted for as a reaction both to the attempt to transfer power from educators to government and other external parties and to the method of so doing, by imposition. But it can also be seen as a response to the proposed shifting of emphasis within the curriculum to vocationalism. Since curriculum practice in England has traditionally been based on an 'essentialist' conception of liberal education (Holmes and McLean, 1989), in which vocational preparation has been afforded inferior status, government efforts to give it greater prominence and parity of esteem could be seen by many as a threat to established and cherished values.

For management education itself, the immediate background to current concerns consists of the series of critical reports which appeared during the 1980s on the state of current provisions (Constable and McCormick, 1987; Handy, 1987; Mangham and Silver, 1986) and the subsequent establishment of the Management Charter Initiative (MCI). However, it is perhaps worth noting that criticism of and debate about management education is nothing new. In America, for example, controversy over the proper form of management education has been in evidence throughout its relatively long history (Hugstad, 1983), and in Britain vigorous debates took place in the 1970s over the 'relevance' of management education to vocational interests (see for example McClelland's (1971) response to Livingston (1971)). It seems, indeed, that while history may not be repeating itself it may be rhyming.

Predictably, in the light of the history of management education in Britain (Locke, 1989; Thomas, 1980), the MCI has met with a mixed response from both business and the education system. The more grandiose proposals for the creation of a management profession based on a hierarchy of qualifications leading to chartered manager status seem largely to have failed. But the creation of a certification system, linked to National Vocational Qualifications and with the controversial notion of management 'competences' as its central idea, appears to have made substantial headway. According to the MCI, it has more than 1600 members representing around 25 per cent of the workforce (MCI, 1993: 3) and its 'strategy has been to focus on the practical needs of the employer' utilizing standards 'derived not from theory, but from an analysis of best practice' (MCI, 1993: 4). Indeed, it is the fear that such a system may come to dominate provisions in universities that has in part moved some management academics to call for a more concerted reaction to such developments (Willmott, 1994).

'Powerful interests' have thus clearly been at work in management education. Government and business have sought to intervene more directly in educational affairs than hitherto and with a considerable degree of success. The question of 'what knowledge is of most worth' (Holmes and McLean, 1989) has increasingly been answered not by teachers but by business and the state. Since those educational provisions that have been controlled by institutions dominated by employers, such as City and Guilds craft qualifications and the BTEC National and Higher National certificates and diplomas, have been characterized by a narrow vocationalism (Holmes and McLean, 1989), with little or no pretence of educational value, anxieties about the growing influence of business interests over management education seem well justified from an educational point of view. Thus an MCI survey of 507 UK organizations with more than 20 employees concluded that: 'All the evidence points to the fact that firms are moving away from the academic route to management training and development and towards practical, work-based training linked to the value it can bring to the organization' (MCI, 1994).

Some Conceptual Issues

Put crudely, current concerns among management educators about management education as education can be formulated in something like the following terms. Management education has to date included an educational aspect and a non-educational aspect (perhaps a training aspect – we will return to a discussion of such terms in a moment). The educational aspect is diminishing and may well disappear or be marginalized to such an extent that management education will cease to be educational. This prospect, in addition to quite possibly putting many management educators out of work or at best diminishing their status and job satisfaction, might lead to a situation in which (a) the raising of 'critical' issues will become less possible (Willmott, 1994); and (b) managers will become less effective managers than they might otherwise be (Burgoyne, 1993), possibly because of (a). Stated even more starkly, the worry is that management education might be reduced to management training. To the extent that training is non-educational, management education might thus become uneducational. Are such concerns justified?

We can approach this issue in two ways. First there is the matter of conceptual distinctions. If 'training' and 'education' are synonyms, then any concern about the former being substituted for the latter might seem misplaced, reflecting merely a confusion over terms. If not, then the reduction of education to training is a logical possibility. Secondly, there is an empirical issue. If management education can in principle be educational, can it be so under current and likely future conditions? In the rest of this section we address the conceptual problem – what does it mean for some learning process to be considered educational?

To explore the nature of education and the educational is a philosophical enterprise, but since we are not professional philosophers and space is limited our discussion will necessarily be somewhat unsophisticated. We also acknowledge Jack London's (1947: 18) stricture that philosophers 'have left the real and solid earth and are up in the air with a word for a flying machine'. But in the peculiar situation in which university teachers, almost alone among professional educators, are exempted from any requirement for systematic exposure to educational thinking as a preparation for their vocation, even a crude overview of the issues may be of value.

Most of us will intuitively recognize a distinction between 'education' and 'training', and this intuition is comfortingly reinforced by philosophers of education, such as Peters (1970) and Dearden (1990). Education and training are conceptually distinct although not mutually exclusive terms.

Peters (1970) argues that for a learning process or activity to be designated as 'education', it must meet the following criteria.

First 'that "education" implies the transmission of what is worth-while to those who become committed to it' (Peters, 1970: 45). The notion of 'worthwhile' does not imply any particular content, only that whatever the content is must be regarded as valuable. Thus to say that someone has been educated but learned nothing of value is a contradiction. In addition, the learner must be committed to worthwhile knowledge; to be educated is to value whatever is learned. Notice also the rather obvious point that education presupposes learning.

Secondly, 'that "education" must involve knowledge and understanding and some kind of cognitive perspective, which are not inert' (Peters, 1970: 45). Education must involve knowledge and understanding and not simply the mastery of skills, for 'we do not call a person "educated" who has simply mastered a skill' (Peters, 1970: 30). Nor is knowledge of facts sufficient; a body of knowledge, a conceptual scheme, some understanding of principles and of explanation is necessary. The learner must also acquire a 'cognitive perspective', being able to appreciate specialized knowledge in a broader perspective which goes beyond narrow competence. Education also implies that the learner changes as a result of the learning experience; education is that which alters the learner's way of being. We can add that, while training also involves a change in the learner, the only requirement is a change in behaviour. Thus Keep (1989: 177), quoting Hesseling (1966), refers to training as a 'sequence of experiences and opportunities designed to modify behaviour in order to attain stated objectives'. 'Behaviour modification' is not a sufficient criterion of education, since it may be attained by means of, for example, drugs or surgery. Education implies the acquisition of concepts rather than merely changes in behaviour, a distinction ignored by stimulus-response theories of learning (Lewis, 1973).

Thirdly, 'that "education" at least rules out some procedures of transmission, on the grounds that they lack wittingness and voluntariness on the part of the learner' (Peters, 1970: 45). People who have learned as a result of such processes as conditioning or brainwashing cannot be regarded as having been educated. Education presupposes an awareness on the part of learners that they are engaged in an educational enterprise and some freedom of thought and action in its pursuit.

As Peters indicates during his discussion of his second criterion, the development of skills is not sufficient grounds for designating some learning process or activity as education. To the extent that training is conceived of as centrally concerned with skills acquisition, it need not be educational. As Dearden (1990: 89) has argued, it 'might well be that a particular training programme had no educational value whatever, without on that account alone necessarily ceasing to be training'. However, that does not mean that a training programme cannot be educational. Nor need an educational programme be unconcerned with skills. The acquisition of knowledge and understanding may require the development of certain skills – how to conduct an experiment, how to use a library, how to carry out computations – and may also develop skills indirectly – those of inquiry, criticism and judgement. Education and training are different, but learning with educational value and the acquisition of skills may both result from the same learning activity. Dearden concludes:

> The point of learning under the aspect of vocational training is to secure an operative efficiency; the person will be able to operate the word-processor, give first aid, administer the injection, or run the shop. The point of learning under the aspect of education is to secure breadth and depth of understanding, a degree

of critical reflectiveness and corresponding autonomy of judgement. Are the two compatible? There would seem to be no a priori reason why they should not be. A process of training could be liberally conceived in such a way as to explore relevant aspects of understanding, and in a way which satisfies the internal standards of truth and adequacy. Training for the liberal professions is often like this. (1990: 93)

One meaning of 'vocational education', he proposes, is 'vocational training that is liberally conceived' (1990: 93). A liberal conception of education has, as we have seen, been a central element of the 'essentialist' tradition of English, if not British, education. But could such a conception be applied to management education?

In an exceptionally clear and well-argued paper, Watson (1993) has provided a cogent rationale for a system of management education which embraces both the 'aspect of vocational training' and the 'aspect of education'. He argues that the skills and qualities required of 'good' managers, although insufficiently understood, are nonetheless understood well enough to provide an underpinning for such a system. These skills and qualities are closely associated with those articulated by Newman (1852) in his advocacy of a liberal conception of education. Comparing the qualities mentioned by Newman with Mintzberg's (1973) specification of managerial roles and skills, Watson notes that there are substantial similarities as well as some differences. Newman ignores such qualities as decision making under ambiguity, resource allocation and entrepreneurialism, whereas Mintzberg tends to ignore, or take for granted, the intellectual skills of criticism, analysis and synthesis without which managers cannot expect to achieve competence. In addition, managers also need to be 'culturally literate' (Hirsch, 1987), 'to understand the culture in which they are operating, and the other cultures which may impinge on their organization, in order to be able to understand the presumptions and expectations of those with whom they work, be it colleagues, employees, customers, suppliers or government officials' (Watson, 1993: 21–2). In general, Watson argues:

a satisfactory education for management should lead to three distinct characteristics: first, those skills of intellectual analysis and social competence which Newman argued were the outcome of a good liberal education; secondly, those additional interpersonal skills seen as necessary by Mintzberg; and thirdly, the possession of a body of knowledge about organizations, and their analysis. (1993: 23)

To state what is perhaps obvious, there seems no reason in principle why management education cannot be educational. Even if it were to become focused on training, then that training, liberally conceived, might still be of educational value. But since principle and practice rarely coincide in an imperfect world, we are still left with the question of whether management education can in fact be educational. It is to this difficult issue that we now turn.

The Educational Value of Management Education

These conceptual considerations suggest that to be educational the activities and processes of management education must at least promote learning, knowledge and understanding of what is worthwhile. This immediately raises a key issue: what is it worthwhile for managers to learn? Or, to put it another way, is what managers learn through management education worthwhile? In addition, recognizing that the outcomes of institutional learning depend on the character of the 'learning milieu' (Parlett and Hamilton, 1972), which includes the orientations which learners and teachers bring to their tasks, some attention to those orientations seems appropriate. In the next section we take up the latter theme.

Education versus Qualification Earning

Dore (1976) draws attention to a key distinction between 'schooling that is education' and 'schooling that is qualification-earning'. He argues that the effect of schooling, the formal pursuit of study, on learners depends not only on the object of learning and the way it is learned, but also crucially on learners' orientations to learning, on *why* they are attempting to learn.

> Most people, when they speak of 'education', have in mind a process of learning – be it by disciplined training or by freer more enjoyable methods of experiment – which has mastery as its object . . . whether the mastery is an end in itself, or whether the knowledge is mastered for use, and whether that use is a practical one or mere self-indulgent pleasure, it is mastery of the knowledge itself that counts. In the process of qualification, by contrast, the pupil is concerned not with mastery, but with being certified as having mastered. The knowledge that he gains, he gains not for its own sake and not for constant later use in a real-life situation – but for the once-and-for-all purpose of reproducing it in an examination. And the learning and reproducing is all just a means to an end – the end of getting a certificate which is a passport to a coveted job, a status, an income. If education is learning to *do* a job, qualification is a matter of learning in order to *get* a job. (1976: 8)

An orientation to qualification earning does not preclude learning, for learners must still learn enough to enable them to pass the assessments leading to qualification. But what is learned, other than the message of the 'hidden curriculum' (Snyder, 1971) that qualification earning pays, is superficial and short term and does not affect the person's being in any significant way. In Peters' (1970) terms it induces no commitment from the learner to what is learned; it amounts not so much to drinking from the fountain of knowledge as merely gargling. Not only is the learning experience 'ritualistic, tedious, suffused with anxiety and boredom, destructive of curiosity and imagination; in short, anti-educational' (Dore, 1976: ix), but the claim to having 'qualified' is at best partial and at worst empty. Qualification, then, need not indicate mastery or competence, although it may do so.

In the drive to expand the quantity of training in management, much significance has been given to the importance of qualifications which have been seen as important to motivating managers to make personal investments in their development and as a way of raising the status of management to a 'professional' level (Banham, 1989; Frank, 1991). It has also been noted that the wider availability of qualifications would improve managers' mobility chances in internal and external labour markets (Handy, 1987). What has seldom been considered, however, is the possible effects on the orientations of managers to learning. Although both the fairness and theoretical rationale of competence-based assessment schemes have been questioned (Collin, 1989; Proctor and Powney, 1991), their unintended effects on learners' orientations seem not to have been. Since qualification earning can be seen as anti-educational in Dore's terms, the 'bait' of qualifications might well turn out to be counter-productive, diverting managers' attention from their real problems and from a quest for mastery in favour of ritualistic displays geared to the satisfaction of the demands of an externally devised scheme. Wickens (1992), at least, seems to have recognized this possibility.

The prospect of obtaining a qualification has, as we have seen, been offered as an important, perhaps *the* important, basis for encouraging managers' commitment to learning. But there are alternatives which can be drawn to the attention of anyone who wants to know why they ought to learn. Drawing again on Dore (1976), it can be said that one ought to learn: 1. in order to acquire knowledge and skills as ends in themselves, 2. in order to be able to use skills and knowledge. The rationales for 1 include 1(a) because the process of acquiring knowledge and skills is a source of pleasure; 1(b) because it is one's moral duty or innate to one's development as a human being to develop one's capacities to the full; 1(c) because to possess knowledge and skill gives one prestige. And for 2, 2(a) because the application of knowledge and skills is pleasurable; 2(b) because one can obtain power, income or respect from others by skilled performance; 2(c) because one can obtain the same by possessing a qualification; 2(d) because by applying one's knowledge and skills one can make one's community or nation a better place.

It seems unlikely that in management education, when conceived in vocational terms, many learners will be motivated purely by the desire to learn as an end in itself. As educators we might aspire to promote 2(d) while recognizing that what counts as a 'better place' is open to argument, and it seems unwise to ignore 2(a) and 2(b) and, indeed, 1(a)–(c). However, 2(c) is pernicious, which leaves us wondering whether the drive to link management learning increasingly to management qualifications, and the growing tendency to treat courses and colleges as commodities, might lead to the substitution of management qualification earning for management education.

The spread of qualification earning is by no means, of course, a possibility restricted to the new forms of competence-based qualification that have been widely promoted in recent years. Indeed, it would seem that when access to positions in the occupational system comes to depend heavily on the possession of certificates (Collins, 1979), and especially when competitive pressures, fuelled by fears of unemployment, are acute, learners' orientations may well be driven in this direction. Overloaded syllabi inducing a survival mentality, uninspiring teaching and, in the case of vocational courses, a lack of perceived relevance, can also be taken to be contributory factors. Yet it could be different. Might not, for example, MBA programmes be much more effective vehicles for learning if they were participatively designed and offered no promise of a qualification? Might not the participants (if there were any!) then pursue their studies with a view to deep rather than superficial learning, driven by their internal 'need to know' and supported by all the resources the learning institution could muster? Might they not then develop a 'fascination' for learning (Jourard, 1967) which would enable them to become, and to want to become, the lifelong, independent learners managers are now supposed to be? Might they even become better managers?

Management versus Education

The record so far suggests that the prospects for such changes are not good. In Britain there is a tradition of resistance not only to the form but to the fact of management education. Locke quotes the British journal *The Engineer* reacting to a proposal that business and management studies should be added to university curricula:

> if we had to choose between an extension of the college course and workshop training, we should unhesitatingly select the latter . . . we do not believe that any amount of college education in [business and management studies] can ever take the place of the day-to-day touch which is given by a few years as an apprentice or pupil. (1989: 106–7)

This suspicion of 'college education' may be an inheritance of British empiricism, a respect for hard facts, the school of hard knocks and the university of life; but if it is, it cannot easily be met by squabbling over the curriculum content when it is the thing itself, education as such, that is rejected by the client. The educator is challenged to demonstrate at once both the value of education and its practical relevance to the business in hand, but employers' objections to the content continue. Their protests, voiced jointly by the BIM and the CBI, 'at the growing unease and doubts about some developments in the rapid expansion of undergraduate and postgraduate courses in business education' (Locke, 1989: 179) might have been shrugged off as the prejudice of ignorance until they were subsequently and more powerfully expressed by Mintzberg (1989). He wonders:

> what does the word 'professional' mean in the context of managing? It surely does not mean the same as in medicine or engineering, for these fields have certified methods for diagnosing and for solving practical problems in particular contexts. We certainly have techniques in management, no shortage of those, but

none certified in that way. Indeed, we know a lot more about the failure of our techniques . . . than we do about their successful applications. In other words, we have almost no systematic evidence on the successful practice of management.

And, turning to the universities, he concludes that:

formal education can hardly be considered a prerequisite to practising this so-called profession. No one identifies successful managers on the basis of holding an MBA (apart from the fact that it starts them off on the fast track). Indeed, if the success of the Japanese in practising management compared with their reluctance to teach it is any indication, then conventional MBA training should be considered part of the problem, not part of the solution. (1989: 348-9)

In other countries, particularly Germany and Japan, managers have been more highly educated, but not necessarily in management and certainly not *first* in management. Locke describes the university circuit in Germany in which graduates in engineering or science acquired the proficiency in mathematics to enable them to comprehend business economics and to turn themselves into *Wirtschafts-Ingenieur*, the economics-engineer. The prospects in Britain for this kind of academic background to a career in management were never as good. Devoid of German *Technik*, 'personality considerations and especially social skills are more important in choosing, and advancing, managers in Britain' (Lawrence, 1984: 142).

It seems to be the relationship between theory and practice, between education and what in other spheres would be called professional competence, that bedevils both management and its education in Britain. We have already heard that the clear distinction between education and training is not very helpful because the latter, 'liberally conceived', might have educational value. There might be a case for saying that all education, liberal or otherwise, contains an element of training. The conviction that work and thinking must be associated, that each was an inseparable element in education, continued to influence British educational philosophy until recent times, but it may not carry much conviction with status-conscious British managers. The close association that it sets out between theory and practice – or praxis – and its foundation in technical competence is, however, very close to Lawrence's account of German management's emphasis on *Technik*. Locke, referring to Lawrence, attributes to it the German conviction 'that the product is the thing and superior performance means superior products' (Locke, 1989: 264). Mintzberg, emphasizing the craft-like quality of management, says that 'no craftsman thinks some days and works others. The craftsman's mind is going constantly, in tandem with her hands. Yet large organizations try to separate the work of minds and hands' (1989: 31).

Technik, or the craft element in management, also underlies authority over subordinates and respect for their managers: 'the sense of *Technik* presides over the community of workers. It provides the ideology of community motivation, the common purpose' (Locke, 1989: 268). Authority rather than power, if it is not founded in magic or tradition (Weber, 1968), often depends on respect for some form of competence or learning; it is, for example, the central thread of professional relationships. That has provided a model for much of the development of management education and training in this country in the pursuit of recognized qualifications for the practice of management but, it would seem, without much effect on the actual practice of management. The complexities and problems attending this search have been described by Reed as threefold: internal conflict and competition, dependence on employers, and the problem presented by 'the existing knowledge-base available to managers' (Reed, 1989: 163). Once again, there are suspicions that the pursuit of professionalization is more concerned with status than competence or authority (Child et al., 1983). *Technik*, or something very like it, might have been developed from the foundation of British manufacturing industry and its legacy of apprenticeship in the nineteenth century (Anthony, 1986), but it was abandoned in a partial and unsuccessful pursuit of 'professionalization'. Whatever the consequences for managers, there is little doubt that the model of 'professional' management has done its 'professors' a power of good.

Management Education as a Market Segment

The developing professions of management and of management education are apt to be too easily confused. Such confusion is dangerous because it introduces two perspectives in judging the value of management education: whether it is good for the managers or for their teachers. The distance between the two is illustrated by the activities of the British Academy of Management (BAM). BAM is a nascent form of professional closure of the kind so graphically described by Illich (Illich et al., 1977). Its professional or market autonomy offers the prospect of some comfort and security from the painful dilemmas of the business and academic worlds. The published proceedings of the 1994 BAM conference run to 551 pages. There are over 300 papers or presentations. Of the 600 or so who attended the conference 438 were there to present papers, sometimes twice, often in the space of 20 minutes with a further 10 for 'discussion'. On the one hand, this could hardly be described as an academic exchange; on the other, as a distinguished member was heard to remark, much of it had little to do with the practice of management.

The construction of an academic market in professional management requires size and synergy in order to secure its safe separation from managers, but it must, at the same time, preserve some indirect relationship with them in order to demarcate its academic stakeholding. This delicate marketing strategy is pursued by moving to a meta-level: the educators begin to concern themselves with what managers are rather than with the techniques of what they need to know and practise. There are (at least) two useful traditions to be exploited.

The first and most academically respectable is to address not the practice of management, but the relationships of power which they reveal, the sociology of management. The academics working this particular seam are scholarly and admirably qualified for their important work, a necessary vocation, because it contributes to an understanding of social relationships and power in organizations. Understanding, however, often gives way to unmasking, in the service of which the critical theories of post-modernism are recruited. An array of theorists from Derrida to Daudi, Foucault to Habermas are presented to uncover the concealed ironies in managerial pretension and the rhetorical disguises of managerial power. This is, no doubt, a perfectly respectable academic activity, but the intentions in exposing managers to it may sometimes be doubted. Leaving aside elementary questions about intelligibility, there must be some concern as to whether the purpose is to discomfort and undermine rather than to facilitate understanding and performance (see also Roberts, this volume). If the unmaskers were to be unmasked by their own techniques, they might, in some cases, be revealed as concealing their hostility to the managers they have to teach.

The second tradition is the growing fashion for eclecticism, demonstrated – with apologies to the valuable work of Gareth Morgan (1986) – in the use of metaphor, parable and comparison. Insight into the significance of what management is can be obtained from hermeneutics, theology, science fiction, pop art, philosophy or literature. Brief but impressive forays are made into distant academic disciplines. There are advantages in these hasty importations to what would seem to be the remote field of management which it is their intention to illuminate; they escape the need for scholarly knowledge and they do not occupy the foreign field long enough to risk argument or refutation.

None of this is to suggest that the understanding of management as a social process and as a relationship of power is not a study of urgent importance, but it is about management, not managing. Perhaps the time has come when the two activities should be separated in an effort to achieve some clarity about the purpose and content of management education. The study of the process of management might be better conducted in those academic departments that carry the intellectual capacity to pursue it and which do not rely on a prospectus designed to attract students who expect to be taught how to manage. The result might be that the financial support for such studies would be reduced, but at least, on the one hand, the scholarly commitment and integrity of those who survived to teach the management process would be assured while, on the other, those labourers in the field of teaching managers might be expected to demonstrate some essential empathy with their students.

The removal of these higher reaches of critical studies to another place would leave us with a concern to direct management education at managers rather than at each other in our own closed, segmented market. But we should not conclude that all theory can be abandoned, because it is the apparent divorce between theory and practice, leaving the latter for lower levels of education or training, that has bedevilled the education of British

managers. Even if we regarded management education as severely vocational, practice cannot be unrelated to theory, whether it be of engineering
or medicine. Once again we are left with the problem of determining how
this education should be conducted.

Managing Education versus Educating Managers

We, the educators, must address the question against the stark possibility
raised earlier that management education might cease to be educational.
Perhaps we have to face an even more severe question: whether it would be
of the slightest consequence, other than to ourselves, if management
education ceased altogether. There is little reliable evidence that management education in general and the MBA in particular contribute to
improved managerial performance: there is some argument that it causes
actual damage (Anthony, 1986; Leavitt, 1983; Mintzberg, 1989; Rose,
1970; Whitley et al., 1981).

The problem facing management education may be composed of two
distinct elements. The first is the reasonable supposition on the part of
clients in any vocational programme of education that it should contribute
to improved performance. In the case of the established professions, this
expectation is sustained by legal requirement and assurance of competence.
Management education has set out to simulate this provision largely by
equipping managers with a mastery of techniques in decision making,
statistical skill, strategic analysis and so on. That basis has been challenged
on three grounds: the skills are easily acquired by intelligent and educated
people after their recruitment to organizations; they can easily be bought
in; and, in turbulent times, they are likely to change so rapidly as to make
the educational preparation redundant. This hard core of the curriculum is
increasingly discounted in favour of two ingredients of the successful
practice of management: knowledge of the business or even of the specific
organization (Kotter, 1982; Mintzberg, 1989) and the capacity to cope with
change, the one certainty in an uncertain environment.

The first cannot be provided by any general educational programme: it
comes from that old enemy of the pedagogue, experience. Perhaps the old
protests of the accountants and the engineers were, in this respect, right.
What remains is the need to equip, or at least to help in acquiring, the
capacity to learn from experience and to harness it to adaptability. This
may require a 'cognitive perspective' and the development of a critical and
reflective capacity to avoid becoming enslaved by the experience that is also
so necessary. Education can be expected to provide an environment that
encourages the development of open and objective discussion, perhaps
something like the openness of the Japanese *ringi*, an accepted forum for
discussion of the sort that has always been so stoutly resisted by British
managers when faced with any proposal to formalize participation, like the
recommendations of the Bullock Report (1977). British managers' comparative lack of education may, in fact, have resulted in this one disabling

weakness, not so much an incapacity to think but to debate, to see different perspectives, different conceptions of truth and right. If so, all our recent efforts to reinforce the power – not the authority – of an uneducated management will make things worse, more encased and isolated in its secure and protected status.

But at least we may have lit upon a form of educational provision that could actually be related to improved managerial performance. It is, of course, as we have said, very like Newman's 'Idea of a University'. It must be confessed that it is also very like the education of the British Civil Service and that may be an idea that many people will find difficult to swallow. Our objections to the education of the all-rounder may have become confused with a quite proper distaste for the class-bound nature of both the product and the educational route from which it has emerged. The two, the education and its pattern of provision, are not necessarily inseparable. There is not too much reliable criticism of the competence of the British Civil Service; a great deal of it is directed at its class-based isolation. It resembles, in some respects, the preparation of both Japanese managers and civil servants, a good, often first-class, education followed by thorough grounding in organizational experience and technique. The attack on the British, amateur, generalist tradition has become familiar to the point of tedium (Wiener, 1981) but it is, itself, too general. There is not much evidence that a good general education damages subsequent managerial performance. There is growing argument to suggest that it may contribute to managerial abilities the relevance of which have been concealed by ill-founded management theory. There is mounting evidence which suggests that a specialized management education does nothing or does harm. We may have attributed consequences to the wrong cause; it is not the value of a general education but the belief in the importance of a general managerial career pattern that weakens British management:

> The British emphasise the generalist approach to management, and a British manager is proud to call himself a 'good all-rounder'. There is a corresponding emphasis on variety of experience – between functions, between companies, and even between industries. (Lawrence, 1984: 142)

The second potential linkage between education and managerial performance is related to the capacity to deal with change. We have all heard enough, from more than one source, about the importance in this respect of the management of culture, the disabling contradiction of which, in dealing with change, is that it is difficult and can take 15 years (Kotter and Heskett, 1992). Education is likely to be more effective because, if it is well founded, it will concern conceptual understanding, 'a breadth and depth of understanding' and a capacity to synthesize within a sustained intellectual framework. The educated person is less likely to be shocked by the new, more likely to be stimulated to an understanding of change. In the arts or the sciences, theoretical grounding and the experience of critical dispute encourage the active pursuit of challenge.

There is a third respect in which education can be of value in the practice of management. Locke concludes his study of *Management and Higher Education since 1940* with a discussion of motivation. He says that, in contrast to the examples of British and French relationships between education and management, 'the German system of higher education supports the community motivation that is embodied in the organizational culture', that it 'fostered the disappearance, at the operational level, of the contradiction between thought and action' and 'blurred the distinction between staff and line' (Locke 1989: 274). He maintains that the relative poverty of British managers' education contributes to a loss of community motivation in their organizations and that:

> education is not just a part of the solution to the management problem but a part of the problem itself . . . In Great Britain there persists, as a result of the educational system, a great prejudice against education throughout every level of society. This means, at the mass level, that people who must work do not value education per se: education is good for them only when they see how it affects their ability to do their specific job. (1989: 281)

Locke constantly reminds us that any educational solution must be culturally specific, grafted into the values of its society. If British managers are incurably utilitarian, their educators must demonstrate the profitable advantage in education. The paradox is that it is only by concern with broader goals, only by taking our eye *off* the ball, that education will prove to be useful. What seems to be required is some sleight of hand, some deception whereby we appear to give the clients what they want, while we work to our own conception of what they need. But that is where we began this discussion, with educators addressing an agenda in isolation from managerial practice. It is precisely this educational conviction that has led to the construction of an entirely prescriptive theory of management, at odds with praxis and divorced from reality (Reed, 1989). The division between teachers and taught finally widens to the point at which the arrogance of the former is reinforced by the avoidance of contact, not only with management practice, but with managers.

Real management – as it has been researched and defined by Dalton (1959), Kotter (1982), Mintzberg (1973), Stewart (1967) and Watson (1994) – engages social, political and conceptual abilities that are far beyond the reach of the current battery of analytical techniques. If we were to research more effectively – remembering the significance of organizational specificity – the complexity of occupational and organizational (not corporate) cultures (Anthony, 1994) and the environments in which managers practise their arcane arts, then we might find a base on which to build theory and teaching. There is some anecdotal evidence that managers respond to an approach that recognizes where they start from rather than where their educators want them to go, and which accords them some respect for the trades they practise. There are certainly the foundations of a tradition of research and theory in real, rather than prescribed, management practice on which a management education might one day be built.

Conclusion

The values that have been argued here as contributing to a necessary flexibility of mind in order to cope with inchoate experience, change and a sense of community purpose come from an education, not from management education as it is currently defined. They could come from literature, philosophy or physics, but they might be more acceptable to managers if they appeared to be cognate to their activity, if they concerned, say, economics or engineering. Alternatively, we could begin the patient reconstruction of management education curricula – there are already indications of positive progress in this direction (see Thomas, 1993; Watson, 1993).

During the course of research into management relationships in a large district health authority (Anthony et al., 1988), a very senior consultant told his interviewer that he, the consultant, had no respect for management as a discipline, that its pretensions to science were vacuous (cf. MacIntyre, 1981) and that its practitioners 'should go away for fifty years and return when they had something valuable to say'. He might have been right. As things stand, it seems that it might be a matter of no great consequence if management education as we know it simply came to an end. Even if there is to be, not an end, but a hiatus and a radical rethinking of management education, the outcome will be a matter of some consequence for the educators. Any reform project must overcome a real obstacle – the threat to the interest of the providers, the educators. No doubt we shall overcome it in a true spirit of objective concern for the best interests of our clients and of our society. We are, after all, educators because we demonstrate the importance of the values that underlie what we teach. There should be no problem.

References

Al-Maskati, H. and Thomas, A.B. (1994) 'Why managers don't learn', paper presented to the Annual Conference of the British Academy of Management, University of Lancaster.

Anthony, P.D. (1986) *The Foundation of Management*. London: Tavistock.

Anthony, P.D. (1994) *Managing Culture*. Buckingham: Open University Press.

Anthony, P.D., Reed, M. and Murray, A. (1988) 'Report to the District General Manager of the South Glamorgan District Health Authority of a study of managerial roles and relationships in the Authority'.

Banham, J. (1989) 'On professionalism and professions: the Management Charter Initiative', *Journal of the Operational Research Society*, 40: 315–21.

Bullock, Lord (1977) *Report of the Committee of Inquiry on Industrial Democracy*, Cmnd. 6706. London: HMSO.

Burgoyne, J.D. (1993) 'The competence movement: issues, stakeholders and prospects', *Personnel Review*, 22: 6–13.

Child, J., Fores, M., Glover, I. and Lawrence, P. (1983) 'Professionalization and work organisation in Britain and West Germany', *Sociology*, 17: 63–78.

Collin, A. (1989) 'Managers' competence: rhetoric, reality and research', *Personnel Review*, 18: 20–5.

Collins, R.K. (1979) *The Credential Society*. New York: Academic Press.

Constable, J. and McCormick, R. (1987) *The Making of British Managers*. London: British Institute of Management.

Dalton, M. (1959) *Men Who Manage*. New York: John Wiley.

Dearden, R. (1990) 'Education and training', in G. Esland (ed.), *Education and Training and Employment, Vol. 2: The Educational Response*. Wokingham: Addison-Wesley. pp. 84–95. First published in *Westminster Studies in Education*, Vol. 7, 1984, Oxford: Carfax. pp. 57–66.

Dore, R. (1976) *The Diploma Disease: Education, Qualification and Development*. London: George Allen and Unwin.

Esland, G. (1990) 'Introduction' in G. Esland (ed.), *Education, Training and Employment, Vol. 2: The Educational Response*. Wokingham: Addison-Wesley, ix–xvii.

Frank, E. (1991) 'The UK's Management Charter Initiative: the first three years', *Journal of European Industrial Training*, 15: 3–12.

Gallie, W.B. (1955/6) 'Essentially contested concepts', *Proceedings of the Aristotelian Society*, 56: 167–98.

Griffiths, B. and Murray, H. (1985) *Whose Business? A Radical Approach to Privatise British Business Schools*, Hobart Papers No. 102, London: Institute of Economic Affairs.

Handy, C. (1987) *The Making of Managers*. London: MSC, NEDC, BIM.

Hesseling, P.G.M. (1966) *Strategy Evaluation Research*. Assen, Netherlands: Van Gorcum.

Hirsch, E.D. (1987) *Cultural Literacy*. Boston: Houghton-Mifflin.

Holmes, B. and McLean, M. (1989) *The Curriculum: a Comparative Perspective*. London: Unwin Hyman.

Hugstad, P.S. (1983) *The Business School in the 1980s*. New York: Praeger.

Illich, I., Zola, I.K., McKnight, J., Caplan, J. and Shaiken, H. (1977) *Disabling Professions*. London: Marion Boyars.

Jourard, S.M. (1967) 'Fascination: a phenomenological perspective on independent learning', in G.T. Gleason (ed.), *The Theory and Nature of Independent Learning*. Scranton: International Textbook Co. pp. 79–101.

Keep, E. (1989) 'A training scandal?', in K. Sisson (ed.), *Personnel Management in Britain*. Oxford: Basil Blackwell. pp. 177–202.

Kotter, J.P. (1982) *The General Managers*. New York: Collier Macmillan.

Kotter, J.P. and Heskett, J.L. (1992) *Corporate Culture and Performance*. New York: The Free Press.

Lawrence, P.L. (1984) *Management in Action*. London: Routledge and Kegan Paul.

Leavitt, H.J. (1983) *Management Education in the West: What's Right and What's Wrong*. London: London Business School.

Lewis, B.N. (1973) private communication.

Livingston, J.S. (1971) 'Myth of the well educated manager', *Harvard Business Review*, Jan/Feb: 79–89.

Locke, R. (1989) *Management and Higher Education since 1940*. Cambridge: Cambridge University Press.

London, J. (1947) *The Iron Heel*. London: T. Werner Laurie.

MacIntyre, A. (1981) *After Virtue: a Study in Moral Theory*. London: Duckworth.

Management Charter Initiative (1993) *MCI Fifth Anniversary Review: Improving Performance Today and Tomorrow*. London: MCI.

Management Charter Initiative (1994) *Management Development in the UK: 1994*. London: MCI.

Mangham, I.L. and Silver, M.S. (1986) *Management Training: Context and Practice*. London and Bath: ESRC, University of Bath, DTI.

McClelland, W.G. (1971) 'Myth squared', *Management Education and Development*, 2: 58–63.

Mintzberg, H. (1973) *The Nature of Managerial Work*. New York: Harper and Row.

Mintzberg, H. (1989) *Mintzberg on Management*. New York: The Free Press.

Morgan, G. (1986) *Images of Organization*. Beverly Hills: Sage.

Newman, J.H. (1852) *The Idea of a University*. London: Longmans Green.

Parlett, M. and Hamilton, D. (1972) *A New Approach to the Study of Innovatory Programs.* Occasional Paper No. 9, University of Edinburgh: Centre for Research in the Educational Sciences.

Peters, R.S. (1967) 'What is an educational process?', in Peters, R.S. (ed.), *The Concept of Education.* London: RKP. pp. 1–23. Reprinted in A. Finch and P. Scrimshaw (eds) (1980) *Standards, Schooling and Education.* London: Hodder and Stoughton. pp. 10–26.

Peters, R.S. (1970) *Ethics and Education.* London: George Allen and Unwin.

Proctor, J. and Powney, J. (1991) 'The standard of qualification in management education: unresolved questions', *Higher Education Review*, 23 (3): 31–40.

Reed, M. (1989) *The Sociology of Management.* Hemel Hempstead: Harvester Wheatsheaf.

Rose, H.R. (1970) *Management Education in the 1970s: Growth and Issues.* London: HMSO.

Snyder, N. (1971) *The Hidden Curriculum.* New York: Knopf.

Stewart, R. (1967) *Managers and their Jobs.* London: Macmillan.

Thomas, A.B. (1980) 'Management and education: rationalisation and reproduction in British business', *International Studies of Management and Organization*, X: 71–109.

Thomas, A.B. (1993) *Controversies in Management.* London: Routledge.

Watson, S.R. (1993) 'The place for universities in management education', *Journal of General Management*, 19 (2): 14–42.

Watson, T.J. (1994) *In Search of Management.* London: Routledge.

Weber, M. (1968) *Economy and Society* (3 vols). New York: Bedminster Press.

Whitley, R., Thomas, A.B. and Marceau, J. (1981) *Masters of Business? Business Schools and Business Graduates in Britain and France.* London: Tavistock.

Wickens, P. (1992) 'Management development is dead!', *Target – Management Development Review*, 5 (5): 3–7.

Wiener, M.J. (1981) *English Culture and the Decline of the Industrial Spirit, 1850–1980.* Cambridge: Cambridge University Press.

Willmott, H. (1994) 'Management education: provocations to a debate', *Management Learning*, 25: 105–36.

Wilson, T. (1991) 'The proletarianisation of academic labour', *Industrial Relations Journal*, 22: 250–62.

3

Mapping the Intellectual Terrain of Management Education

Jannis Kallinikos

... the modern character of science ... forms men of a different stamp. The scholar disappears. He is succeeded by the research man who is engaged in research projects ... The research worker necessarily presses forward of himself into the sphere characteristic of the technologist in the essential sense. (Martin Heidegger, 'The Age of the World Picture' from *The Question Concerning Technology and Other Essays*, 1977: 125)

Management as World Orientation and Technique

The term 'management' is widely used today to refer to the social practice of administration, the body of knowledge, tools and techniques that are supposed to bear on its exercise and the problems and prospects facing formal organizations. It is the status of this corpus of knowledge and its academic affiliation which will mainly concern us here. Attempting to clarify its meaning[1] does not, however, seem to be an easy task. On close scrutiny, the notions of management and its scientific status appear slippery, indeed obscure. Like a spectrum of colours, they keep vanishing under the approaching light. How are we to understand these terms? Is management a science or a hodgepodge of fragments of social sciences[2] lacking the coherent core set of assumptions constitutive of a scientific discipline? Can it be considered simply as an ensemble of tools and techniques with practical preoccupations, or does it constitute a general societal orientation, a phenomenon that permeates the entire society and needs to be explained by recourse to a social-historical matrix of relations? Does its claimed fragmentation reflect a lack of intellectual depth and seriousness, or is it a manifestation of a deeper transformation which the process of knowledge acquisition is undergoing in the late industrial world? These, I contend, are questions that need to be faced and eventually answered if the phenomenon of management is to be appreciated and taught in non-superficial ways.

It is quite common to regard the emergence of management as a recognized academic field at the beginning of the twentieth century, as being connected with the increasing compartmentalization, interdependence and complexity of modern life. Such a view is not entirely unconvincing.

After all, it is tempting to consider the growth and proliferation of administrative tools and techniques as the response to such a deepening differentiation and the resulting complexity of the modern world. On this view, the emergence of management as an academic discipline signifies no more than the conscious effort to codify and systematize practical wisdom, and to develop both a set of tools and a body of knowledge that can be transferred from the detached contexts of the academic world to employment in contemporary working life. The causal or temporal sequence is one of increasing social and economic complexity and accumulating practical problems that create the need for the systematization, development and codification of experientially based knowledge (see Engwall, 1992; Hopwood, 1987; Perrow, 1986).

If the notion of management is reserved for the ensemble of administrative techniques that are conventionally subsumed under this term, then the above sequence could be considered as largely valid. But if the term is opened up to embrace the very basic assumptions on which the entire *orientation to manage* rests, then the whole story appears to be considerably more complex, and causality, if there is any, would seem to run both ways. Management implies and reproduces compartmentalization and fragmentation as a means of mastery and control. For, in order to be managed, the totality of physical and social processes, whether within limited instrumental contexts or in society as a whole, needs to be broken down into narrow domains that can be inspected, measured and handled. On this view, differentiation as well as complexity and interdependence are the effects of cognitive and behavioural predispositions that inhere in management, rather than the other way around. It would seem, then, that we need to make a distinction between management as an overall *world orientation* and management as an ensemble of *techniques* motivated by and directed towards the nexus of ordinary problems confronting formal organizations. A critical evaluation of what is subsumed under the notion of management demands the consideration of both phenomena and the explication of their relationship.

Although perhaps difficult to recognize from the present historical horizon, management, as a practice and an academic discipline, is closely connected with the overall orientation towards the objectification and technicalization of knowledge that pertains to modernity. The technical tenor of the industrial world often appears as reasonable, or even natural, and, in this respect, tends to escape the scrutinizing gaze of critical interrogation. At other times it is inappropriately confused with and confined to the actual machinery of industrial production and the processes of transformation of the physical world. However, science, technology and management are allied phenomena and can be interpreted as different manifestations of the same underlying world view (Heidegger, 1977). They constitute a complex tangle of orientations that mark and reproduce an attitude whereby society and nature are looked on as if they were things to be made and remade, changed and transformed, corrected, amplified, destroyed, reconstructed, etc. This broad orientation towards objectification and mastery is implied by, or even intrinsic to, management. It lies at the heart of the compartmentalization of the material and social world, the growth and academic institutionalization of administrative techniques, and also the constitution and reproduction of particular sets of beliefs, priorities and ideas that help define the basic orientations of contemporary human beings (see also Derrida, 1982).

The inscription of management within the whole network of technical and instrumental orientations pertaining to modernity and the industrial world does not need to imply that the advent and current practice of management, and the values attached to it, are viewed as an inevitable and irreversible trend to be met with distanced passivity. Let me acknowledge, from the outset, that this chapter is indeed critical of much of what goes under the terms 'management' and 'management education'. However, such a critical attitude is not denunciatory, but rather searching and interrogative. It is prompted by the recognition that any attempt to understand and evaluate the advent and growth of administrative techniques and management education must endeavour to locate them within the wider social and historical context. To do so reveals management both as a general societal orientation and an ensemble of practical techniques concerned with the systematization and codification of objectified knowledge, and its utilization for the purposes of designing and directing goal-oriented activity along controllable and predictable lines. It is necessary to understand management at both levels: at the level of general societal orientation where it forms, together with science and technology, a particular world view, and at the level of concrete, mundane techniques and practices concerned with the codification of experience and the reappropriation and utilization of knowledge produced within the wider domain of the social sciences. The explication of the relationship between the two levels can account, I will claim, for the fragmentation of management studies (Whitley, 1984). Only against the background of the general can the particular show its distinctive character.

The present chapter, then, attempts to explore the intellectual terrain of management education, rather than discuss the forms of social learning subsumed under different pedagogic strategies and approaches. Obviously, content and form influence each other and the abundance of sterile methods of learning, encountered in management education, is related, in one way or another, to its heavy vocational inheritance and its fragmented intellectual content. As I will claim later on in connection with the Swedish experience in management education, the friction between academic and vocational training creates a series of contradictions and a context where the assimilation of experiential, context-embedded knowledge characterizing the successful practice of management ('knowing how') with the formal and codified methods of management education ('knowing what') becomes difficult to accomplish. Formal knowledge on the one hand and tacit, experiential knowledge on the other have, since Polanyi (1958), been considered as different domains of human learning relating to intellectual and action skills respectively. Accordingly, they suggest the need for different methods of teaching and exposition (see also Dreyfus and Dreyfus, 1986; Zuboff, 1988). These contradictions have as a rule been reconciled in past and current management education by a heavy emphasis and reliance on management techniques that have created the impression (or illusion) of an education combining practical relevance with rigorous scientific procedures. An important consequence has been the lack of a critical attitude towards the epistemological status of the assumptions underlying the dominant management tools and techniques, which seems, in turn, to have reinforced the original fragmentation of the various domains of knowledge that constituted management education in its early years. But pedagogy itself is an issue that will be left aside in this chapter (although explored in many other contributions to this volume).

Instrumental Epistemology and the Cartesian Inheritance

It emerges from the preceding section that I view management as a characteristically modern phenomenon: management implies a world view that coincides with the emergence of modernity and the industrial world. Certainly, organized, goal-oriented activities have always been present in human civilization, and human history shows that pre-industrial societies were able to accomplish tasks and run large and complex undertakings with a success that still arouses admiration. But to confuse the modern notion of management with the organization and co-ordination of human effort in general runs the risk of overlooking its distinctive character. It is, therefore, necessary to look somewhat more closely at how the disposition to manage is related to overall shifts in framing and perceiving the world that coincide with the emergence of modernity. As noted, it is the very orientation towards objectification and mastery and the conception of the world as an object to be managed that characterize modernity.

In the context of the West, mastery and objectification coincide with a subtle yet radical shift in ontology and epistemology which Heidegger (1977) attributes to the rendering of representation as the dominant way of thinking and acting on the world (see also Derrida, 1982). The radical turn of representational ontology and epistemology is very often overlooked, and representation is conflated and confused with the very act and means of knowing. Representation, as it is used here, does not simply refer to the mental mapping or symbolic encoding of the world. It is distinct from other modes of conceiving and acting on the world in that it implies the proactive bracketing, selection, perception and investigation of particular and limited aspects of the world. Perception is always guided by conception. Representation is, to use Heidegger's (1977) word, *projective* – which means that the world is enacted and organized in terms of a set of assumptions or particular schemata of conception and interpretation that help to select specific aspects of the world.

It is this perception and observation of limited aspects of the world, made from particular angles, that characterize representation. Physics and geology, for instance, are concerned with different aspects of inanimate nature; economics and psychology with different aspects of human behaviour. Selection always implies a standpoint or a network of standpoints from which the world is re-presented, vicariously put in front of an agent with a view to understanding it (the world) in ways that allow for intervention, mastery and change. Again, desire is differently conceived by psychoanalysis and consumer behaviour, but common to both is the principle of selective (aspected) objectification that renders psychic life, in the former case, amenable to interpretation and cure in terms of a set of assumptions regarding psychic functioning and health, and, in the latter case, an object of fulfilment and joy by means of material or symbolic consumption. The psychological objects of psychoanalysis and consumer behaviour are dramatically different. Psychology and economics, and any discipline whatsoever, neither care about nor record the ceaseless parade of the world. The so-called objective facts are fabricated facts (which does not, of course, mean unreal in the sense of fictive), that are only rendered observable by virtue of the network of assumptions that single out and objectify particular facets or domains of human life.

It is important to underline here the crucial significance of the initial assumptions or preconceptions on the basis of which scientific representation constitutes itself and singles out limited and particular domains. *Homo oeconomicus* is as important to economics as motion is to mechanical physics. There cannot be any science of economics without the web of assumptions hidden behind the fiction of *homo oeconomicus* that prescribes the overall way in which social life can be seen, reduced and studied as economic action. Initial assumptions provide the conceptual apparatuses that selectively attend to the world whose openness is thereby closed up; the world is represented in ways that render it amenable to observation, calculation and mastery. Needless to say, calculability and mastery acquire different forms within the intellectual terrain of the various disciplines. Furthermore, whereas the initial assumptions are subject to periodic reformulations that may result in the reorganization of scientific boundaries (Kuhn, 1964), the very *principle* that demands and makes use of them remains unquestioned (Heidegger, 1977).

I would like to emphasize strongly the significance of the initial assumptions, particularly in the face of certain misconceptions as to what defines an object of study and a disciplinary territory. What is commonly referred to as a firm or an organization, for instance, cannot, in itself, make up a scientific object of study and define a disciplinary territory ('management studies') as is sometimes assumed. Just as humans, nature or life can be and are studied by many disciplines, so too a firm or an organization can be studied from many angles, such as those of economics, sociology, psychology or anthropology, even though the concepts 'firm' and 'organiz-ation' might already imply a certain predilection for the investigation of particular aspects of the phenomenon in question. Representation and scientific objectification are concerned with partial or 'aspected' facets of the world.

There is an amusing reference by Foucault to Buffon's astonishment at the naturalist Aldrovandi's way of looking at nature that helps exemplify the logic of representation. There is a long quotation of Aldrovandi's description of the serpent that includes everything from the etymology of the word, to fables and tales, proverbs, death and wounds, riddles, heraldic signs, size, modes of poisoning and many elements that together form, in Foucault's words, an *extricable mixture*. The embarrassment and disorientation that arise when confronting Aldrovandi's description are the result of a mode of being and thinking that has definitively stepped into the abstracting specializations underlying the age of representation. Aldrovandi's logic of 'total', exhaustive description defeats the projective and aspected logic of representation; a logic that is concerned with selective aspects of a phenomenon so that the latter can be put in front of a subject in ways that make it masterable, conceptually and materially. Little wonder that Buffon exclaimed: 'there is no description here, only legend' (Foucault, 1970: 39).

On this view, the scientific quest for objectivity actually emerges as a quest for objectification, that is for representation, the putting of the world in front of the subject in ways that make the world masterable and manipulable. It comes as no surprise, then, that the rendering of the world as an object cannot but presuppose the other for whose sake objectification takes place, namely the subject. Despite positivist rhetoric or the lament of humanism, subjectivism is the inevitable concomitant of objectifying the world, of always viewing it from the standpoint of a set of solidified intentions whose texture makes up what we refer to as the subject. This is the meaning, Heidegger insists, of the Cartesian *cogito ergo sum*. And this is what separates ancient episteme and medieval doctrina from modern science or, for that matter, the pre-industrial from the industrial world. Detached contemplation and religious belief are superseded by a world view that places Man at the centre of the physical and social world, rendering the latter an object of objectifying representation amenable to mastery and control. Objectification and subjectification imply and feed on one another (Foucault, 1978; Gordon, 1980). Notions of the subject as consumer, producer, economic agent etc. refer, of course, not to particular individuals but the ontological and epistemological requirements that prescribe and constitute a mode of being and operating. To quote Heidegger:

> The fundamental event of the modern age is the conquest of the world as picture. The word 'picture' (*Bild*) now means the structured image (*Gebild*) that is the creature of man's producing which represents and sets before. In such producing, man contends for the position in which he can be that particular being who gives

measure and draws up the guidelines for everything that is . . . There begins the way of being human which means the realm of human capability as a domain given over to measuring and executing, for the purpose of gaining mastery over that which is as a whole. (1977: 132–4)

It would seem as though we are far away from the territory of administrative sciences. And yet, the understanding of the phenomenon of management needs to be situated within this wider socio-historical context that constitutes and reproduces the controlling administrative orientations and techniques of modern humans. When I claimed above that management is a characteristically modern phenomenon, distinct from a general idea of organized or co-ordinated action, I meant to imply that the instrumentation of controllable and predictable activities, the standardized and regulated world that we refer to as bureaucracy, cannot exist in cultures that do not operate on the ontological and epistemological premises of representation (Kallinikos, 1992, 1995). Bureaucracy is not simply a system of social relationships governed by rational-legal authority and superimposed, as it were, from the outside on an anterior division of labour. Bureaucracy conceives and constructs the world as divided. It is implicated in the division of labour which it reproduces and enhances (Cooper, 1989). Bureaucracy is the institutional vehicle that embodies that world view which conceives accomplishment as work and individuals as labouring bodies (Arendt, 1958). It is here that we can clearly see the co-extensive territory between scientific objectification, technology and management. Each one presupposes and reproduces the other. Again, this should not be taken to imply that the world completely succumbs to and follows the iron order of objectifying technologies. Nevertheless, neither the modern age nor the significations conveyed by management can be understood and critically evaluated without recourse to representational technologies and the visions they attempt to impart on the world.

It is common to conceive, in Weber's spirit, of the weakening of old bases of legitimation, in the face of the advent of science, as the major turning point in the development of the instrumental orientation of the modern world and the transformation of the practice of management to an academic discipline (Zuboff, 1988). Education transforms the manager from an authoritative figure (traditional authority) to a knowledgeable figure (rational-legal authority). The manager becomes an expert. On this view, management education emerges as a mechanism which produces and legitimates stratification and hierarchy in organizations by recourse to the functionality of the expert. This picture is certainly valid, but again defines management in narrower terms than those implied by management conceived as a world view, a general societal orientation. It describes how management reappropriates scientific findings subsuming technical and ethical-social issues in the apparatuses of administration. Management and management studies emerge as attuned to the *requirements* of the external world rather than as *constitutive* of them. However, management as a modern phenomenon is inescapably connected with the advent and establishment of representation as the basic mode of being, knowing and acting on the world. The description of the evolution of management as a transition from norm to expertise, from morality to technique, fails to consider the ontological premises and the socio-cognitive means that sustain the practices and operations of contemporary work contexts and render such a transition possible. The erosion of old bases of legitimation is inextricably bound up with the radical changes of world orientations prescribed by representation and its conception of the world as an object to be mastered and managed.

Shorn of all intellectual embellishment, the advent of management studies reflects the sheer instrumental orientation of the contemporary world. Interpreted from the horizon of a wide social and cultural technicalization, management practice and education appear as natural consequences of a particular way of conceiving and acting on the world. The reaction of the erudite scholar, the humanist or the artist who feels appalled by everything that the word 'management' signifies is perhaps the response of a world that is dying away. Romanticism, as Mumford (1934) claimed 60 years ago, was never an alternative to the machine, the emblem of instrumentality and dry knowledge. The humanistic criticism of management and technology is indeed incapable of understanding the technicalization of the contemporary world. Not without reason, for humanism is itself the product of such a technical orientation (Heidegger, 1971, 1977). Disciplines as distant from management as psychoanalysis and literary theory are the products of an epistemological (and ontological) view wherein psychic life and linguistic imagination are regarded as objects to be represented, analysed, examined and (in the case of psychoanalysis), changed. But neither psychic life nor poetry needs psychoanalysis or literary theory in order to exist. The latter are as much technologies as management. The Tavistock Institute's involvement in the management of working life is far from an accident and bears witness to a fundamental and common orientation that pertains to all scientific thinking, namely the objectification, codification and utilization of knowledge for functional purposes. Shortly after the appearance of Taylor's *Principles of Scientific Management*, psychology emerged as a major vehicle for and a source of the disciplining and subjugation of the worker and the technicalization of behaviour in work settings. Systematic and codified knowledge of the worker's interior life is, according to Mayo (1945), an indispensable complement to the hard core of knowledge provided by finance and engineering. A largely similar role is assumed today by the anthropology of work going under the names of organizational culture and symbolism, where common values and basic assumptions, supposed to underlie work ethic, knowledge and behaviour, are brought under scrutiny (see for example Schein, 1985). Although channelled through the set of formal activities that we subsume under the notion of management, the organiz-ation and control of the social component of instrumental action is, by and large, the accomplishment of methods derived from social science disciplines (and mathematics) and reappropriated by management and management studies in the service of this purpose (Donzelot, 1991).

The Case of Swedish Management Education

What has been said so far seems to suggest that scientific objectification, bureaucracy and management represent a concurrent and allied set of phenomena coinciding with the emergence and dominance of the representational world view. If science and scientific practice are interpreted from the Heideggerian horizon, then the intellectual status of management studies cannot perhaps justify consideration as a scientific discipline proper. Management is largely preoccupied with the conception and positing of the world in terms that render the latter calculable and masterable. Yet such a task is instrumented and accomplished by disciplines with clearly demarcated and objectifiable domains (economics, psychology, sociology, communication theory, cognitive science, mathematics, etc.).[3] Management does not provide the set of assumptions constitutive of an empirical (objectified) domain. To give an example, the salient contributions made by Simon and March (see Simon, 1959; March and Olsen, 1976) cannot but be located within microeconomics and cognitive or social psychology. They have been developed as a response to the assumptions on human behaviour put forth within these disciplines. In management and business studies there exist neither models of human nature, nor a core set of assumptions, in the sense described above, to be revised.

Management studies, then, emerges as a complex field where the postulates, findings and applications of empirical sciences are carried over, reappropriated and mixed to produce a body of knowledge that is supposed to bear on the conception, planning and instrumentation of goal-oriented activity. In Foucauldian fashion, we might consider the emergence and development of social sciences as a huge enterprise in the governance, control and administration of increasing populations and diversified operations within the extended territories of the newly created national state coinciding with the advent of industrialism (Foucault, 1977, 1978, 1980). In this sense, the orientation to master and manage, implied by representation, creates the historical conditions of possibility for the human sciences. Management studies emerge out of this fragmented territory of knowledge with the determination to distil its findings for the general purpose of an immediate functionality cleansed of 'irrelevant' theorizing and 'costly' conceptual perplexity. Thus reappropriated, the knowledge produced by the social sciences will undergo a profound mutation to serve as both the raw material and the intellectual embellishment for the creation and legitimation of the emerging business schools and university business departments.

The Swedish record of management education provides both a challenge to and an exemplification of the arguments put forth so far.[4] Research on the history of management education in Sweden reveals three distinct periods that lead from fairly simple vocational training to training within business schools and thence to academic higher education (Engwall, 1990, 1992; Guillet de Monthoux, 1991). Modern management education finds its forerunner in small private schools that were exclusively dedicated, during the nineteenth and early twentieth centuries, to the development of commercial skills necessary for conducting business. Often supported by chambers of commerce and trade associations, training in these schools comprised an ensemble of techniques essential to office work, such as bookkeeping, banking, stenography, foreign languages, business correspondence, etc. This initial period of a kind of management education is thought to have extended until 1909, when the first school in higher education in business and economics, the Stockholm School of Economics, was established. Management education at its dawn consisted of a hodgepodge of practical techniques. Its contents grew out of and was almost completely adapted to the contingencies of everyday business activity. Clearly, it is hard to conceive of any coherent body of thought sustaining management education during this period.

The second period was heralded, as noted, by the establishment of the Stockholm School of Economics in 1909, followed 14 years later by the foundation of the Gothenburg School of Economics. Earlier attempts to build an academic affiliation for business economics (mainly accounting and finance) had met the hostility of academia and the indifference of the state (Engwall, 1992). Accordingly, the foundation of both business schools owed a great deal to private funds and the lively interest of the industrial and commercial world. During this stage, the intellectual poverty of the first period was gradually overcome and teaching programmes were broadened to embrace other disciplines. Political economy, statistics and law were added to curricula, conferring an aura of academic credibility that helped heighten the status of the whole enterprise. Curricula at the end of this second stage included as a rule a mix of economics, finance and accounting, economic geography, commercial law and statistics – which still form a considerable part of business education today (Engwall, 1992; Guillet de Monthoux, 1991). An important contrast, however, emerges between teaching programmes at the beginning and end of this period. The dominant part played by economics during the first half of the second period (c. 1909–30) receded, gradually being replaced by management studies, which by the mid-1950s had almost achieved the prevalent curriculum position it still enjoys today. The formal and scientific status of economics had served, as Engwall (1992) seems to suggest, as one means for overcoming the resistance or indifference of an academic world still influenced by Humboldtian ideals, and for legitimating the scientific status of the emerging intellectual terrain. After this goal was at least partially accomplished, however, balance had to be restored to orient and gear management education to the requirements imposed by economic or business reality.

Despite a definite step towards the 'scientification' of curricula, during this second period pedagogy remained entangled in its vocational origins and teaching tended to have a normative and almost an ideological orientation (Guillet de Monthoux, 1991). Research programmes were almost absent (the award of the first doctor's degree had to await the end of the 1940s). Guillet de Monthoux summarizes the period as follows:

> In political economy, as in other subjects taught, any intellectual development occurred at the universities and very seldom in connection with 'higher' business studies. This fact added to the difficulties of business education. Basic reasonings, original presentations of problems and the foundations of abstract models were often ignored. There remained a kind of shorthand logical skeleton which was swotted up by the students in stenographic textbooks, in which assumptions remained obscurely implicit. Had it not been for the hope of getting a well-paid job, students would have despaired of the point of it all. Regarded seriously, as something more than a game of graphs and equations, such an education might well turn into something mystical. Like Latin sermons in a Swedish country church. A matter not of knowledge but of blind faith. What except a question of belief can an economic message detached from its scientific and historical context ever be? (1991: 33)

But intellectual impoverishment was, according to the same author, only part of the story. A second and highly ambiguous step involved the definite transition to a detached and decontextualized body of knowledge that, as noted in the introduction, had neither the rigorous character of scientific endeavour nor the quasi-artistic quality and relevance of practical knowledge developed through years of experiential involvement. This difficulty might be said to be intrinsic to the entire enterprise of education, but the other human disciplines are nevertheless a step removed from everyday accomplishment and never claimed to transmit directly applicable knowledge. The problems posed by the decontextualized character of education in general seem to be accentuated by the Janus-faced character of management education (see, for example, Whitley, 1984). Vocational training and intellectual development do not always coincide. As claimed by Guillet de Monthoux in the above passage, scientific developments seldom occurred 'in connection with "higher" studies'. I find it hard to believe, as he seems to do, that this is simply the consequence of a weird anti-scientific mentality coinciding with the asserted practicality of the Swede in general, and Swedish business schools and university business departments in particular. The unequivocal imprint of a dry, deproblematized, functional knowledge, cut from its contextual and historical origins, is a phenomenon that haunts management research and education in general (see Astley, 1984; Engwall, 1992; Pfeffer, 1982; Whitley, 1984).

The answer, I believe, is not to be sought, at least not solely, in the cultural specificity of management education, but in its general characteristics. The fact that intellectual developments took place in the university, within the institutional and conceptual framework of the established disciplines, and not in the business schools, strikes me as natural, and badly in need of interpretation in terms of cultural characteristics. As I have repeatedly noted, intellectual development is subverted, and the sterile and fragmented intellectual landscape of management and management education accounted for, by the absence of a clear core of assumptions that could help to demarcate a particular intellectual terrain, a scientific object of study and an appropriate methodology for that study. In this respect, the institutional affiliation of research, the question of whether it is conducted within university departments that represent established disciplines or in business schools, is not the major issue. A more positive interpretation of the academic status of management studies is suggested by Simon (1969), notably his view that management forms, together with medicine and engineering, law and education, an ensemble of normative intellectual tasks that need to be judged in terms different from those of analytical or empirical disciplines. I will return to this issue later on.

The third period might be said to start at the end of the 1950s, with the creation of chairs in business economics and the establishment of business departments, first in Uppsala and Lund universities, and gradually in the other major educational institutions around the country. The period can be said to be characterized by an impressive and steady increase in the number of students, professionals and administrative staff. Changes in the curricula were rather minor, however, and the basic structure of the second period can, by and large, describe this period as well. The more spectacular change perhaps was the definite 'academization' of business studies with the development of research programmes. From a handful of PhD holders by the end of the 1950s, the number of people who had defended a doctoral thesis in business administration rose by the end of 1985 to 270.[5] Approximately 85 per cent of them defended their theses after the end of the 1960s (Engwall, 1990, 1992). It is rather difficult to give a definite interpretation of these more recent tendencies. As far as postgraduate studies are concerned, Engwall's account identifies a definite trend, whereby research on organizational and administrative issues has been claiming an increasingly greater proportion of doctoral theses at the expense of marketing, finance/accounting and managerial economics. Dissertations with an orientation towards organization theory reveal the heavy theoretical influence of the Carnegie Institute of Technology (Cyert, March, Simon). There are signs of important changes since Engwall's investigation (the survey was made in 1985), but there is no available study which captures these more recent developments.

It would be possible, then, to discern from the empirical observations a clear trend towards an increasing 'academization' and intellectualization of business or management education. But what does such a trend actually signify? Does it imply that management education is advancing forward towards its consolidation and solidification as a scientific discipline? Data, of course, do not speak for themselves. The growing influence of organization studies during the 1970s and 1980s could be interpreted in positive terms, as implying a 'paradigm' shift and a definite step away from the vocational predilection of management education. Undeniably, organization theory and behaviour convey an intellectual aura not to be found in the other subfields of management studies. Engwall's (1990) data seem, however, to suggest that such a shift is not to be taken, at least not solely, as an unequivocal sign of intellectual maturity, since people with a background in marketing and finance tended, and still tend, to leave university for high-paid jobs in industry and the private sector.

It would seem that the wide gap between undergraduate and post-graduate education is of greater importance. Whereas this chasm is known to characterize the entire system of higher education in Sweden, it is probably more noticeable within management education. Undergraduate students have very little contact with research and are seldom taught what is occurring on the other side of the divide. The quality of undergraduate teaching is still, as Guillet de Monthoux (1991) observed, highly normative and almost ideologically biased. Strange as it may seem, the content of undergraduate education is presenting an inverted picture of the themes and research orientations of postgraduate programmes, with the great majority of undergraduates choosing finance/accounting as specialization, several marketing, and only a tiny fraction organization studies. These are, by and large, the major specializations of university business departments.[6] Even if the share of accounting teaching has gradually diminished (Engwall, 1992), the emergence and proliferation of other management subfields often had to take place within the specializations of accounting and finance.

Decoupled from the overall context of representation and scientific objectification, these findings may seem striking, or even bizarre. As has been argued above, management education has always had a double identification: a close adjustment to the practical requirements of everyday business activity, on the one hand, and an academic identification, on the other hand. By becoming 'higher', management education faced a new reference group in the institutional world of academia, composed of single but coherent and demarcated disciplines with a long history and well-developed teaching and research procedures and administrative rituals. Emulation can promote homogenization. The chasm and spectacular differences between undergraduate and postgraduate programmes in Swedish management education can certainly be illuminated by recourse to this double identification, in such a way as to bring to mind Meyer and Rowan's (1977) interpretation of the double structure of general education (see also Whitley, 1984).

Be that as it may, I have insisted, throughout this chapter, that socio-logical interpretations of this kind do not suffice to explain why management education still has such a strong vocational affiliation and such a fragile scientific territory. The fragmented character of management studies has been observed by many students of the field (Astley, 1984; Engwall, 1992; Pfeffer, 1982; Whitley, 1984). Whitley's account, in particular, seems to me accurate and suggestive. Yet his interpretation, caught in terms of a sociological model, fails to observe how the intellectual terrain of management studies is epistemologically flawed. The very characteristics he identifies as crucial for explaining the current situation in the field – low control over performance and significance standards, the dispersion of critical resources and the heterogeneity of the target audience – seem to me to be but the consequences or accompaniments of the lack of a clear disciplinary focus. The anarchic dance of concepts, methodological tools and research problems that characterizes management studies is the result of an intellectual terrain that has been, or was unable or perhaps never intended, to define its scientific boundaries. The question as to whether management studies has ever made any important and distinctive contribution to the human and social sciences appears disturbing. Neither is management's relatively recent ascent into the institutional world of science adequate to explain the current situation. For there exist novel disciplines that exhibit well-established disciplinary missions and rigorous theoretical and methodological procedures (such as cognitive science). Again, in order to account for the scientific status of the field we need to go back to consider the idea of representation, scientific objectification and the related core of assumptions that defines a disciplinary territory.

As I have claimed throughout, management research and education reappropriate the findings of other disciplines and extend their applications, but lack an explicit disciplinary focus, a selective (aspected) objectification of the world. There lie the roots of the prevailing situation. The intellectual arrogance with which the social science disciplines still face management education, despite their common representational and functional inheritance, can perhaps be attributed more to the latter's lack of a unifying core set of assumptions than to its vocational origins. Be that as it may, it would seem that both these characteristics – the absence of a clear disciplinary focus, and the vocational origin and affiliation of management education – are ultimately interdependent and have put a definite stamp on the way it is conducted. Little wonder, then, that the pedagogical forms in this domain have always suffered from a sterile reproduction of practical recipes and a de-philosophized, de-theoreticized and de-problematized transference of knowledge accomplished in other disciplinary fields. The Swedish experience seems to me, by and large, to recount this story.

Conclusion

Is, then, the academic experience of management education to be interpreted solely in negative terms? Do management studies represent but a flawed model of scientific research? I have sought, throughout this chapter, to suggest an answer with respect to the fragmented nature and precarious scientific status of the intellectual terrain occupied by management studies. These characteristics have been observed by many students of the field and it would be hard to deny them. However, what has been said above does not necessarily imply an unequivocally negative attitude towards management studies. To be sure, there is much in the field, as no doubt in every field, that does not deserve serious consideration. Popular management books are not in any way representative of what is going on in the field, for all that they may emerge from the academic world.

In a sense, the characteristics of management education described here – fragmentation and vocationalism – might be looked on as recounting, *mutatis mutandis*, the academic experience of engineering and medicine (Simon, 1969). All three represent academic arrangements that seek to reappropriate and combine the analytical methods and results of well-demarcated disciplines with a view to applying them to achieve desired practical ends.[7] The tension and unstable equilibrium between established scientific standards and the demands of vocationalism or professionalism epitomized by the academic experience of all three are not an accidental epiphenomenon. They could certainly be explained by the previously mentioned ideals of the modern university and the attempt to purge vocational training from its curricula. But it could also reflect the kind of mastering demands created by the changing texture of the late modern world (Lyotard, 1984; Vattimo, 1989).

The infiltration of engineering by physics, medicine by biology and management studies by economics reveals, as Simon (1969) observes, the failure to understand the vocation of and the demands made by what he calls the emerging science of design. In his view, the latter is distinct from the analytical mission of established disciplines concerned with the creation and sustenance of artificial systems to be developed in the boundary area between natural laws and human purpose. The sciences of the artificial are not concerned with the analysis of the internal functioning of a system (such as the human brain), but with the selective reconstruction and design of certain key attributes (such as automated computation) that allow the resulting artificial system to respond to a range of environments and tasks. It is the 'thin interface', as Simon puts it, between system and environment, the 'inner' and the 'outer', rather than the exhaustive analysis of internal relations of a system, that is the focus of design and the sciences of the artificial (see also Cooper, 1983; Kallinikos, 1989).

Of course, Simon insists, the sciences of the artificial in general and the practice of management research and education in particular cannot violate scientific laws, but nor can they be evaluated by exclusive reliance on them, for they represent an enterprise with a pronounced normative orientation that constructs rather than simply reflects reality and truth. The construction of 'intelligent' machines, for example, should not be evaluated by comparing them with humans and human imagination in general, but in relation to their stated purposes and aspirations, which are none other than the duplication or simulation of certain human mental attributes.[8] The failure to respond properly to such a vocation, together with the misconceptions as to what defines a scientific territory, might well account for the prevailing situation in management education. Simon's moral is, then, that management education is not to be evaluated by standards derived from the analytical or empirical disciplines. Institutional pressures to adopt and imitate an ideal, and often a stylized, model of scientific research might produce the semblance of a proper academic discipline devoid of meaning and practical purpose.

Thus the very characteristics that seem to account for the fragmented and precarious status of management studies – the absence of a core set of assumptions and proximity to economic reality – might be interpreted in a different and more positive way. There is in the pursuit of academic management studies a pluralism of perspectives, a criss-crossing of intellectual boundaries and themes, an ability to explore alternative conceptual frameworks and improvize with different research questions, a different relationship with the lay public and practitioners alike, which, when compared with the secluded and detached world of more established disciplines, presents a picture that might hold considerable promise. In this respect, the academic experience of management studies might gestate, albeit incompletely a novel model for conducting research that reflects the demands of the intellectual tasks of design and artificiality, thereby breaking with the clear boundaries of the age of representation and the Humboldtian ideals of academic research and education, and favouring instead local and shifting alliances of concepts, methodological tools, problems and solutions (Donzelot, 1991; Lyotard, 1984).

True, these same characteristics have often favoured scientific dilettantism, sometimes bordering indeed on frank charlatanism. I will not deny that and I have sought throughout this article to give an interpretation of the fragmentation and the relatively lowly scientific status of management education. Yet I am not sure whether the remedy is to be sought in the adoption of standard models of scientific research. When I claim, in these concluding remarks, that the experience of management education might produce a novel and promising model of scientific research, I stress the term 'might'. Such a speculation is itself based on the idea of a profound mutation of those characteristics that define the status of knowledge and the processes of knowledge acquisition in the late modern world. There is some evidence that the standard model of scientific research practised in the age of representation cannot any longer respond, in an adequate way, to the nexus of problems and questions facing contemporary life. The rigid distinctions of subject from object, of normative from descriptive statements, of ethics from truth seem to confront their own limits, in this changing context of the contemporary world (Heidegger, 1977; Lyotard, 1991; Vattimo, 1989). However, only systematic investigations that take seriously these ideas can really tell whether management studies bear the germ of new possibilities, a novel model, so to speak, for the pursuit of academic research and education in this late age of modernity.

Notes

1 I will use the terms 'management', 'management education' and 'management studies' to refer to the alliance of subfields commonly made up of accounting, finance, organization theory and behaviour, marketing and managerial economics.

2 I avoid the question of whether the social disciplines themselves can be considered as scientific domains in the sense of the natural sciences. I will, however, make a distinction between, say, management and education (the discipline of education) on the one hand and economics or psychology on the other. The difference, I will claim, can be traced back to an initial set of assumptions that help to define a scientific or disciplinary territory, a limited domain of ideas and observations. It is not obvious whether management studies and education, for instance, are defined by such a core set of initial assumptions.

3 The question of how the subfields that make up management studies reappropriate the findings of other disciplines is a complex one and demands extensive argumentation that cannot be supplied here. It is enough to note that finance and operational research can be thought of as applications of economics and mathematics respectively (Whitley, 1984). Similarly, marketing reappropriates basic assumptions from economics and psychology (mostly behaviourism), while organization theory and behaviour can be looked on as applications of concepts and notions drawn from sociology and social psychology (Burrell and Morgan, 1979).

4 In the presentation of the Swedish record on management education, I will draw heavily on the work of Engwall and his associates. However, the interpretation of the empirical data, which they have meticulously gathered over many years, is entirely my own.

5 With slightly over eight million inhabitants, Sweden is, in terms of population, a relatively small country.

6 The dominance of accounting/finance appears to be diminishing during the 1990s, although again this is an *ad hoc* observation, not a conclusion based on systematic empirical data.

7 This may also be true of other disciplines, such as law, education and architecture (see Simon, 1969: 55–8).

8 This subject does, of course, raise questions of immense complexity, such as how normative and descriptive statements can be combined or reconciled. Obviously, these are questions that cannot be dealt with here. It is enough perhaps to say that Simon's overall technocratic solution of *modal logic* – a branch of logic that attempts to combine descriptive and normative statements – can only be applied under specific and very limited conditions. The Heideggerian view outlined earlier seems to suggest that the whole edifice of the scientific project, not simply the applied disciplines, is permeated by strong normative elements that construct rather than reflect reality and truth.

References

Arendt, H. (1958) *The Human Condition*. Chicago: The University of Chicago Press.

Astley, G.W. (1984) 'Subjectivity, sophistry and symbolism in management science', *Journal of Management Studies*, 21: 259–72.

Burrell, G. and Morgan, G. (1979) *Sociological Paradigms and Organizational Analysis*. London: Heinemann.

Cooper, R. (1983) 'The other: a model of human structuring', in G. Morgan (ed.), *Beyond Method*. London: Sage.

Cooper, R. (1989) 'The visibility of social systems', in M.C. Jackson, P. Keys and S.A. Cropper (eds), *Operational Research and the Social Sciences*. New York: Plenum.

Derrida, J. (1982) 'Sending: on representation', *Social Research*, 49 (2): 294–326.

Donzelot, J. (1991) 'Pleasure in work', in G. Burchell, C. Gordon and P. Miller, (eds), *The Foucault Effect: Studies in Governmentality*. London: Harvester.

Dreyfus, H.L. and Dreyfus, S.E. (1986) *Mind over Machine*. New York: The Free Press.

Engwall, L. (1990) 'Västhagen and after', *Working Paper 90/7*. Department of Business Studies, Uppsala University.

Engwall, L. (1992) *Mercury Meets Minerva: Business Administration in Academia, the Swedish Case*. Oxford: Pergamon Press.

Foucault, M. (1970) *The Order of Things*. London: Tavistock.

Foucault, M. (1977) *Discipline and Punish: the Birth of the Prison*. London: Penguin.

Foucault, M. (1978) *The History of Sexuality: the Will to Know, Vol. 1*. London: Penguin.

Foucault, M. (1980) *Power/Knowledge: Selected Interviews and Other Writings*. New York Pantheon.

Gordon, C. (1980) 'Afterword', in M. Foucault *Power/Knowledge: Selected Interviews and Other Writings*. New York: Pantheon.

Guillet de Monthoux, P. (1991) 'Modernism and the dominating firm: on the managerial mentality of the Swedish model', *Scandinavian Journal of Management*, 7: 27–40.

Heidegger, M. (1971) *On the Way to Language*. New York: Harper and Row.

Heidegger, M. (1977) *The Question Concerning Technology and Other Essays*. New York: Harper and Row.

Hopwood, A. (1987) 'The archeology of accounting', *Accounting Organizations and Society*, 12 (3): 207–34.

Kallinikos, J. (1989) 'Play and organizations', in M.C. Jackson, P. Keys and S.A. Cropper (eds), *Operational Research and the Social Sciences*. New York: Plenum.

Kallinikos, J. (1992) 'Digital songs: aspects of contemporary work and life', *Systems Practice*, 5 (4): 457–72.

Kallinikos, J. (1995) 'The architecture of the invisible: technology is representation', *Organization*, 2 (1): 117–40.

Kuhn, T. (1964) *The Structure of Scientific Revolutions*. Princeton: Princeton University Press.

Lyotard, J.-F. (1984) *The Postmodern Condition: a Report on Knowledge*. Manchester: Manchester University Press.

Lyotard, J.-F. (1991) *The Inhuman*. Cambridge: Polity Press.

March, J.G. and Olsen, P.J. (1976) *Ambiguity and Choice in Organizations*. Oslo: Universitetsförlaget.

Mayo, E. (1945) *The Social Problems of an Industrial Civilization*. Boston: Harvard University, Graduate School of Business Administration.

Meyer, J. and Rowan, B. (1977) 'Institutionalized organizations: formal organization as a myth and ceremony', *American Journal of Sociology* , 83 (2): 340–63.

Mumford, L. (1934) *Techniques and Civilization*. London: HBJ.

Perrow, C. (1986) *Complex Organizations: a Critical Essay*. New York: Random House.

Pfeffer, J. (1982) *Organizations and Organization Theory*. Boston: Pitman.

Polanyi, M. (1958) *Personal Knowledge*. London: Routledge.

Schein, E. (1985) *Organizational Culture and Leadership*. London: Jossey-Bass.

Simon, H.A. (1959) 'Theories of decision making in economics and behavioral science', *American Economic Review*, HLIX: 253–83.

Simon, H.A. (1969) *The Sciences of the Artificial*. Cambridge, MA: The MIT Press.

Vattimo, G. (1989) *The End of Modernity*. Cambridge: Polity Press.

Whitley, R. (1984) 'The fragmented state of management studies: reasons and consequences', *Journal of Management Studies*, 21 (3): 331–48.

Zuboff, S. (1988) *In the Age of the Smart Machine: the Future of Work and Power*. New York: Basic Books.

4

Management Education and the Limits of Technical Rationality: The Conditions and Consequences of Management Practice

John Roberts

In his article 'Towards a Rational Society', Habermas (1971) draws a distinction between two forms of rationality: 'work' – instrumental action 'governed by *technical rules* based on empirical fact'; and 'interaction' – communicative action which generates and enforces binding reciprocal norms. In his more recent work (Habermas, 1989) this distinction has been recast as 'action oriented to success' and 'action oriented to achieving understanding'. For Habermas the defining characteristic of advanced capitalist societies is that subsystems of instrumental action have escaped the influence of what was previously an encompassing and limiting institutional framework grounded in a normative order. The linking of science and technology has led to a self-feeding expansion, which provides its own legitimation. The consequence of this for Habermas is the development of a technocratic consciousness which effectively eliminates the 'distinction between the technical and the practical' (1971: 113). The need for unrestricted communication about the goals of life activity, the norms that should direct the organization of work and the directions taken by science and technology 'disappear behind the interest in the expansion of our power of technical control' (1971: 111).

Drawing on this analysis and other aspects of critical social theory, I want, in this chapter, to develop a critique of what I will argue is the continued dominance of technical/instrumental rationality in the content and conduct of management education. In particular I will focus on the inadequacies of technical rationality for developing students' understanding of the conditions and consequences of their practice as managers. I want to argue that, for all their claims to practical relevance, technicist approaches to management education typically leave students' 'practical consciousness' – the usually tacit and habitual knowledge that informs actual practice – both unquestioned and unreformed.

Leading on from this, I will suggest a number of reorientations in management education that are necessary if our claims to practical relevance are to be taken seriously, and sketch out some of the ways in which we have attempted to embody these in the new MBA programme at Cambridge University. Rather than merely oppose managerial instrumentalism with a critique that is focused on the domination of nature and other people, my concern here is to explore how, within the context of management education, the instrumental and moral domains can be brought back into relation with each other. In turn, this implies seeking to generate some understanding in students about the social processes of organization, and in particular the role of their own immediate practices in the production and reproduction of organizational life.

The Reduction of Management Practice to Technique

I want to argue, following MacIntyre (1981) that orthodox management education proceeds from the assumption that the manager is no more than a 'morally neutral technician' and that this assumption then structures both the content and conduct of courses. One obvious manifestation of this assumption is the emphasis that is given within management programmes to the teaching of analytical techniques. For example, Anthony in his review and analysis of British management education notes that programmes are 'heavy on techniques of financial analysis, marketing, decision analysis and the like' (1986: 120). Now of course there is nothing wrong with the teaching of these techniques in themselves, but it is necessary to make explicit the form of rationality that seems to inform this particular version of management education. It embodies what Weber (1978) called instrumental rationality – the restless calculation of means in relation to ends. As such the business school can be seen as one of the vehicles of what Weber saw as the progressive rationalization of the social world. In disseminating 'best practice' to successive generations of students there is a usually implicit belief in the possibility of the progressive rationalization of action; a ready embrace of the modernist assumption of the progressive and cumulative character of knowledge.

It can be argued that some of the subjects taught in business schools can only be taught in this form for they are no more than techniques and lack any disciplinary base (see Kallinikos, this volume). However, the dominance of instrumental rationality is more clearly evident in the manner of use and presentation of material drawn from other more established disciplines – economics, psychology and sociology. Typically it is the more positivistic streams of thought within these disciplines that are drawn on and in this way many of the conflicts, debates, tensions and uncertainties within these disciplines are glossed over and hidden from sight. Knowledge which is clearly the product of the human imagination is in this process of translation reduced to a set of 'objective' facts to be digested as truth by the student.

Nowhere are such translations more evident than in the teaching of organization behaviour. The very title carries with it the reification of the collectivity of 'organization' and the passive assumptions of behaviourism. That it appears as just one subject among others implies that 'employees' are just one more resource to be managed by the untheorized manager, rather than the source of all the activity involved in the process of organizing. Now it could be argued that following in the wake of the excellence literature (Peters and Waterman, 1982) there has been a decisive shift away from such a naive orientation to behavioural control. My own sense, however, is that, although the focus of attention in this literature has seemingly shifted from the technical to the social dynamics of organizations, the prescriptions for salvation that are offered still express and appeal to an interest in the more efficient realization of unquestioned organizational ends (duGay and Salaman, 1992). Something similar can be said about the explosion of courses and literature concerned with business ethics, where typically this new interest in ethics is justified precisely in terms of the threats and opportunities to corporate self-interest.

In seeking to understand the dominance of this technical rationality it is important to take account of the instrumental interests that shape the actual conduct of management education. The hope embedded and offered in this dedication to the teaching of technique is that, armed with such techniques, the MBA student will be better able to control organizational reality and thereby better able to realize his or her own interests through the realization of the 'organization's' objectives. There is thus an easy alliance between the instrumental interests of students in getting an MBA, a label of legitimacy or expertise necessary to promote their future career interests, and the assumptions embodied in how students are taught. The self- or company-sponsored nature of most courses introduces an element of consumer power into the classroom, and with it the passive yet demanding attitudes of consumption. There is often a strong pressure from students, a sort of impatience that all knowledge should come to them in a predigested and immediately usable form. Against the backdrop of job insecurity and growing organizational uncertainty, it is possible that what is being demanded here is comforting certainty.

There are likewise practical interests at work for the teacher that tend to push him or her towards the transmission of knowledge as fact. In our consumer-led culture where the customer is king and, in the case of MBA students often have more experience of business than the teacher, the classroom can easily become a potentially hazardous place. The resort to the certainties of technique arguably offers the teacher a place of relative security. As a technical expert there is a good chance that the teacher will 'know' more than the student and on this basis can command their attention. At the same time, techniques and fact readily lend themselves to formal examination and thereby become the means whereby individualized control can be established over the potentially threatening student body (see Grey et al., this volume).

In the above I have sought to suggest the dominance of technical rationality in both the form and content of management education, a dominance that is reinforced by the instrumental interests of students, teachers and sponsoring organizations, although the latter are often nervous of losing their newly trained executives. Anthony argues that such an orientation is 'perpetuated and defended in the name of the practical' (1986: 137), defined in terms of what managers believe they need to realize the goals of their organizations. It is in this way that practice comes to be equated with the application of technique. In the section that follows, I want to argue directly against this equation, by drawing on various critiques of instrumental reason. Notwithstanding the practical consequences of the dominance of technical views of management practice, I want to argue that such views offer a distorted and inadequate view of the actual conditions and consequences of management practice that paradoxically weakens its effectiveness (Nord and Jermier, 1992).

Beyond a Technical View of Practice

The practical consequences of the dominance of technical reason in management are numerous. The acquisition of technical expertise is precisely the basis on which managers make claims for the legitimacy of their exercise of power; through the use of techniques decisions can be justified and potentially mystified by reference to the 'objective' facts that they generate. At the same time, since such objectivity can only be established through empirical method; ideas and values which by their nature cannot be verified in this way are reduced to the status of being merely subjective. Thus technical reason becomes self-legitimating, and increasingly immune to normative challenge or direction.

The dominance of instrumental reason can be seen to feed and foster what Habermas calls a 'technocratic consciousness' in which the relationship to the body, self, others and the world comes to be seen exclusively in instrumental terms; as Marcuse put it, 'the liberating force of technology – the instrumentalisation of things – turns into a fetter of liberation; the instrumentalisation of man' (1964: 159).

It was for this reason that Marcuse argued that domination is implicit within technological rationality. One aspect of the instrumentalization of humans involves the naturalization of the present. In this respect he is particularly critical of 'managerial thought' in empirical social sciences, which he argues 'terminate in methods of improved social control' (1964: 108). In such work the negative critical power of thought, he argues, is translated into a form of operationalism which is placed in the service of exploring and improving the existing social conditions. Within the unquestioned framework of existing social institutions such work appears as neutral if not positively therapeutic in its intentions. But if the very structure of society is made the object of critical enquiry, then the political and ideological character of such work becomes evident precisely because it involves a 'deceptive objectivity that conceals the factors behind the facts' (1964: 141).

It is important to recognize the power effects of technical rationality: its capacity to legitimate managerial power, as an overarching ideology that disarms critical thought and as a source of techniques for the pursuit of managerial control. Here, however, I want to focus on the adequacy of these techniques for realizing the purposes for which they are designed.

One of the most powerful critiques of managerial mystique is to be found in MacIntyre's *After Virtue*. MacIntyre casts the manager as one of the 'central figures' of our age, whose claims to legitimate power rest in large part in their assumed expertise in realizing organizational effectiveness. This effectiveness is 'inseparable from a mode of human existence in which the contrivance of means is in central part the manipulation of human beings into compliant patterns of behaviour' (1981: 71). Social science through the medium of management education has clearly served as one of the main sources of 'knowledge' on which such claims to expertise are based.

The force of MacIntyre's critique lies in his attempt to disclose such expertise as a fiction; specifically a moral fiction. He seeks to undermine the whole project of behavioural control with the simple assertion that, 'Our social order is in a very literal sense out of our, or indeed anyone's, control. No-one is or could be in charge' (1981: 101). He points to the inherent sources of unpredictability in social life, not least those created by individuals' attempts to escape the predicative behaviour of others.

If MacIntyre's assertion is accepted, the implications for management education are genuinely radical. Negatively it suggests that the claims to expertise that are the basis of management teachers' authority are shattered along with those of the students who have paid so much to be introduced to the secrets of administrative control. The desire for means to control others may be there, along with techniques which claim to be able to realize such control. Nevertheless, they cannot realize such organizational order in their own terms. Positively, MacIntyre's assertion implies that in place of the illusory comfort of manipulative techniques, the most important product of a management education should be an insistence that the student recognize that he or she is not in control and instead begin to develop the habits of mind and action consistent with the reality of organizational interdependencies.

In order to explore further MacIntyre's assertion of the fictional character of management expertise I intend to look more closely at the nature of management practice. Here I will draw on Giddens' (1984) structuration theory as a source for what I will argue is a more adequate account of practice than that assumed in technicized forms of management education, and in this way begin to point to the overlap between critical views of management and the realities of management practice.

Giddens' work seems particularly appropriate for the themes that I am attempting to develop here, since his work seeks to develop a synthesis of streams of social thought that have themselves generated on the one hand uncritical managerialism and on the other unrelenting criticism of the role of management. Rather than attempt a full summary of structuration theory here, I merely wish to draw out some of the most significant implications of this theory for our understanding of the conditions and consequences of management practice.

Giddens (1979, 1984) characterizes his own work as an attempt to map out an analytical ground that avoids the dual extremes of what he terms 'voluntarism' and 'determinism': those who view the agent as a mere cypher for social structural forces and action theorists who emphasize the creative character of agency. It can be argued that these two extremes are themselves both represented in the pursuit of behavioural control that is the allure of much management education; the would-be manager seeks the knowledge with which to render others predictable in the service of their own unreflected and assumed autonomy of action. In place of these dualisms Giddens develops a view of what he calls the 'duality of structure'. In an attempt to avoid the elision of the terms system and structure that is found in functionalist theory, Giddens reserves the use of the word system for an understanding of the practical interdependencies that characterize social and organizational life. Stable patterns of interdependencies in organizations and societies are to be explained in terms of the 'virtual order' of structures of signification, legitimation and domination. These structures, rather than determining action, are instead described as 'the medium and outcome of action'. Through being drawn on in interaction, structures provide the knowledge, rules and resources that shape relationships and their outcomes. However, these structures are themselves only produced and reproduced through action.

What is attractive in this formulation is the central yet always conditioned role that is given to agency. The allure of techniques is that their application will immediately render practice more efficient. It is as if efficacy lies in the power of the technique, for which the manager is merely a vehicle – a neutral technician. What Giddens' formulation of practice makes clear is that like all knowledge, technique does not translate directly into practice, but rather what is key is the manner and context in which these techniques are drawn on by the agent. Techniques, themselves the historical product of interested labour, are merely a resource for the manager and in this way the neglected character of the manager as agent comes into central view.

Technical instrumental reason typically takes for granted the ends that action serves. There is also a tendency to assume a mechanical form of causality, as if means will automatically produce the desired result if applied appropriately. Finally, within instrumental reason there is often an implicit assumption of the separation of the acting subject from the object of action. The view of practice that emerges in structuration theory undermines each of these assumptions. It is a view of practice as profoundly creative. Not just plans and projects but the whole of organized social life is only produced and reproduced through action. The 'organization' and others are not the given context for action, but rather action contributes to the creation of this context. In place of mechanical causality there is an insistence on what Giddens calls the 'recursive' nature of knowledge; through action we reshape the world in the image of our knowledge of it. Analytical techniques such as accounting which purport merely to reflect the 'objective facts' of organizational life are from this perspective constitutive of these facts (Hines, 1988; Roberts and Scapens, 1985). There is no place for the individual outside the social order; both action and refraining from action are events in the world. At the same time, by insisting that the agent is self-conscious and constantly 'reflexively monitoring' their own and others' actions, this is a view of practice in which there are no passive victims or masters. The reduction of others to the status of predictable objects, which is the promise of so many techniques, is immediately revealed as an omnipotent phantasy. Simultaneously, critical theorists who make an easy identification with the oppressed are forced, as was Burawoy (1979), to explain individuals' active participation in their own exploitation.

While the view of practice that emerges from structuration theory is more profoundly creative than that implicit in technical views of practice, the relationship of the agent to their practice offers a number of important qualifications to the ideal of objective rationality that is the goal of such techniques. In place of objective rationality Giddens talks of the 'rationalisation of action': the reasons we give to others and ourselves for what we do. Giddens is keen to avoid what he calls the 'derogation of the lay actor': the tendency within social science for the expert to dismiss the subject's own understanding of themselves and their situation. In this regard, much of management theory can be seen as an attempt to develop techniques that circumvent the subjectivity of others; so that the manager already knows the motives of his or her staff better than they do. At the same time, the efficacy of management techniques and their enduring appeal can begin to be understood not in terms of these producing the organizational predictability and control that they superficially promise, but rather in the way that they provide the manager as agent with legitimate rationalizations for their actions. In this light the efficacy of technical knowledge is principally ideological (Pfeffer, 1981).

But while such rationalizations of action are under certain circumstances the best guide to understanding the action of ourselves and others, Giddens insists that they are in no way exhaustive. There is always a tension between how action is rationalized and the practical understanding embodied in what we do. What Giddens calls 'practical consciousness' spans the awkward divide between what is preconscious and hence in principle accessible to consciousness and what is truly unconscious and hence resistant to self-reflection.

Let us look first at the nature of preconscious knowledge. Giddens insists that most practice is habitual, routine and based on tacit, taken-for-granted knowledge. It could be argued that it is precisely the progressive intention of technical management education to bring such habitual action under the inspection of reason and thereby to enhance its rationality. Here, however, I would argue that in its emphasis on technique (objective) to the relative neglect of the student (subject) who might make use of such technique, such education actually compounds rather than advances the cause of rationality. Classroom teaching, even with the help of case studies, is unavoidably discursive in character and thereby easily encourages the student to believe that understanding has been realized if only knowledge can be repeated or regurgitated; in other words, has itself become routinized. That techniques are typically taught with little or no questioning of the ends they might serve, or indeed the taken-for-granted beliefs and assumptions of those who might use them, further reinforces the lack of critical reflection. In sum, the danger of much technical management education is that it gives students the rhetoric of objective rationality, while leaving their practical rationality both unexplored and unreformed. It encourages an escape from the potential perils of subjectivity rather than a full understanding of its creative possibilities and inevitable limits.

The taken-for-granted character of individuals' practical consciousness is reinforced by deep and largely unconscious attachment to ways of seeing and the routine and habits that support them. Giddens suggests that routine and habit have as one of their main effects the maintenance of a sense of personal security and well-being. Learning at the level of practical consciousness is therefore likely both to encounter resistance and to generate anxiety. Such unconscious sources of practical motivation in their assumed irrationality are of course an affront to the promise of professional neutrality and objectivity that is the goal of most management education. But I think that it is more profitable to think about the unconscious in terms of the powerful sources of affect which arise within the context of our practice and relationships (Craib, 1989). Viewed in this light, the pursuit of the ideal of objectivity and technical rationality can be seen itself as a form of irrational defence that wishes to sanitize practice, and through the promise of the certainty of control rob experience of the discomfort and uncertainty inherent in our practical dependence on others (Hirschhorn, 1988; Reed and Palmer, 1972). As Adorno and Horkheimer (1979) suggest: 'Man imagines himself free when there is no longer anything unknown'; the illusory comfort of objective fact and techniques of control is that they will banish uncertainty and unpredictability and the fear that goes with this from the realm of practice.

This last point brings me to a final set of issues around the nature of practice. Giddens talks of the 'paradigmatic' character of action: we act in relation to tacit models of self-world. The instrumental orientation to action that is fed in much of management education proceeds from and helps reproduce individualism; a belief in the essential separateness and solitariness of the individual ego. From within such an assumption there is only an external and instrumental orientation to others and the world. Causality is uni-directional and mechanical (Berger and Luckman, 1966). The problem with this form of reasoning is that it repeatedly fails to consider the effects of our own actions within the model of the world in terms of which we act.

In contrast to this rather disconnected image of action implicit in technical reason, structuration theory insists on the relational character of practice; on the essentially interdependent character of action. Practice involves us immediately in relationship with self-conscious others. The problem with instrumental action is that it is seldom present to itself. In its highly focused attention to particular future plans and projects it readily loses sight of the unintended consequences of action and the negative circularity of much social causality; of the numerous ways in which today's solutions generate tomorrow's problems. Action and those on whom it impacts are merely means to an end and in this way the unintended consequences of action are only recognized when means fail to achieve desired ends. However, the use of control techniques is rationalized, the manipulative intentions that they embody are unavoidably expressed in our practice, and discernible to others over time in the disjunction between what is said and done. Others' response to such manipulation then becomes part of the future conditions for our action, even if we do not recognize our own part in generating such conditions. Even in the absence of manipulative motives our actions almost inevitably escape our intentions, because action involves a dependence on other self-conscious subjects with different perceptions, interests and experiences. Techniques of control seem to offer a way around these dependencies, and indeed the history of much of management theory seems to have taken the form of ever more elaborate and extensive attempts at control (Clegg and Dunkerley, 1980). But the reality of interdependence points to the impossibility of the realization of such control.

It is in relation to this interdependent character of practice that instrumental reason seems to be particularly blind. To illustrate this point more fully I want to draw on the analytical categories of structuration theory: domination, signification and legitimation, as they relate to the management literature.

It is in terms of the theorization of power that there is perhaps the sharpest contrast between managerial and critical views of management practice. In one sense within the managerial literature power is simply taken for granted. It is that which is necessary for those with the role of co-ordinating social systems to secure the actions of others. This is the Parsonian view of power as a sort of system lubricant; since power is exercised in the interests of the system as a whole it is immediately conflated with authority. Given such assumed legitimacy, any resistance to the exercise of power is itself cast in the form of deviance. Within this overall set of assumptions about the legitimacy of managerial power, the organizational literature then restricts its attention to struggles within management for individual and departmental dominance.

By way of contrast, the more naive forms of critical theory insist that managers are no more than cyphers for the interests of capital (Braverman,

1974). Commercial organizations are the seat of unavoidable contradictions between the interests of labour and capital, and at best the manager is torn between the need to elicit co-operation and the need to exercise control (Littler and Salaman, 1984). What such managerial and critical perspectives share unwittingly is a rather passive view of the employee. Giddens' insistence on the ubiquitousness of self-conscious agency immediately questions this passivity. Giddens links his own analysis of power directly to agency; he talks of the transformative capacity of power, of the 'power to' do. (This linking of power and agency is parodied in the technologies of empowerment as if this were something that could be given or demanded.) Such a view of power then informs his view of the dynamics of power relationships. In interaction, power in the form of rules and resources is drawn on by both parties to the relationship. In opposition to the technicist vision of perfected administration Giddens argues for what he calls a 'dialectic of control'. Whatever the relative 'balance' of power, he argues that within the course of a relationship there is always autonomy and dependence in both directions.

What comes into sight here is the self-defeating character of power dynamics in many organizations. The effectiveness of technical control can claim superficial empirical support from the reality of others' conformity. However, as I have argued elsewhere (Roberts, 1984), techniques of control are effective not because they give the manager control over the behaviour of others, but by encouraging in subordinates a similarly individualistic and instrumental orientation. While such individualism may apparently secure relative advantage for management, what it often also achieves is something like a negation of collective power. Within the terms of individualism power is always talked about in relative terms, as something that one person has over another. However, the reality of practical interdependence is such that attempts to make a reality of this misconception over time serve only to add further twists to the cycles of control and counter control that characterize so much of organizational life, and weaken the interdependencies on which the collective survival of the organization depends (Knights and Roberts, 1982). As Daudi describes:

> While the first exercise 'their' coercive power, the second develop contra-coercive mechanisms of protection which take the shape of various strategical actions. This often results in a vicious circle. Among the 'antagonists' a spirit of low trust may develop, accompanied by losses of energy since attention is channelled into pseudo-activities, into intrigues and various attempts to contract each other's space of action. (1986: 2–3)

An at least tacit recognition of the negative dynamics of hierarchical power seems to have informed the recent interest in the concept of organizational culture. Managers are invited to become 'managers of meaning'; to move in Walton's (1985) terms from 'control to commitment'. While hierarchy emphasizes compliance based on threats and inducements to individualized interests, the emphasis of cultural analysis seems to be on the tacit shared meanings that invisibly bind organizational members. As an instrument of self and organizational understanding the concept of culture has considerable potential, and yet technical reason has immediately sought to transform such understanding into an instrument of executive control (Smircich, 1983). Culture becomes just another, albeit more subtle set of variables to be manipulated (Ray, 1986). Thus Peters argues that, *'these devices – vision, symbolic action, recognition – are a control system, in the truest sense of the term.* The manager's task is to conceive of them as such, and to consciously use them' (1987: 486, original emphasis).

In a paper that is particularly pertinent to the views being developed here, Willmott suggests that such 'Corporate Culturism' embodies an attempt to bring instrumental reason to bear on the control of the 'affective domain'. In his view it involves 'the *systematizing and legitimizing* of a mode of control that purposefully seeks to shape and regulate the practical consciousness and arguably the unconscious strivings, of employees' (1993: 523, original emphasis). 'Strong' cultural values communicated through the complementary technology of 'transformative leadership' (Bass, 1990) offer the 'beguiling' promise of both personal autonomy and shared purpose, as long as these purposes are those espoused by the leader.

While acknowledging the totalitarian quality of the aspiration to manage the affective domain, and indeed the practical organizational transformations that are attempted in the name of culture, I want here to point to what I see as the inherent limitations of such technicized cultural imagination. Precisely because managerial studies of culture, such as those of Peters, are communicated as new technologies of control, my sense is that they preclude in those who would imitate the 'excellent' those vital moments of critical reflection on both self and what is already taken for granted in the organization. Such critical reflection might reveal the contradictions between what is being said and done, or call into question assumptions into which the manager has long been socialized. Instead millions are invested in culture change programmes and the formation of corporate statements of vision and values, that often leave what is communicated in practice untouched; they thereby add no more than further confusion and distrust to already distorted patterns of communication within an organization.

In fairness, the more sensitive managerial accounts, even if they cling to a rather homogenous view of culture, emphasize the importance of practice. Schein's (1989) account of culture, for example, insists on the tacit, taken-for-granted character of assumptions and on the difficulties involved in bringing such assumptions to awareness. Practice is thereby seen more properly as the unconscious carrier of cultural beliefs. In a similar vein, Argyris' (1990) analysis of 'defensive routines' is alert to the tension between what is merely espoused and 'theory-in-use', and traces the distortions of internal communication to the actual practice of managers. Although neither of these writers can be said to feed the illusion of omnipotence that informs technical approaches to management education, both can be criticized for presenting an overly psychologized conception of organizational life, in their neglect of the economic inequality that conditions interests in manipulation and defensiveness.

Nowhere in the managerial literature on culture is the structure of ownership and inequality that is reproduced in capitalist organizations itself called into question. At best attention is deflected from this by appeals to the arguably limited and instrumental values that all might share. The promise of cultural control is that peer pressure to conform to 'shared values' and self-discipline will relieve the manager of much of the burden of the external control of staff behaviour. But the conditions and consequences of economic power are still evident in practice and all too easily assert themselves to reveal precisely what is not to be shared.

Here it is necessary to speak of what I will call the laziness of the powerful. Perhaps the emphasis on technique in management education in part reflects a belief that power in the sense of others' compliance can be taken for granted. The imbalance of resources is such as to render obedience almost automatic. The effectiveness of economic power can be simply assumed, or at best thinly concealed beneath a collective rhetoric of common endeavour. Such beliefs about power can readily be discerned in the practical contempt for subordinates that often seems to be expressed in managerial practice; indeed that informs the technocratic imagination. To achieve a position of power offers the chance of making one's own meaning and interests count over others and can be grasped as an alternative to engaging seriously with others' meanings. In this sense the acquisition of power over others is inimical to learning, for with luck power will allow the consequences of both an individual's incompetence and greed to be displaced onto others (Rueschemeyer, 1986).

Within the limits of the technocratic imagination, talk of practical interdependence is both preposterous and frightening, and yet what critical studies of the actual consequences of culture change programmes suggest is that nowhere are their consequences quite what is intended. Instead what is produced is dramaturgical compliance, managerial isolation or personal retreat (Anthony, 1990; Kunda, 1992). In other words, the attempt at cultural control runs foul of the reality of interdependence.

The reality of interdependence brings me to the question of managerial legitimacy. Technical management education is clearly in the business of providing the symbols of legitimacy to managers: the label of an 'MBA', the neutral rhetoric of efficiency and objective necessity, the backing of 'facts and figures'. While the managerial literature simply assumes the legitimacy of the ends that managerial activity serves, and critical approaches easily assume their illegitimacy, the position I would take points back to the creativity of practice. Richard Sennet (1980) talks of authority as the constant breaking and remaking of meaning; in this sense managerial authority can neither be assumed nor denied *ex ante*, rather it is the condition and consequence of managerial action. Or as Anthony writes,

The authority of management must rest upon a moral base, secure in a concern for the integrity and the good of the community that it governs. That authority must be achieved, won rather than imposed: it cannot be sought by coercion or by the deceptive application of psychological tricks . . . Real authority must rest upon real moral concern perceived to be real because its intentions are real. It may, it must be acknowledged, contribute to greater reciprocal commitment but that must not be its purpose. (1986: 199)

For the manager, authority comes both from above in the form of authorization, and below in terms of voluntary co-operation. A critical view of management practice can similarly focus both on the sheer incompetence of much practice, as well as the realities of exploitation that so often accompany such incompetence. Between them these tensions seem to define the space of action that is available to managers, within which there is the opportunity for more or less skillful, and more or less destructive action.

The technocratic imagination seems willing to recognize its dependence on others only as it denies this dependence in an omnipotent attempt to reduce the other to the status of dependable object. The alternative is to recognize the stark reality of this interdependence which includes colleagues and the wider social and physical environment. As Bateson puts it, 'The unit of survival – either in ethics or in evolution – is not the organism or the species but the largest system of "power" within which the creature lives. If the creature destroys its environment, it destroys itself' (1972: 332).

Implications for Management Education

In the above I have sought to expose the limitations of technical views of management practice through drawing on the arguably more sophisticated view of practice that Giddens has developed in his structuration theory. I now want to consider the implications of this view of practice for management education. The above analysis suggests that if management practice is to be seriously addressed by management education, then what is required is a series of 'turns' or reorientations in both the content and manner of the conduct of such education.

From Morally Neutral Technician to Agent

The first reorientation that I want to consider could be characterized in terms of a shift from a focus on the manager as neutral technician to a focus on the manager as self-conscious agent. An obvious problem with a great deal of formal education, including management, is the way that it tends to ignore or marginalize the lived experience of the student. Teachers, in their desire to legitimate their knowledge with the status of objective science, eschew the subjectivity that nevertheless informs both the choice of what it is relevant to know and the interpretation of the 'facts' such knowledge generates. For some students too there seems to be a desire to escape the limitations of their own subjectivity by an embrace of objectivity. There seem to me to be good reasons to resist these tendencies in management education.

It is easy for education to treat students as mere empty vessels waiting passively to be filled with expert knowledge. The above discussion of practice, however, makes very clear that action is shaped by the accumulated experience and understanding of a lifetime. Moreover, the knowledge that informs action, practical consciousness, is almost entirely taken for granted. Each individual student brings to the class, and to their practice as a manager, deeply engrained habits of thought, feeling, perception. The hope of much technically oriented education seems to be to supplant this understanding with something more rational, and yet by engaging only with the assumed instrumental interests of the student as would-be functionary I believe that the more usual outcome is that the student's practical consciousness is left unexplored and untouched.

A Reflexive Turn

All this implies the need for a reflexive turn in management education: that it should attempt both to bring to awareness and then reflect on what the student brings to the class; that it should encourage them to look more closely, or look again at what they thought they knew. Rather than displace their subjectivity with objective fact, they should work to develop their capacities for critical self-understanding.

The implication here is that to be meaningful there is a need to move away from education as mass consumption. As in the management of any change there is a need to unlearn, and this requires first that the student should become aware of what he or she already knows. Such a reorientation to education has of course long been part of the project of those who advocate some forms of experiential learning. The recent interest in the 'learning organization' has typically included some element of 'self' or 'personal development' (Pedler et al., 1990). I see this as preferable to approaches that leave the manager's subjectivity unexplored. Nevertheless, in line with the earlier discussion of culture, it is easy for this reflexive turn to involve no more than the progressive instrumentalization of the self; the extension of new forms of 'self-discipline' over the productive self (Rose, 1989). I think that the content and form of what is taught here is all important.

To escape this limitation it is necessary for a reflexive turn in management education to offer more than new ways to criticize and discipline the self, and to open the way for students to explore their own experience of work more seriously. The smooth, planned and programmatic image of rational organization that inhabits the textbooks is typically at odds with the muddle and conflict that is the meat of work experience. The illusory promise of technique is that it can supplant the muddle and conflict. An alternative is to encourage students to take their experience more seriously and for education to attempt to support this critical self/world understanding rather than displace it with objective fact.

The most naive forms of Marxist analysis tend to cast the manager in the role of agent of capital, and locate the main division of interests within work organizations along the management/workforce divide. This has its mirror within the managerial literature in the tendency to address students as if they were to be part of the glamorous and most powerful cadre of senior managers. By encouraging students to reflect on their own lived experiences of work it is likely that the divisions within management will come into sight. The recent decimation of middle management in 'downsizing' exercises implies that the managerial role can no longer count on corporate protection. Multidivisional and multinational structures frequently create a corporate capacity to attempt to secure their perceived interests at the expense of individual and business unit survival. Technical approaches to management education in feeding the promise of control simply deny the reality of this experience of dependence, or easily cast it as a matter of shame or personal failure. In emphasizing the sovereign autonomy of the rational individual – managers' right to manage – their own domination by others and the ways in which their own actions unwittingly contribute to this are ignored.

From Autonomy and Independence to Interdependence

The attraction of most MBA courses seems tacitly to depend on the insecurities of egoistic ambitions of the students. The MBA is viewed not only as the necessary if not sufficient condition for those that aspire to senior positions, but increasingly has come to be embraced as a potential defence against the widespread insecurities of the managerial labour market. The paradoxes of such individualism are twofold. In pursuit of individual security or ambition individuals are drawn increasingly into conformity with the expectations of powerful others. The promise of future autonomy becomes the justification of present conformity. The organizational consequences of such individualism are at best mixed. On the one hand, it results in the subordinate's nervous preoccupation with the perceived interests of distanced powerful others; in other words, it realizes and secures hierarchical control. On the other hand, it tends to create sharp lateral divisions between individuals and groups; divisions that weaken and distort the integration of task dependencies both within and across different functional groups (Roberts, 1991).

In arguing for a shift in management education from an emphasis on independence and autonomy to a focus on interdependence, I am suggesting only that the practical conditions for effective organization are taken seriously. To encourage the illusion of omnipotent control simply blinds students to the practical conditions and consequences of what they do. Reed's (1985) distinction between the collaborative system and the control system offers some sense of the main dimensions of such interdependencies. On the one hand, there is the system of hierarchized and individualizing domination where in the name of some distanced power – the market, senior management – we come to practise power on ourselves and each other. On the one hand, there is what Reed calls the collaborative system, the practical interdependencies within and beyond the firm that make up the 'transformation' of production. In regard to the latter, Anthony (1986) argues that MacIntyre's critique of technical management has confused the textbook with reality; management practice is often part of the nascent 'community' that forms around the activities of production.

The inescapable reality of organizational interdependencies, and the redefinition of the management role in more systemic terms, are now strongly represented in the managerial literature; for example in the work of Peter Senge (1990) and Larry Hirschhorn (1991). But while the rhetoric is there, it has yet to be embodied in much of the practice of management education.

One can point to the highly individualistic and competitive classroom climate that is the consequence of the continued use of examinations as the primary mechanism for student appraisal. As Foucault (1977) notes, the exam is one of the modern instruments of disciplined subjectivity. It is the main instrument for the control of the student body, and yet its effect within the classroom and beyond is to reproduce a highly individualized mentality. The negative consequences in educational terms are several. Understanding is pursued not for its own sake but only where marks or grades are at stake. While competition has its place, it tends to set the students against each other and thereby weakens the degree to which each serves as a resource for others' learning. Competitive debate displaces the potential for creative dialogue. The ability to demonstrate the appearance of learning replaces the deeper appraisal of substantive shifts in self-understanding. Finally and most importantly, since 'results' are individual, little or nothing is learned about the conditions for effective practical co-operation with others. It is no surprise that MBA courses are often in effect vehicles for the production of analysts and consultants, experts who work at a distance from organizations, rather than a training for individuals who are effective at working with others within organizations. This outcome is simply a reflection of what has been emphasized within management education; distanced 'objective' analysis and technical expertise rather than the skills of practical engagement.

Sketch for the Teaching of Management Practice

In the previous section I suggested a number of reorientations or turns that are needed if the teaching of management is to get closer to the reality of management practice. Here I want to sketch out the way in which we have attempted to embody these concerns in the new MBA programme at Cambridge University.

In many respects the programme has a similar content to almost any other MBA; all the functional disciplines are there, all the analytical techniques are taught. However, it is in the framing and delivery of this content that we have attempted to make a number of innovations.

Unusually, we attempt directly and explicitly to address the nature of management practice through a course that runs through all three terms. Professional views of the nature of management occupy the middle term of this course, but this is framed by terms that focus on the personal and ethical character of practice. Students typically arrive expecting to be taught only how to manage others. Against this expectation, we begin with a course that insists that students reflect first on how they 'manage' themselves in one-to-one relationships and in groups. Our intention here is to break the fiction that practice can be sanitized of all subjective or personal content. We begin conventionally enough by a simple introduction to communication skills. Skills are important, and if taken to heart can readily transform practice, but our experience suggests that the understanding that shapes practice is simply not open to this form of prescriptive training. To illustrate this gap, and to begin to engage with students' practical understanding, we spend most of the term working with unstructured groups that attempt to reflect on the process of the group's formation and development. These are supported by lectures and seminars that reflect on students' prior experience of work and organization.

What we are attempting here is to make use of immediate classroom experience as a direct resource for learning. The class provides a context in which individual motives are revealed directly in the collision and collusion of different individuals' wants. The uncertainty inherent in this kind of learning inevitably surfaces the accumulated emotional as well as cognitive habits that individuals bring to their relationships with others. Contemporary management writers suggest that such uncertainty will be the defining characteristic of both individual and institutional experience in the coming decades; Peters (1987) even suggests that we should learn to 'thrive on chaos'. Classroom and organizational experience suggests that practical uncertainty is met more typically by massive but largely unconscious individual and group defences that rapidly overwhelm all pretences to rationality. The classroom thus provides both the experience of uncertainty and an opportunity to reflect on the individual and collective responses to such uncertainty. As the student group dynamic unfolds there are opportunities to experience and reflect on the dynamics of dependence and omnipotence. Whatever the material benefits of power, psychologically it can easily take the form of a sort of group seduction that ultimately harms both the individual and the groups they lead. To alert students to the unconscious and driven character of the desire for power, to cast it as a defensive reactivation of infantile omnipotence, potentially offers them a more rational sense of their own limitations and potentials. As the preoccupation with relative power subsides, so then attention can shift again to processes around the formation of group culture and the possibilities of consensus grounded in dialogue.

Experience to date suggests that the learning in this part of the course is difficult and slow; seemingly as much is learned from the frustration of expectations as from their fulfilment, but this inevitably implies a rather lively relationship between class and facilitators. Whatever its difficulties, making use of the classroom context in this way immediately confronts students with a realistic sense of the conditions and consequences of their own and others' practice. While psychology is often introduced into MBA courses in the form of manipulative techniques, here its focus is oriented to reflection and to self-understanding. The habitual nature of practice, the tacit nature of most knowledge, the reality of individual differences of perceptions, the uncertainty, difficulty and causal circularity of reciprocal dependence, are all encountered directly and offer a stark contrast to the comforting yet illusory promise of techniques for the prediction and control of others.

Only in the second term, when we hope that students have at least some ability to distinguish between their own needs and assumptions, and the needs and perceptions of the other individuals and groups on whom they depend in their work, do we move on to look at professional views of management practice. Much of the literature here is focused on theories about the control of staff, but again we explicitly contrast this with critical views of the management role, and a direct consideration of the bases of managerial authority. Overall the view of practice here is drawn from systems theory and uses the language of boundary management to define the nature of management practice (Hirschhorn, 1991). The emphasis is on the management of interdependencies as a condition for the realization of the organizational task, within which coercion and exploitation can be seen to have a largely disruptive effect. At the very least we hope to leave students with a sense of the contradictory pressures that they will have to balance in creating their own space of action within an organization, and the ability to distinguish between leadership as self-serving rhetoric and genuine institution building (Mant, 1983).

This distinction is then opened out in the final term through a stream of classes that focus on both corporate and individual ethics. Courses on the physical environment and on the social, moral and political consequences of work attempt to explore the consequences of management activity from beyond a managerial frame of reference. Such material cannot be taught in expert mode. It is an area for judgement and individual choice. We believe, however, that there is value in creating a space within the course where such questions can be raised legitimately. Habermas (1971) insists that the problem with instrumental reason is that ethics as such disappears as a category of life. All choice is reduced merely to the calculation of means and ends. Again, classroom dialogue, the legitimation of the personal voice against the seeming imperative of organizational need, is intended to model the behaviour and processes whereby institutional objectives might be moderated by individual ethical concerns.

Along with other more conventional aspects of taught material, the learning from this part of the course is constantly reinforced through a series of work-based assignments. The course is taught over three terms, but runs for a total of 21 months. Between the first and second terms the students spend a year working full-time back in their host or sponsoring organizations. This structure allows for a constant iteration between the taught content of the course and the students' direct experience of management work within their own organizations. By means of organizational assignments the conceptual content of the course is reinforced and developed by requiring students to use this to understand their own immediate work situation.

Although the assignment work ends with a focus on the management of change, the basis for this is set through largely diagnostic work that requires students to investigate, reflect on and describe both the context and process of work. The outer context is studied in terms of macro-economic influences, and the competitive strategy of the business. The inner organizational context is mapped using a form of 'soft-systems methodology' that has the advantage of fracturing the assumed unity of 'organization' into the partial and interested perspectives of different functional groups, customers and suppliers. The very process of researching this context models the interpersonal and intergroup dependencies that constitute the organization, and at the same time usually reveals the points of intersubjective dissonance that are the condition and consequence of the organization of the task system.

The merit of this structure seems to lie principally in the way in which it deepens the level of students' learning. Because of the gap between explicit knowledge and the tacit knowledge that informs practice, there is always a danger that purely academic courses will leave practical understanding untouched. The assignments necessitate that the students digest concepts in order to be able to use them to describe the organizations in which they work. At one level this could be seen as no more than an insistence that students 'apply' the understanding that they have 'acquired' in the classroom to the management of their own organizations. In practice, however, the process of 'application' is anything but mechanical. In being asked to use concepts students are obliged to learn again what they thought they had already learned. In looking at their own organizations through the lens provided by such concepts they are similarly challenged to view afresh an organizational world that they had come to take for granted.

Conclusions

In the above I have sought to explore just one way in which we are attempting to break the stranglehold of technical rationality in management education. As Alvesson and Willmott put it, 'Management is too potent in its effects upon the lives of employees, consumers and citizens to be guided by an instrumental form of rationality' (1992: 1). In doing so I feel that one is necessarily working against the grain. MBA courses inevitably appeal to students' instrumental interests in securing their own future career. Thus their initial explicit orientation is one in which the world and others, including staff, are seen primarily as means or obstacles to the realization of their personal wants. Such a mentality is reinforced by the insecurities of labour and product markets. To confront such an orientation seems only to court rejection; it seems necessary instead both to feed and to challenge it, within its own terms and in terms of wider ethical concerns. As I stated in the introduction, rather than merely oppose the technical with the moral my concern is to bring these two spheres into closer relation with one another. Collective action is typically weakened by the deflections of energy involved in domination and individualistic resistance. Incompetence as well as exploitation both carry the weight of moral responsibility.

It seems to me that technical views of management practice are open to criticism both from within and beyond instrumental reason. From outside such views can be seen to embody the intention to dominate others and can be criticized as such. From within instrumental reason there is no evidence that the application of techniques of control actually realizes the control that it seeks. Even management writers such as Drucker (1974) are wise enough to recognize that 'controls weaken control'. In other words, technical views of management practice are both amoral and ineffective within their own terms of reference. In either case a more complex view of practice seems to be required. Nevertheless, a great deal of management education still seems to play on the insecurities and greed that wish to believe in the possibility of such managerial omnipotence, and enormous amounts of energy and suffering are generated in the attempt to make an organizational reality of such illusions.

The alternative to these illusions seems to be to recognize the social, relational and political character of practice; to acknowledge the reality of practical interdependence and to learn the disciplines of acting within such limits. This in turn implies an education that is addressed to the person who will be a manager, rather than to the manager as functionary.

I believe that it is important to teach that systems are only produced and reproduced through individual action and interaction, and to point to the space of action that this implies. What I have in mind here is what Deetz (1992) calls 'responsive micropractice'; the possibilities for individuals to recognize their own collusion, to speak against their fear, to challenge thought, to act from a sense of care for others – in sum, to take responsibility for the creativity of their immediate actions. Only in such attention to the minutiae of everyday practice is there hope of disentangling the destructive forms of organization from the productive. In this respect the classroom is potentially a safer setting than the workplace to reflect, experiment, challenge and demand; a place to begin to build a skilled awareness of everyday practice. Management education might thereby find for itself a fuller role as a resource to help the individual acknowledge and confront the dilemmas of managerial work, both instrumental and moral, rather than escape to the illusory neutrality of the technician.

References

Adorno, T. and Horkheimer, M. (1979) *Dialectic of Enlightenment*. London: Verso.

Alvesson, M. and Willmott, H. (eds) (1992) *Critical Management Studies*. London: Sage.

Anthony, P. (1986) *Foundation of Management*. London: Tavistock.

Anthony, P. (1990) 'The paradox of the management of culture or "he who leads is lost"', *Personnel Review*, 19 (4): 3–8.

Argyris, C. (1990) *Overcoming Organizational Defenses*. New York: Prentice-Hall.

Bass, B. (1990) 'From transactional to transformational leadership: learning to share the vision', *Organizational Dynamics*, Winter: 19–31.

Bateson, G. (1972) *Steps to an Ecology of Mind*. New York: Ballantine Books.

Berger, P. and Luckman, T. (1966) *The Social Construction of Reality*. New York: Doubleday.

Braverman, H. (1974) *Labor and Monopoly Capital*. New York: Monthly Review Press.

Burawoy, M. (1979) *Manufacturing Consent*. Chicago: University of Chicago Press.

Clegg, S. and Dunkerley, D. (1980) *Organization, Class and Control*. London: Routledge and Kegan Paul.

Craib, I. (1989) *Psychoanalysis and Sociology: the Limits of Sociology*. Hemel Hempstead: Harvester Wheatsheaf.

Daudi, P. (1986) *Power in the Organisation*. Oxford: Blackwell.

Deetz, S. (1992) *Democracy in an Age of Corporate Colonization: Developments in Communication and the Politics of Everyday Life*. New York: State University of New York Press.

Drucker, P. (1974) *Management: Tasks, Responsibilities, Practices*. Oxford: Butterworth-Heinemann.

duGay, P. and Salaman, G. (1992) 'The cult(ure) of the customer', *Journal of Management Studies*, 29 (5): 615–33.

Foucault, M. (1977) *Discipline and Punish: the Birth of the Prison*. Harmondsworth: Penguin.

Giddens, A. (1979) *Central Problems of Social Theory*. London: Macmillan.

Giddens, A. (1984) *The Constitution of Society*. Cambridge: Polity Press.

Habermas, J. (1971) *Towards a Rational Society*. London: Heinemann.

Habermas, J. (1989) *The Theory of Communicative Action. Vol. 2*. Cambridge: Polity Press.

Hines, R. (1988) 'Financial accounting: in communicating reality, we construct reality', *Accounting, Organizations and Society*, 13 (3): 251–61.

Hirschhorn, L. (1988) *The Workplace Within*. Cambridge, MA: MIT Press.

Hirschhorn, L. (1991) *Managing in the New Team Environment*. Reading, MA: Addison-Wesley.

Knights, D. and Roberts, J. (1982) 'The power of organization or the organization of power', *Organisation Studies*, 3 (1): 47–63.

Kunda, G. (1992) *Engineering Culture: Control and Commitment in a High Tech Corporation*. Philadelphia: Temple University Press.

Littler, C. and Salaman, G. (1984) *Class at Work: the Design, Allocation and Control of Jobs*. London: Batsford Academic and Educational.

MacIntyre, A. (1981) *After Virtue*. London: Duckworth.

Mant, A. (1983) *Leaders We Deserve*. Oxford: Blackwell.

Marcuse, H. (1964) *One Dimensional Man*. London: Routledge.

Nord, W. and Jermier, J. (1992) 'Critical social science for managers? Promising and perverse possibilities', in M. Alvesson and H. Willmott (eds), *Critical Management Studies*. London: Sage.

Pedler, M., Burgoyne, J. and Boydell, T. (1990) *The Learning Company: a Strategy for Sustainable Development*. London: McGraw-Hill.

Peters, T. (1987) *Thriving on Chaos*. London: Macmillan.

Peters, T. and Waterman, R. (1982) *In Search of Excellence: Lessons from America's Best-run Companies*. New York: Harper and Row.

Pfeffer, J. (1981) *Power in Organizations*. Cambridge, MA: Pitman.

Ray, C. (1986) 'Corporate culture: the last frontier of control', *Journal of Management Studies*, 23 (3): 287–97.

Reed, B. and Palmer, B. (1972) *An Introduction to Organisational Behaviour*. London: The Grubb Institute.

Reed, M. (1985) *Redirections in Organizational Analysis*. London: Tavistock.

Roberts, J. (1984) 'The moral character of management practice', *Journal of Management Studies*, 21 (3): 287–302.

Roberts, J. (1991) 'The possibilities of accountability', *Accounting, Organizations and Society*, 16 (4): 355–68.

Roberts, J. and Scapens, R. (1985) 'Accounting systems and systems of accountability: understanding accounting practices in their organizational contexts', *Accounting, Organizations and Society*, 10 (4): 443–56.

Rose, N. (1989) *Governing the Soul*. London: Routledge.

Rueschemeyer, D. (1986) *Power and the Division of Labour*. Cambridge: Polity Press.

Schein, E. (1989) *Organisational Culture and Leadership*. Oxford: Jossey-Bass.

Senge P. (1990) *The Fifth Discipline: the Art and Practice of the Learning Organization*. New York: Doubleday.

Sennet, R. (1980) *Authority*. London: Secker and Warburg.

Smircich, L. (1983) 'Concepts of culture and organizational analysis', *Administrative Science Quarterly*, 28: 339–58.

Walton, R. (1985) 'From control to commitment in the workplace', *Harvard Business Review*, March–April: 77–84.

Weber, M. (1978) *Economy and Society*. CA: University of California Press.

Willmott, H. (1993) 'Strength is ignorance, slavery is freedom: managing culture in modern organisations', *Journal of Management Studies*, 30 (4): 515–52.

5

Critical Theory and Management Education: Some Strategies for the Critical Classroom

J. Michael Cavanaugh and Anshuman Prasad

Over the last decade, critical theory has emerged as a subdiscipline of considerable promise. This comes at a time when the number of critical scholars in the academy is on the rise, new theoretical modalities are flourishing, and when even conventional academicians are experiencing doubts about the explanatory power of the rationalistic project. Yet, in spite of these encouraging signs, it is our sense that critical discourse continues to exert only a marginal influence over the management curriculum, owing primarily to the inability of its proponents to tie it to 'the mundane but important world of management' (Alvesson and Willmott, 1992: 17).

This apparent disparity between theorizing and practice should be of particular concern to those interested in critique because the business classroom represents a key, arguably *the* key, location for implanting and validating a critical programme for developing alternatives to economistic understanding. Although many factors have contributed to the theory/practice 'gap', in this chapter we propose that criticism's problematic of application derives from an institutional failure to engage in self-examination. Accordingly, we speculate about the roots of this problem, and conclude with a provisional empirical framework designed to aid instructors and students in the reflexive project.

Management and Criticism

> I consider it to be an urgent task to disengage from concepts that are being deadened by routine; use the meaning that they regain both from a re-examination of their history and from a reflexion on their subjective foundations. That, no doubt, is the teacher's prime function. (Lacan, cited in Norris, 1991: vi)

In so far as management scholarship in the United States is concerned, criticism[1] won a recognized, albeit begrudged, niche in the academy with the publication of Peter Frost's seminal *Academy of Management Review* article (1980). Indeed, although some pioneering work (for example Baran and Sweezy, 1966; Benson, 1977; Braverman, 1974; Brown, 1978; Burawoy,

1979; Clawson, 1980; Clegg, 1979; Clegg and Dunkerley, 1977; Edwards, 1979; Greenfield, 1979; Heydebrand, 1980; Nord, 1974; Perrow, 1979; Silverman, 1970) had preceded the Frost piece, the outpouring of critical work since constitutes critical theorizing as a subdiscipline of considerable power and promise.

The rise of criticism in disciplinary status seems all the more remarkable when one considers the terminal objectives of critical and conventional scholarship. Unlike conventional analysis, emphasizing inductive and deductive argument useful for goal setting and problem solving within the literature's reigning instrumental 'explanatory form' (Kahn, 1990; Shalin, 1992; Wise, 1980), critical discourse is meant to be *practised* as an *act* of resistance to any 'free-standing' (foundational) theoretical institution unwilling or unable 'to think about thought itself and to consider possibilities in addition to actualities' (Sack, 1992: 40). Besides offering alternative frameworks, the critical discourse aims to 'unsettle' the prevailing empiricist management agenda by enrolling it in the contemporary debate about the proper perspective for examining 'things' (Knights 1992; Sack, 1992; Smart, 1976).

The Perceived Crisis of Criticism

> criticism today lacks all substantive social function. It is either part of the public relations branch of the literary industry, or a matter wholly internal to the academies. (Eagleton, 1984: 7)

We are concerned, however, that, in spite of the inroads made in the academic literature, critical thinking as such has yet to penetrate standard organizational behaviour and management texts (and, by extension, corporate practice). Nor, to our knowledge, is criticism a standard course component in business school curricula at any level in the United States or Canada. Not surprising, perhaps, considering the attention-shaping power of the prevailing management (technical) paradigm (Forester, 1985). But, while ideological and discursive factors deserve attention (Said, 1978), an exclusive emphasis along these lines fails to acknowledge criticism's role in the creation of its own fugitive status.[2] Thus, the interest here is in formulating an empirical framework to stimulate reflection on criticism's crisis of relevance, our contribution to it and what might be done about it.

Self-examination, however, is reputedly not a pain-free procedure; and will require, if it is to have any chance of success, that we refrain from wearing our 'isolate individuality' (the private contemplative access to 'hidden' meanings) on our sleeves (compare with LaCapra, 1989; Lentricchia, 1980). Too much is at stake here. Indeed, pressure for self-criticism arises from a suspicion from within that criticism as a practice is rapidly becoming superfluous (Cain, 1984; Eagleton, 1984). (Interestingly, some mainstream academicians are openly having second thoughts about the empirical relevance of their own literature as well (Cavanaugh and

Prasad, 1994).)[3] It seems to us, then, that articulating a reflexive mechanism of some kind represents an institutional need of the first order.

Since the basic purpose of this chapter is to spur discussion regarding the development of a reflexive business school curriculum, we have chosen to organize it along the following lines. We begin with a discussion of what we have termed criticism's mutually reinforcing problems of placelessness, accessibility and reflexivity, in order to problematize some long-standing institutional and conceptual features shaping the critical project; and second, a sample of pedagogic strategies is offered as a means to enrol the business student and instructor in transforming the business classroom into a site of intellectual engagement as opposed to one of closure as currently practised. This, hopefully, will not only create a collaborative forum for testing technicist understandings, but the plausibility of critical modalities as well.

Placing Ourselves under the Microscope

The Problematic of Placelessness

Forsaking the classroom not only means that criticism as an institution is left without a site to (re)produce its understanding of the world, but that it abandons its validating practical mandate to make a difference through intervention in practical life (Eagleton, 1984).[4] As Atkins (1989: 3) observes, 'Clearly, the classroom is one of those (contesting) places, arguably the most important one, where the future of theory is being played out' (compare with Freire, 1970). We concur with Atkins (1989) and other commentators (Cain, 1984; Eagleton, 1984; Said, 1978), who fear that if critical theory's rhetoric–action gap is not closed in the classroom, and soon, the critical project runs the risk of seeing itself reduced to yet another self-occupied form of 'intellectual work' isolated from matters of real-world concern.

Critical theorizing's crisis of (under)representation (curricular irrelevance) is attributed by various observers to a number of factors, including the claim that university reputations are built first on publication as opposed to teaching records; the institutionalization of critique, that is when concern for praxis is superseded by careerism, specialization and routine (Cain, 1984; Graff, 1985); the reputed eclipse of critical theory's arch-nemesis, positivism, within the philosophy of science – what point in kicking a proverbial dead horse? (Bernstein, 1988; Caldwell, 1982); and, perhaps most significantly, the legacy of personal and programmatic weightlessness (Weberian *Angst* – compare with Shalin, 1992) following the Frankfurt School's loss of faith in the idea of the working class as reflective subject.

Arguably, the practice of criticism was most impacted by this last factor. First, to this day theorists grope for an adequate theory of politics (Best and Kellner, 1991) as well as a setting for its implementation (the problem of placelessness). And second, the yawning theoretical hole left by the loss of the working class as historical agent could be interpreted to mean that reflexivity, more or less by default, was hereafter the exclusive preserve of *homo-academicus*. Reflexivity, in effect, was 'a matter wholly internal to the academies' (Eagleton, 1984; compare with Lash, 1993). Willy nilly, Marx's worst fears seemed to have materialized; that is to say, criticism had suffered a Hegelian-like intellectualization. The upshot seems to be a quiet redefining of discursive horizons involving a more or less discrete retreat from criticism's traditional programme of establishing an inclusive social arena for enlightened critique (Eagleton, 1984) to an individualist (privatized) and vicarious emphasis on the rehabilitation of ruling-class self-consciousness (*Selbstbewußtsein*) (compare with Burrell and Morgan, 1979; Meszaros, 1989; Shalin, 1992; Wellmer, 1971).

The Problematic of Accessibility

Gaining a basic appreciation, not to mention a level of competence, in the critical mode is more difficult than it needs to be. Perhaps this can be attributed in part to the process of academic proprietorship cited above. What does it say, for example, when someone of the intellectual where-withal of Anthony Giddens struggles with Habermas' prose (Giddens, 1979)? Arcane disquisitions on epistemic and ontological fitness, albeit intellectually absorbing to specialists, are not likely to win many student converts. However, if including students in the critical conversation is a worthy social and institutional goal, then a genuine effort must be made to show students how criticism is relevant to their everyday lives. This does not necessarily mean that core concepts must be thrown overboard or watered down. On the contrary, but a critical pedagogy will demand a new commitment to formulating vocabulary, models and techniques that support an inclusive process.

Another way to think about this is to ask if scholarship is sufficient in itself as an agent of social change. We, obviously, have our doubts. Accordingly, the task before us, we believe, is to inaugurate a practical programme for bringing the critical 'programme', to ground – for elaborating a 'plane of action' (Koestler, 1984). In our view, this entails an undergraduate and graduate curriculum/pedagogy based on re-establishing critique's ties with everyday issues of life and human happiness (Putnam, 1978). Theorizing's problematic, abstract and fugitive status aside, can anyone doubt, particularly in business schools, the need to provide students with the means to step back from indoctrination? That is, to equip students *via what we write and teach* with the intellectual *Selbstbewußtsein* to form their own judgements so that they might come to understand their own connections with the issues that confront us as a society.[5]

Perhaps an example will make this strategy clearer. We typically introduce criticism's core notion of opposition as a contest over discursive/ creative space and the construction of self-identity, 'the ways we think, feel and act' (Harding, 1986: 19). In our experience, student interest rises when

critique is shown to be about the control of individual life opportunities –
for example, the core issues of who is healed first, who is housed first,
whose children get immunized, who dies first, who marries the doctor, who
gets to be the doctor, who removes the asbestos . . . in short, how each of
us will be treated and the resources available to us (Best and Kellner,
1991). Specifically, we try to demonstrate how the logic of instrumental
reason constrains life's chances by constraining discursive spaces. Indeed,
instrumentalist thinking conceives of progress as the moving away from
meaning (interpretation). Progress, in effect, is accomplished by nailing
objects down. The expansive object of critique, on the other hand, entails
the self-conscious process of back-filling or the recovery of discursive space
and choice (Smart, 1976). Through representations such as these, students
are encouraged to work out the normative implications of the ontological
suppositions shaping these competing traditions.

Specifically, each tradition is assessed on how it affects our ability to
respond (to feel, to act); particularly in terms of political and communal
action (Winner, 1986). Students, in effect, are pressed to identify the kinds of
social relationships promoted by each of these thought forms. Briefly, the
logics driving each are analysed in the following manner. Beginning with the
notion of a consistent and factual social world, instrumental reason relies on
techniques of abstraction to penetrate appearances and unearth the truth it
knows to be there (Evernden, 1992). But in the process of creating a 'literal',
two-dimensional landscape (Evernden, 1992) the de-'valuing' (decontamina-
tion) of discursive space is carried to an extreme. On one level, the urge to
abstract, to 'purify', to 'wrest the object of the external world out of its
context', itself entails a radical reduction of reality (Evernden, 1992: 68). On
another, the desired outcome of abstraction – the achievement of absolute
values (certainty) – precludes further discussion by naturalizing itself
(Knights, 1992; Young, 1993). In addition, because the strength of the
decontextualized object lies in its self-containment and completeness (its
'closure' – Knights, 1992), only those initiated in the application of
abstraction are privileged to speak for it. Such are the ways instrumental
discourse works to condense discourse in scope and participation.

One normative correlate of abstraction, students discover, is a regressive
fatalism before the aura of finished products. Individual agency tends to
shrink before the awesome necessity of nature. In its quest for formal truth
the 'dissociated point of view' not only reduces all subject matter to *objets
trouvés*, but circumscribes the field of moral and political action as well
(Sontag, 1977). As Young (1993: 10) puts it, 'In its hermetic and personal
vision, abstraction encourages private visions in viewers.' This symptomatic
retreat into self-absorption, plus the 'objectifying' distance underwriting the
privilege of radical simplification freezes the status quo through a strategy
of enervation, that is by 'making one less able to react in real life' (Sontag,
1977: 41). Not only is the consideration of other possibilities precluded
through a process of self-censorship, but having transformed the social
world into inevitable forms (a state of political impoverishment), everyone,

including the experts, becomes a bystander before their own creations (Sontag, 1977). The upshot is:

> the real relationship between man and his world is reversed in consciousness. Man, the producer of a world, is apprehended as its product, and human activity as an epiphenomenon of non-human processes. Human meanings are no longer understood as world-producing, but as being, in their turn, products of the 'nature of things' (Berger and Luckmann, 1967: 89).

In other words, ontological agency (one's politics) is constituted by the balance between the proportion of one's consciousness believed fixed, or indisputable, and that produced, or reworkable (see Figure 5.1). Critique, we offer our students, functions as a kind of alter ego by inverting instrumentalism's propensity for 'estrangement' (Israel, 1971). Suspicious of abstraction's bare surfaces, the critical theorist's task (and now the student's), therefore, is to plumb the invisible at close range in order to restore the denied empathy (human involvement) articulating subjects and objects (Gombrich, 1971; Smart, 1976). Discursive space (and consciousness) is recoupled by ascribing authorship to instrumentalism's naturalized universe. In this manner, self-transformation (praxis) takes place as one learns to interrogate 'objects'. As Rosen explains:

> The self is a social self, a social construct acquiring identity in relationship to the object. In the process of transforming the object, the self is also transformed. Hence, praxis involves transcendence of the subject/object dichotomy in that it involves not only the epistemological categories of theory and critique, but also the ontological categories of experience and doing. (1987: 578)

The Problematic of Reflexivity

> Most of us are capable of at least one meta-perspective, but I suspect few of us are capable of sustaining a meta-meta-perspective very successfully or for very long. (Hull, 1988: 9)

As illustrated in Figure 5.1, the praxic project to subvert the self-other duality by expanding the definition of agency (Colletti, 1972; Heydebrand, 1983) rests on shifting the canonical line leftward. The presumption is that simple awareness of the socially and historically constituted nature of the canonical line, represents the first step in (re)gaining the leverage necessary to change life's circumstances. Praxis, in this model, is less a discursive rupture than an incremental passage.

Nevertheless, a pedagogical agenda of reengagement is not likely to occur until enough of us realize that the argument here is first of all about ourselves (Walzer, 1987). Thus, in the spirit of self-examination, we address a third and last problematic. Specifically, it is our view that the concept of radical detachment (reflexivity) has compounded the elitist disposition noted earlier because, oddly enough, of the tendency to play it out on empiricist terms. That is, critique's claim to epistemic authority has been predicated – not unlike empiricism – on philosophical detachment – moments of 'unmediated' seeing. Both, it seems to us, rest on the undefensible

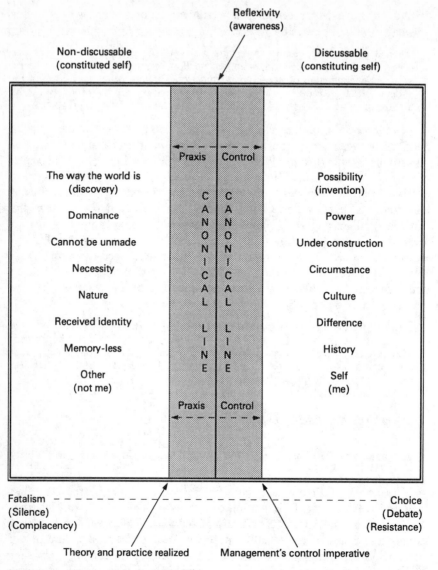

Figure 5.1   *The organization of subjectivity*

foundationalist premise that social connection invalidates criticism (undercuts subversion, in the case of critique). Critique's claim to self-deconstruction notwithstanding, we are concerned that this privileged claim to textual privatization only serves to essentialize critical discourse. The 'uninitiated' student, therefore, is left to guess how this *privileged intuitive authority* is acquired. The real question, then, becomes not whether students can be taught to think reflexively; but do we want to teach them?

Presuming the willingness is there, perhaps the question should be reframed to read, what can we do in the classroom to foster awareness of the existence and meaning of canonical line(s)? How, in other words, do we teach the perspective that thought is a product? This will entail, we propose, that reflexivity as a 'magical device' (Best and Kellner, 1991) for achieving 'a higher level of generality' (Adorno, 1977: 126) be supplanted by a demystified (operationalized), localized and on-going revaluation of the formation of oneself as thinker and moral agent.

There is no need to start from scratch, however. Taking our cue from Adorno (1977, 1989) and Foucault (1972), we challenge students to undo aspects of the solidified realm of being depicted in Figure 5.1 through analysis of the material conditions of discourse – or what we call the construction of authorship.[6] Memory, historiography, genealogy, immanent critique . . . each offers students an avenue to begin constructing their own perspectives through the juxtaposition (comparison) of the 'given' with the layers and dimensions of constructed 'memory' (historical specificity). Mindful of Habermas' discomfort with immanent critique (Habermas, 1987), it should be noted that the object here is not to recover concrete historical ideals to replicate in the present, but to create grounds for engagement through referentiality. The critical perspective that emerges from this dialectical give and take between thought figures provides the basis for a mediation (*Vermittlung*) that highlights the constituting forces and connections grounding a given phenomenon (Best and Kellner, 1991).

In the process, students gain an appreciation of the contingent relationships between the meaning of 'objects' and emotional epistemological context (Benson, 1983; Rosen, 1987). Specifically, students come to realize that the re-creation of social possibilities (as well as domination) depends on one's relative capacity for deconstructing and reconstructing objects (Adorno, 1977).[7] Thus, historicist constructs serve to problematize representation by fabricating 'ideas that illuminate and apportion the mass of the simply existing' (Adorno, 1989: 4). Students, in effect, are presented with an opportunity to expand and reinvigorate their own (perhaps monolithic) working texts by reinvesting previously unassailable knowledge with the memory of their origins. The agonistic process that sometimes results makes it possible to draw back into view the processes on which knowledge/ memory/choice are being constructed – coming to acknowledge that memory, for example, cannot exist outside of those people doing the remembering (Young, 1993). Additional classroom micro-strategies for facilitating the transition from dualities to dialectics are discussed in the next section.

Demystification and Engagement in the Academic Workplace: a User's Manual

The task of the critical researcher is to explicate the instances and processes of organization and its components – such as power, control, rules, goals, resources, production, and so on – in their socio-historical context. (Rosen, 1987: 576)

It should be no mystery by now that we are convinced that reflexivity (thinking about authorship and the agenda of authorship) cannot be passed on simply by talking about it. Indeed, the didactic approach only serves to mystify and privatize demystification. After all, we are asking business students, no less, to remake efficiency into a problematic, *the* problematic! Students, like the rest of us, need tools to work with. The material below, then, amounts to a user-friendly guide.

To begin, sooner rather than later, students need to be shown why unveiling authorship is so important. What useful social function does critique promote? Why do it in the first place? Depending on the class, we compose an explanation based on some of the following topics:

1   our concern that demystification will remain the exclusive preserve of academic theorists – thus mystified and elitist (Eagleton, 1984);

2   the *a priori* (objectifying and alienating) vocabulary composing the management discourse, that is, 'bond markets', 'price trends', 'accounting practices', 'technology', 'management', 'efficiency', 'the economy', 'stock exchange prices', 'interest rates', 'value chains' and the like, needs to be unpackaged if the marketization of seemingly every aspect of human experience is to be checked;

3   the power corporations wield over economic policy, democratic tradition – over subjectivity, no less (Deetz, 1992) – mandates that we scrutinize these undiscussable concepts out loud;

4   the 'second contradiction of capitalism' pitting unbridled consumption ('progress') and the ecology against one another (O'Connor, 1988) – that is, the corporation as a geophysical force;

5   the global mobility of capital and with it the intensification of Dickensian (junk bond, debt-driven and maquiladorian) capitalism in newly industrializing nations;

6   the marked decline of the typical employee's wages, benefits and standard of living over the last two decades. Or, you can follow Nancy Fraser's (1989) example and pull no punches:

> suppose that among other candidates for core elements of this framework (in need of contestation) are ingredients like the following: an organization of social production for private profit rather than human need; a gender-based division of social labor that separates privatized childrearing from recognized and remunerated work; gender- and race-segmented paid labor markets that generate a marginalized underclass; a system of nation-states that engage in crisis management in the form of segmented social welfare concessions and subsidized war production. (Fraser, 1989: 107)

Any one of these, we feel, justifies making engagement the core feature of our business courses. But acknowledgement of these issues is only that – an acknowledgement. Experience has taught us that students (or anyone for that matter) need to be walked through the concept of authorship and its corollary, authority.

We customarily split this task into four stages:

1   We devote a session to explaining that interest in unveiling authorship or taking representations on less than their face value possesses a long heritage extending back to Socrates and forward to contemporary organizational theorists like Jeffrey Pfeffer (1982).

2   By the same token, class time is earmarked for discussing our own intellectual indebtedness. This practice serves to underscore the notion that our representations are 'inevitably stamped with our own particular set of local interests, views, standards'. In other words, our students are made to understand that we don't speak from the mountaintop (Barnes and Duncan, 1992).

3   We next introduce a conceptual framework consisting of what we call the three streams of macro-authorship ('theoretical', 'paradigmatic' and 'structural' authorship) as a conceptual aid to students interested in working out a 'historical view' (Graff, 1990).

4   Last, we provide a set of cues in the form of questions designed to aid students recognize authorship at work. The details of this analytical syllabus are presented below.

Step 1 History of Critique: Composing an Institutional Memoir

Critical thinking has a long tradition in the history of human thought, going in some ways back to the Buddha (sixth century BC), Lao-Tzu (fifth century BC), and Socrates (fourth to fifth centuries BC). Confining ourselves, however, to the Western intellectual tradition alone (and bringing the focus of our scrutiny to more contemporary times), one needs to recall that, although modernity has been the target of concerted criticism during recent years (and rightly so, the authors of this chapter feel), the inauguration of modernity in Europe was also accompanied by the emergence of a deeply critical and sceptical sensibility (Connolly, 1993).

As Parekh (1973: 57), among several others, has pointed out, the European transition from the medieval to the modern was marked by intensive discussion, debate and criticism of 'the traditional (Western) view of rationality'. In brief, the 'traditional view of rationality' conceived of human reason as being independent of the thinker's socio-psychological make-up. This immaculate conception of human reason was challenged by several thinkers, including Machiavelli, Hobbes and Francis Bacon.

While Machiavelli, and later Hobbes, brought human reason down from its heavenly heights by arguing that reason's motive force rested in individual interests, Francis Bacon sought to demonstrate the fallibility of reason through his theory of the 'Idols of the Mind'. Similar critiques of reason were carried out by the eighteenth-century philosophers of the French Enlightenment, such as Condillac, Helvetius and Voltaire. In addition to this primarily psychological critique of reason, the medieval European conception of reason was subjected to a socio-historical critique by the German idealists, especially Hegel. These two streams of critique (namely, psychological and socio-historical) of medieval reason were brought to a unique and highly productive synthesis in Karl Marx's critical conception of ideology (compare with Larrain, 1979, 1983).

In some ways, the modern European critical tradition can be said to have 'come of age' (Larrain, 1979: 34) with Marx. After Marx, this tradition has been continued by such thinkers as Georg Lukacs, Antonio Gramsci, Karl Mannheim, the various members of the 'first' Frankfurt School, and many more. During recent years, the critical tradition has been further elaborated and reshaped by structural Marxists like Louis Althusser, by 'post-modern' thinkers such as Jacques Derrida, Michel Foucault and Jean-François Lyotard, and by Jürgen Habermas, 'the heir of the Frankfurt School of critical theory'.

Step 2 Locating Authority: Composing Personal Memoirs

It is also important to introduce students to the idea that our representations reveal as much about ourselves as the worlds they represent (Barnes and Duncan, 1992; Clifford and Marcus, 1986; Morgan, 1983). In other words, a critical understanding of our own politics requires an acknowledgement of the kinds of local interests bearing on personal authorship. We typically use James Clifford's (Clifford and Marcus, 1986: 6) handy checklist to explore some of the factors influencing the intellectual perspectives that both students and instructors bring to the classroom. Following Clifford's example, an effort is made to uncover links between our intellectual 'autobiographies' and current social context. This 'grounding' exercise also signals our intention to create an open, dialogic classroom atmosphere. Early on, then, we break the ice by acknowledging our own intellectual origins, our claim to authority (as academics, for example), and the historical context shaping these factors. We then ask students to 'anchor' themselves in a similar fashion.

Step 3 The Concept of Macro-authorship

We employ the concept of macro-authorship with a view to problematizing certain reified constructs such as 'the author' and 'knowledge'. The twin terms – 'the author' (sometimes the scientist) and 'knowledge' (sometimes science) – are words of extraordinary privilege in today's societies, and can be said to wield an almost mystical and metaphysical cultural authority in the contemporary world. By exposing our students to the idea of macro-authorship (that is to the possibility of something which is analytically prior and hierarchically superior to the individual author), we seek to gain some intellectual purchase for questioning the taken-for-granted authority of 'the author' as well as of 'knowledge'.

Everyday notions of 'the author' revolve around the individual as the autonomous producer of his or her texts. However, we regard it as important to introduce our students to the idea that the individual author may be more usefully thought of as a point of articulation for a series of macro-level forces. Schematically, these forces may be conceptualized, in ascending order of comprehensiveness, as (a) theoretical, (b) paradigmatic, and (c) structural.

Thus, rather than ascribing authorship to the individual whose name appears on the cover of a book, it is possible to show that there is a theoretical author (the theoretical framework of the work), a paradigmatic author (the knowledge frame within which theory is articulated), and the structural author (the social and historical conditions of possibility of a particular knowledge frame).

This may be clarified by a brief example. The author of a text on leadership and group processes is, in an everyday sense, recognized as having produced (authored) the text. But such a text may be understood to have (a) a 'theoretical author': the theory of consensual and co-operative organization (Barnard, 1938); (b) a 'paradigmatic author': functionalism (compare with Burrell and Morgan, 1979); and (c) a 'structural author' which includes, among other things, the Great Depression and the associated search for intellectual order that was one of the important conditions for the emergence of functionalism.

The foregoing example is merely suggestive, and is not meant to be a comprehensive analysis of macro-authorship. Even this highly brief analysis of 'authorship', however, successfully suggests that the individual author can more appropriately be regarded as merely enunciating the basic themes that have already been authored by the theoretical, paradigmatic and structural authors. Through this kind of analysis, students learn to recognize the temporality and embeddedness of knowledge.

The idea of macro-authorship is intended to alert students to the context-dependent nature of knowledge and, in the process, to bring 'knowledge' down from the mountain top. Far from being transcendent, universal and trans-historical, therefore, knowledge is shown to be always embedded in unique and specific socio-cultural contexts and formations. The result, we hope, is a dereification and demystification not only of the contents of specific bodies (for example organizational behaviour or human resource management) of knowledge, but also of the institutional apparatuses and arrangements that govern, regulate and discipline the processes of knowledge production.[8]

Step 4 Interrogating the Management Literature: Running Alvesson's Gauntlet

The issue here boils down to the following question - how does one recognize authorship when one thinks one sees it? Or, put another way, when should I be on the ideological alert? To assist our students in this regard, we suggest that they subject their management readings to the following question set:

Context Cue Does the author place his or her subject in a historical setting? Are influential events, theories and persons, not to mention a literature's (and an author's) roots, discussed? Does, for example, the author assume that his or her set of recommendations possesses universal application across all cultures? Does the author's context furnish enough information so that the reader can judge whether the author's statements are reasonable (Alvesson, 1987: 177)? More specifically, are descriptions of the actual working conditions of managers provided or not (1987: 175)? Or, is the author focused exclusively on codifying the successful experiences of leading organizational actors? Is interest, in other words, confined exclusively to the psychological (individual) level?

Power Cue Is power expressly discussed? If so, in what way? For example, are the origins of power relationships revealed? Is space devoted to who benefits and loses with the implementation of the author's programme? Or are issues of distribution and conflict ignored because the author assumes a level playing field where self-interest is excluded, and where management's purported intention is for everyone to benefit equally? ('Pluralism' and 'coalitions' are key terms here; see Alvesson, 1987: 184.) In short, are the interests of management and labour assumed to be the same?

Actualizability Cue When interrogating the management literature we ask students not to forget Astley's observation that 'theorists offer managers ideas, which, though they may not have directly instrumental or technical implications, crucially impact managerial practice in an indirect way in their role as symbolic constructs' (Astley, 1984: 269). We then ask them to judge the workability of the author's recommendations. Essentially, *can the author's recommendations be lived* – or are they 'no more possible than a community of saints' (Turner, 1984)? In other words, are detailed steps to implementation in specific situations provided? To answer this one, we ask students to slip on their manager's shoes and ask if IBM's management team, say, could actually implement the author's recommendations with the information provided? For example, is Peters and Waterman's (1982) solution to 'stick to the knitting' operational in any meaningful way? If not, proceed to ask what *is* the purpose of this recommendation.

Closing

> The real contradictions of our lives notwithstanding, the radical academic is not an oxymoron. (Fraser, 1989: 1)

Some may feel the need to complain that the 'micro-strategies and local deconstructions' aimed at de-isolating the critical scholar and the business classroom (Eagleton, 1991) enumerated here are hopelessly modest. And they probably have a point. No question, this *is* a conservative agenda, one bound to disappoint the vanguardist dream that intellectuals are pre-destined to play out in the Leninist tradition of left-wing democratic politics. But such complaints, we feel, tend to miss the point, because, in the meantime, political theory and theorists need and can be put to some practical use. Thus, the need to install an anti-essentialist and historically situated pedagogy in the business curriculum is as much about being a critical intellectual within the academy as it is about the 'conscientization' of the classroom.

Whether we like it or not, we have an institutional need to invite the business student to join in the debate, Our tradition obliges us to equip students with the means to form their own judgements so that they can see their own connection with the issues. Furthermore, the moment is ripe for inaugurating a democratic programme in schools of management. For one, democratically oriented scholarship, even in the US Academy of Management, is on the rise. A critical mass of critical scholars already exists. What is lacking is discussion about some kind of collective agenda. At the same time, the variety of tools at our disposal is without precedent. We are experiencing nothing short of 'a veritable explosion of new theoretical paradigms for political and cultural critique' (Fraser, 1989: 2). Last, recent comments by the incumbent president of the Academy of Management and his most recent predecessor seem to indicate that the academy's leadership, at least, is experiencing its own problematic of (ir)relevance (Cavanaugh and Prasad, 1994). This *Angst* may be our cue for 'redescribing social life' behind enemy lines.

Notes

1 In our view, criticism is the pedagogic route to 'conscientization'. By conscientization we mean that 'process in which men, not as recipients, but as knowing subjects, achieve a deepening awareness both of the socio-cultural reality which shapes their lives and of their capacity to transform that reality' (Freire, 1970: 27).

2 Rosen warns against complacency when he writes that 'Critical theory, therefore, is always critical and not utopian, for it is based on the proposition that although we may understand the limits of a theoretical system or organizational structure through critique, we must dismantle and transcend these limits *and our own opposing position at the same time*' (Rosen, 1987: 576, our emphasis).

3 Some leaders of the Academy of Management seem to be making the Academy's 'relevance' into a problematic. For example, in his 1993 Presidential address, David Hambrick expressed his concern that management scholars are becoming irrelevant to the needs of the 'real' world of organizations owing to the 'incestuous, closed [ivory tower] loop' that they have created for themselves (Hambrick, 1994: 16). Richard A. Bettis based his 1994 candidacy for the Academy's position of Vice President-Elect on the claim that 'The Academy faces a crisis of relevance . . . We need to recognize that we do, can, and should matter – should be important to managers and government policy makers' (Bettis, 1994). Whether this represents a Kuhnian watershed of sorts is anybody's guess at this point. (One might argue, of course, that it is the task of critique to make it into one.) However, even management writers like Etzioni (1989) and Mintzberg (1989) are growing impatient with functionalist remedies.

4 In principle, critique is grounded in the stipulation that ideas must pass muster. That is, theory is ultimately validated by its 'doing'; in this case, by demonstrating a capacity for producing change via research and teaching (Morgan, 1983; Wise, 1980). See also Albrecht Wellmer (1971: 11), who writes that the fate of theory does not hang on 'the judgement of scholars . . . but the assent of men who "speak and act for it"'.

5 This strategy, of course, may represent a real letdown for some Western intellectuals who, unlike their Eastern European counterparts, never got to enact 'the great, unlived romance' – the making of a revolution (Hoffman, 1993: 3).

6 Foucault makes the claim that objectifying forms of reason 'can be unmade, as long as we know how it was they were made' (Kritzman, 1988: 37).

7 With respect to the tug-of-war over the placement of the canonical line depicted in Figure 5.1, dominance is defined as the management of objectification – the inclination to shift the canonical line to the right.

8 The idea of macro-authorship raises some interesting questions in the context of the individual agency/voluntarism versus structural determination debate. A naive and decontextualized reading of the concept of macro-authorship may convey the erroneous impression that the authors of this chapter are arguing in favour of some sort of absolute and vulgar structuralist determinism. That, clearly, is not the case. Indeed, the very fact that we have written the present chapter shows our (qualified) faith in human agency and the possibility of (at least limited) change – a change that we hope goes somewhat beyond the rigid parameters imposed by some structuralist grammar. That being the case, it is more accurate to view this chapter as navigating a middle path between the twin extremes of absolute voluntarism and absolute determinism. For instance, in the early parts of the chapter, the authors emphasize voluntarism and 'social construction of reality' as an antidote against the managerialistic construal of social and organizational reality as an ontological given. However, it is important to note here that the conventional texts and writings of management are deeply complicit (consciously or unconsciously) in this construal of managerial reality. Indeed, it may not be an exaggeration to contend that the primary purpose of the various texts of management is to reaffirm this managerialistic construal of reality. If that be the case, it becomes imperative that the critical management scholar *subvert* the authority of the purveyors of conventional management knowledge. This chapter seeks to further this agenda of subversion by pointing to the *limits* to authorial autonomy, and by adopting the somewhat structuralist device of the three aspects of macro-authorship.

References

Adorno, T.W. (1977) 'The actuality of philosophy', *Telos*, 31: 120–33.

Adorno, T.W. (1989) *Kierkegaard: the Construction of the Aesthetic*. Minneapolis: University of Minnesota Press.

Alvesson, M. (1987) *Organizational Theory and Technocratic Consciousness: Rationality, Ideology, and Quality of Work*. New York: Walter de Gruyter.

Alvesson, M. and Willmott, H. (eds) (1992) *Critical Management Studies*. London: Sage.

Astley, G. (1984) 'Subjectivity, sophistry and symbolism in management science', *Journal of Management Studies*, 21 (3): 259–72.

Atkins, G.D. (1989) 'Introduction: literary theory, critical practice, and the classroom', in G.D. Atkins and L. Morrow, *Contemporary Literary Theory*. Amherst: The University of Massachusetts Press.

Baran, P.A. and Sweezy, P.M. (1966) *Monopoly Capital*. New York: Monthly Review Press.

Barnard, C.I. (1938) *The Functions of the Executive*. Cambridge, MA: Harvard University Press.

Barnes, T.J. and Duncan, J.S. (eds) (1992) *Writing Worlds: Discourse, Text and Metaphor in the Representation of Landscape*. London: Routledge,

Benson, J.K. (1977) 'Organizations: a dialectical view', *Administrative Science Quarterly*, 22: 1–21.

Benson, J.K. (1983) 'A dialectical method for the study of organizations', in G. Morgan (ed.), *Beyond Method: Strategies for Social Research*. Beverly Hills: Sage.

Berger, P. and Luckmann, T. (1967) *The Social Construction of Reality*. Garden City: Anchor Books.

Bernstein, R.J. (1988) *Beyond Objectivism and Relativism: Science, Hermeneutics, and Praxis.* Philadelphia: University of Pennsylvania Press.

Best, S. and Kellner, D. (1991) *Postmodern Theory: Critical Interrogations.* New York: The Guilford Press.

Bettis, R.A. (1994) Remarks made in an Academy of Management newsletter dated February 28, 1995.

Braverman, H. (1974) *Labor and Monopoly Capital.* New York: Monthly Review Press.

Brown, R.H. (1978) 'Bureaucracy as praxis: toward a political phenomenology of formal organizations', *Administrative Science Quarterly*, 23: 365–82.

Burawoy, M. (1979) *Manufacturing Consent.* Chicago: University of Chicago Press.

Burrell, G. and Morgan, G. (1979) *Sociological Paradigms and Organizational Analysis: Elements of the Sociology of Corporate Life.* Portsmouth, NH: Heinemann.

Cain, W.E. (1984) *The Crisis in Criticism: Theory, Literature, and Reform in English Studies.* Baltimore: Johns Hopkins University Press.

Caldwell, B. (1982) *Beyond Positivism: Economic Methodology in the Twentieth Century.* London: Unwin Hyman.

Cavanaugh, J.M. and Prasad, A. (1994) 'Legitimation Angst and the problematic of (ir)relevance: or what management theory may have to offer the practice of organizational change', paper submitted to the *Journal of Organizational Change Management.*

Clawson, D. (1980) *Bureaucracy and the Labor Process.* New York: Monthly Review Press.

Clegg, S.R. (1979) *The Theory of Power and Organization.* London: Routledge and Kegan Paul.

Clegg, S.R. and Dunkerley, D. (eds) (1977) *Critical Issues in Organizations.* London: Routledge and Kegan Paul.

Clifford, J. and Marcus, G.E. (eds) (1986) *Writing Culture: the Poetics and Politics of Ethnography.* Berkeley: University of California Press.

Colletti, L. (1972) *From Rousseau to Lenin: Studies in Ideology and Society.* London: New Left Books.

Connolly, W.E. (1993) *Political Theory and Modernity.* Ithaca, NY: Cornell University Press.

Deetz, S.A. (1992) *Democracy in an Age of Corporate Colonization: Developments in Communication and the Politics of Everyday Life.* Albany: University of New York Press.

Eagleton, T. (1984) *The Function of Criticism: From the Spectator to Post-Structuralism.* London: Verso Press.

Eagleton, T. (1991) *Ideology: An Introduction.* London: Verso Press.

Edwards, R. (1979) *Contested Terrain.* New York: Basic Books.

Etzioni, A. (1989) *The Moral Dimension: Toward a New Economics.* New York: Free Press.

Evernden, N. (1992) *The Social Creation of Nature.* Baltimore: Johns Hopkins University Press.

Forester, J. (1985) 'Critical theory and planning practice', in J. Forester (ed.), *Critical Theory and Public Life.* Cambridge, MA: MIT Press.

Foucault, M. (1972) *The Archaeology of Knowledge.* New York: Pantheon Books.

Fraser, N. (1989) *Unruly Practices: Power, Discourse, and Gender in Contemporary Social Theory.* Minneapolis: University of Minnesota Press.

Freire, P. (1970) 'Cultural action for freedom', Monograph Series #1, *Harvard Educational Review* and Center for the Study of Development and Social Change, Cambridge, MA.

Frost, P. (1980) 'Toward a radical framework for practicing organizational science', *Academy of Management Review*, 5: 501–7.

Giddens, A. (1979) 'Habermas' critique of hermeneutics' in J.W. Freiberg (ed.), *Critical Sociology: European Perspectives.* New York: Irvington Publishers.

Gombrich, E.H. (1971) *Norm and Form.* 2nd edn. London: Phaidon.

Graff, G. (1985) 'The university and the prevention of culture', in G. Graff and R. Gibbons (eds), *Criticism in the University.* Evanston, Ill: Northwestern University Press.

Graff, G. (1990) 'Other voices, other rooms: organizing and teaching the humanities conflict', *New Literary History*, 21 (4): 817–39.

Greenfield, T.B. (1979) 'Organization theory as ideology', *Curriculum Inquiry*, 9 (2): 97–112.

Habermas, J. (1987) *Lectures on the Philosophical Discourse of Modernity*, Cambridge, MA: MIT Press.

Hambrick, D.C. (1994) 'What if the academy actually mattered?' (1993 Presidential Address), *Academy of Management Review*, 19 (1): 11–16.

Harding, S. (1986) *The Science Question in Feminism*. Ithaca, NY: Cornell University Press.

Heydebrand, W. (1980) 'Organizational contradictions in public bureaucracies: toward a Marxian theory of organizations', in A. Etzioni and E. Lehman (eds), *A Sociological Reader on Complex Organizations*. New York: Holt, Rinehart and Winston.

Heydebrand, W. (1983) 'Organization and praxis', in G. Morgan (ed.), *Beyond Method: Strategies for Social Research*. Beverly Hills: Sage.

Hoffman, E. (1993) *Exit into History: a Journey through the New Eastern Europe*. New York: Viking.

Hull, D.L. (1988) *Science as a Process: an Evolutionary Account of the Social and Conceptual Development of Science*. Chicago: The University of Chicago Press.

Israel, J. (1971) *Alienation from Marx to Modern Sociology: a Macrosociological Analysis*. Boston: Allyn and Bacon.

Kahn, J.S. (1990) 'Towards a history of the critique of economism: the nineteenth-century German origins of the ethnographer's dilemma', *Man: The Journal of the Royal Anthropological Institute*, 25 (2): 230–49.

Knights, D. (1992) 'Changing spaces: the disruptive impact of a new epistemological location for the study of management', *Academy of Management Review*, 17 (3): 514–46.

Koestler, A. (1984) *Arrow in the Blue*. New York: Stein and Day.

Kritzman, L.D. (ed.) (1988) *Michel Foucault: Politics, Philosophy, Culture*. New York: Routledge.

LaCapra, D. (1989) *Soundings in Critical Theory*. Ithaca: Cornell University Press.

Larrain, J. (1979) *The Concept of Ideology*. London: Hutchinson.

Larrain, J. (1983) *Marxism and Ideology*. Atlantic Highlands, NJ: Humanities Press.

Lash, S. (1993) 'Pierre Bourdieu: cultural economy and social change', in C. Calhoun, E. LiPuma and M. Postone (eds), *Bourdieu: Critical Perspectives*. Chicago: University of Chicago Press.

Lentricchia, F. (1980) *After the New Criticism*. Chicago: University of Chicago Press.

Meszaros, I. (1989) *The Power of Ideology*. New York: New York University Press.

Mintzberg, H. (1989) *Inside Our Strange World of Organizations*. New York: Free Press.

Morgan, G. (ed.) (1983) *Beyond Method: Strategies for Social Research*. Beverly Hills: Sage.

Nord, W.R. (1974) 'The failure of current applied behavioral science: a Marxian perspective', *Journal of Applied Behavioral Science*, 10: 557–78.

Norris, C. (1991) *Spinoza and the Origins of Modern Critical Theory*. Cambridge, MA: Basil Blackwell.

O'Connor, J. (1988) 'Capitalism, nature, socialism: a theoretical introduction', *Capital Nature Socialism*, 1: 16–17.

Parekh, B. (1973) 'Social and political thought and problem of ideology', in R. Benewick, R.N. Berki and B. Parekh (eds), *Knowledge and Belief in Politics: the Problem of Ideology*: 57–87. London: George Allen and Unwin.

Perrow, C. (1979) 'Organizational theory in a society of organizations', paper presented at the *Public Administration: Future Perspectives* Symposium, Quebec.

Peters, T.J. and Waterman, R.H. (1982) *In Search of Excellence: Lessons from America's Best-run Companies*. New York: Harper and Row.

Pfeffer, J. (1982) *Organizations and Organization Theory*. Cambridge, MA: Ballinger.

Putnam, H. (1978) *Meaning and the Moral Sciences*. London: Routledge and Kegan Paul.

Rosen, M. (1987) 'Critical administrative scholarship, praxis, and the academic workplace', *Journal of Management*, 13 (3): 573–86.

Sack, R. (1992) *Place, Modernity, and the Consumer's World: a Relational Framework for Geographical Analysis*. Baltimore: Johns Hopkins Press.

Said, E. (1978) *Orientalism*. New York: Vintage Books.

Shalin, D.N. (1992) 'Critical theory and the pragmatist challenge', *American Journal of Sociology*, 98 (2): 237–79.

Silverman, D. (1970) *The Theory of Organisations*. London: Heinemann.

Smart, B. (1976) *Sociology, Phenomenology and Marxian Analysis*. London: Routledge and Kegan Paul.

Sontag, S. (1977) *On Photography*. New York: Anchor Books.

Turner, S.P. (1984) 'Social theory without wholes', *Human Studies*, 7: 259–84.

Walzer, M. (1987) *Interpretation and Social Criticism*. Cambridge, MA: Harvard University Press.

Wellmer, A. (1971) *Critical Theory and Positivism* (English translation by John Cumming). New York: Herder and Herder.

Winner, L. (1986) *The Whale and the Reactor: a Search for Limits in an Age of High Technology*. Chicago: The University of Chicago Press.

Wise, G. (1980) *American Historical Explanations: a Strategy for Grounded Inquiry*, 2nd edn. Minneapolis: University of Minnesota Press.

Young, J.E. (1993) *The Texture of Memory: Holocaust Memorials and Meaning*. New Haven: Yale University Press.

6

Is a Critical Pedagogy of Management Possible?

Christopher Grey, David Knights and Hugh Willmott

Prologue

The clock hands reached the angle of 90 degrees. As if primed automatically to do so, the students shuffled their notes into neat piles on their desk, exchanged glances that combined relief and mild resentment, and trooped out of the class. The lecture had not been a success.

Sometime later, Dr M, alone in his office, looked back at the afternoon's events and was confused. What exactly had gone wrong? For Dr M was a most conscientious teacher, who prepared his lectures with great diligence. He had been to a staff development course on teaching methods, and was well versed in the use of visual aids and handouts. Indeed, he had expended much effort in producing a detailed handout for each of his lectures. Moreover, he knew that his lectures could not be seen as too abstract or unrelated to practical matters since he always drew on 'real life' examples to illustrate his arguments. He also sought to indicate the implications and benefits of his analyses for the practice of management.

Last year, Dr M had tried using case study materials, but had fallen back on lectures when the students had failed to get involved in discussion, merely waiting for him to supply the correct answers. Still, he drew comfort from the fact that, each year, the students' exam papers showed that they had absorbed the contents of his lectures.

For all that, his students seemed bored in lectures, and when he overheard them talking in the corridor, they had said that the lectures were pointless. Given the time and effort put into the preparation of his lectures, this reaction was depressing. Dr M found himself looking forward to Christmas, when he could forget the students' surly indifference for a few weeks.

Introduction

Although a caricature, the case presented in the prologue draws attention to certain disturbing features of the education process in management and business schools, and perhaps elsewhere. Some teachers of management may identify with aspects of the experience of Dr M and his despair that his efforts to improve his teaching have been counter-productive. Unless indications of students' indifference or hostility to teaching are disregarded or simply taken as 'the norm', they should stimulate critical reflection on pedagogy in management education.

This chapter is the product of a collective process of reflection on, and experimentation in, management education. It draws attention to the character and limitations of conventional approaches to management education and introduces some of the intellectual sources of an alternative critical approach. It also presents an account of aspects of our attempts to operationalize such an approach, and identifies some of the difficulties to which this effort gives rise. Within the literature on education considerable attention has been given to critical pedagogy (for example Freire and Shor, 1987; Giroux, 1983) and, recently, these critical approaches have themselves been subject to critique (de Castell et al. 1989; Luke and Gore, 1992). However, within management education, scant regard has been paid to these debates, a situation we aim to rectify here.

The impetus for writing on this topic arises from the authors' experiences of teaching together in the late 1980s and early 1990s. One of us (DK) had established in the early 1970s the final year undergraduate course we will describe, while another of us (HW) taught on it as a doctoral student and again 10 years later when taking up a lectureship. The remaining author (CG) taught on the course between 1987 and 1993. Although this indicates that each of us made distinct contributions at different times, we were all actively involved in developing and modifying both the content and pedagogy of the course.[1]

In developing our teaching we have been operating on the basis of, and in reaction to, our understandings of more conventional pedagogies in a variety of institutions. In this regard, a note of caution is necessary: we have not undertaken here to provide detailed justifications of our understandings of conventional management education at undergraduate level, and it would be misleading to claim that the development of the course discussed later was informed by anything other than our experience. Nevertheless, as indicated by other contributions to this volume, our work elsewhere (Grey and Mitev, 1995a; Willmott, 1994a) and the work of others (Anthony, 1986), our understandings of undergraduate teaching are not without a reasoned and evidential basis.

Additionally, our pursuit of a critical pedagogy of management has been informed by research work in a whole variety of contexts, and in particular by our orientations towards orthodoxies in managerial knowledge (for example, Alvesson and Willmott, 1992a; Grey and Mitev, 1995b; Knights, 1992; Knights and Murray, 1994). Thus we begin by sketching the broad outlines of our position on managerial knowledge as a contextual prelude to the discussion of a critical pedagogy of management.

Management, Social Science and Positivism

The creation of management or business studies as a distinct academic discipline occurred relatively recently, although its roots can be traced back to the nineteenth century (Engwall, 1992). In recent years there has been a proliferation of departments and institutions concerned with management education, with buoyant demand for their courses.[2]

As an academic discipline, management draws its theoretical and methodological inspiration from the social sciences, and especially economics, psychology and sociology. Social sciences, in turn, can be seen to have emerged from the enlightenment project that has sought to reproduce the systematic study of the physical world in the social domain (see Kallinikos, this volume). A condition of possibility for such knowledge was the belief that human beings could be the object as well as the subject, or agent, of knowledge (Foucault, 1970). Following their natural science precursors, the social sciences were forged and framed around the preoccupation with securing 'objective' representations of human behaviour and social institutions (in other words, scientific knowledge) for purposes of controlling (Habermas, 1970) and/or disciplining (Foucault, 1979) aspects of the social world. Believing there to be no ontological discontinuity between physical nature and human beings, mainstream social scientists have subscribed to a methodology that critical philosophers of social science (Winch, 1958; Habermas, 1970) characterize, disparagingly, as positivist. While this is not the place to enter into an extended discussion of the philosophy of social science, we broadly agree with Giddens (1974: 1–4), where he identifies positivism as exhibiting three characteristics which we summarize here as:

1   the concepts and methods of the natural sciences (for example in terms of experimentation and the generation of general laws) are the most (or exclusively) appropriate for studying human activity;
2   knowledge arises from direct perceptions of the world, and nothing is real which is not knowable in this way;
3   value judgements are not knowable in this way and are inappropriate to scientific enquiry.

Despite a proliferation of critiques (for example Bernstein, 1976; Feyerabend, 1988), positivism continues to inform the social sciences that underpin and legitimize the management disciplines, as it supports and sustains what it presumes are the explicit objectives of practising managers to control and manipulate both employees and consumers for purposes of economic and/or other advantage (MacIntyre, 1981).

The positivism of the management disciplines has its roots in the engineering disciplines that extended their unproblematic belief in machine efficiency into the social domain of management. The shift from machine to social and economic organization was not accompanied by any epistemological or methodological reflection or refinement. From scientific management, through time and motion (T&M) studies to more recent innovations such as total quality management (TQM) and business process re-engineering (BPR), the overwhelming concern has been to *perfect* organizational and working practices in order to advance the goals of corporate management.

Elements of social science have thus been selectively appropriated and applied, but have rarely been deployed to reflect critically on the positivist assumptions and ambitions of managerial theory. Whether it is 'one best way', continuous improvement or customer-oriented process change, all of these approaches accord with the postulates of positivism in which knowledge is a product of direct observation, and where there exists a unitary and objective truth to be understood independently of the judgements of the observer. The basic assumptions of positivism and its associated anachronistic engineering ideology have been maintained and extended in mainstream approaches to management (Alvesson, 1987) and reasserted in the prescriptions of excellence, TQM and BPR (Grey and Mitev, 1995b; Wilkinson and Willmott, 1994; Willmott, 1994b).

These remarks serve to highlight the centrality of the positivist 'mindset' to the development of management theory. We now focus more narrowly on some of the problems for pedagogy that derive from this. To illustrate these we return to our fictional prologue.

Positivism in Teaching

In our prologue we implicitly depicted Dr M as operating within a positivistic universe where he views his teaching role as passing on to his students scientific knowledge about the world, as distilled in the textbooks. For Dr M, the problem of pedagogy is entirely an issue of how these facts can be presented in a way that is effectively consumed by students. However, what he overheard in the corridor worries him because quite clearly many of his students are expressing dissatisfaction with his teaching.

Having recently attended a staff development course, Dr M feels that he has improved his methods of presentation. He has also begun to encourage some student participation in lectures. However, he believes that this must necessarily be restricted since problems are deemed to have well-defined solutions. It may be recognized that there are a number of possible solutions, but the purpose of discussion is to identify the relevant issues and thereby to discover the correct solution of a particular problem. If the central content of lectures is the scientific truth, as established by research about the 'real world', then the only admissible evidence of successful learning is the mastery of these truths. Any questioning of those truths, except when posed in terms of 'relevant' problems, is represented in conventional pedagogies as a failure to understand the subject, or as the importation of irrelevant material. Thus to answer a question about, for example, marketing in terms of the virtues or vices of consumerism as a condition and consequence of the practices of marketing, does not normally constitute mastery of the facts relevant to the marketing domain. From the students' point of view, it is quicker and easier – 'progress' is more likely – when Dr M, buttressed by the authority of the textbook, defines and controls the boundaries of his discipline in a way that enables him to identify the issues, and answer the questions, himself.

Necessarily, we are presenting matters in extreme form. We recognize that students can be induced to be participative under certain conditions. These include being assessed on discussion; believing that discussion of this sort is a useful skill; not realizing that discussion is merely a pedagogical device to get them to identify for themselves that which has already been ordained as relevant.

However, we are sceptical of these devices for generating student participation, both because they are unacceptably manipulative and because they are readily seen as such by students who are likely to respond, at best, with the ritualized appearance of participation. Also, if pursued from within a positivist paradigm, in which knowledge is presumed to have an 'objective' status beyond interpretive discourse, we contend that there is little space, or indeed justification, for genuine student participation. In the face of these difficulties, what options are open to concerned management teachers such as Dr M? In the next section we elaborate on some of the most obvious alternatives.

Approaches to Management Teaching

The Staff Development Approach

In the face of problematical teaching experiences, the first possible response is one which might be characterized as the staff development approach. Our depiction of Dr M suggests that he has begun to pursue this approach, which is one of the dominant ways of addressing teaching 'problems'. The staff development response consists of attempts (whether directly involving staff development agencies or not) to refine and vary teaching methods. There is a whole field of knowledge production here, ranging from books which espouse 'tips for teachers' to elaborate training programmes for lecturers. Recent developments in so-called quality assurance have legitimated and extended these approaches, which often have as their principal objective the delivery of customer (that is student) satisfaction. In management education this commodified rhetoric of education is particularly dominant because it accords with the positivistic, engineering world view of managerialist academics (Grey and Mitev, 1995a).

In the main, what are being offered by 'staff development' programmes are adjustments to the means of communicating or delivering teaching material to students. These take at least two forms. One, which might be called the *hard* version is to stress the 'real-world' practical relevance of teaching through, in particular, the use of case-study material.

Alternatively, the necessary 'realism' of the hard version is achieved through recourse to students' own experience in organizations (especially on postgraduate and post-experience courses). Other attempts at realism involve the use of videos, role plays and so on. In general, this option involves the use of specific examples as a means of generating interest from students, and persuading them of the usefulness of their studies. By incorporating ever more specific 'real world' examples in their courses, teachers generally gain a good reception, not least because the narrative of case studies is easier to understand than abstract principles. Also it is an (albeit distant form of) 'hands-on' learning experience where students participate in simulated exercises to advance solutions to practical management problems. Here the teacher remains completely in control because students' solutions will invariably be critically examined in the light of a 'better', if not perfect, solution informed by the teacher's 'expert' knowledge. Unproblematical expertise, then, is the foundation of this hard version of the staff development approach. When students co-operate with this type of teaching it is often difficult to discern whether this is because they are convinced of the utility of the knowledge, or because they are anxious to secure the qualification.

The second variation of the staff development approach we call the *soft* version. This can take the form of techniques like role playing, but is also represented by the whole gamut of activities from ice-breaking exercises to psychodynamic work with groups of students, where learning is assumed to occur not just in terms of 'facts' to be acquired but also through the processes of working with information in simulated settings. This approach is underpinned by humanistic understandings of students as emotional actors who, as such, require the construction of a certain psychological context for them to learn effectively.

For present purposes, our criticism of both versions of the staff development approach is that they do not problematize the knowledge which they seek to transmit. Instead, the focus is consistently on the development of effective *means* through which management knowledge may be transmitted. The staff development approach *may* yield some success in increasing the perceived quality of the learning experience for students, but it does not constitute a critical pedagogy because it both embodies and transmits knowledge which could, and in our view should, be problematized.

The Discipline Approach

A second teaching approach is less explicitly managerial in outlook, and focuses on content rather than presentation. Here the teacher presents a body of academic knowledge which the student is expected to master. It is taken for granted that management students should acquire this knowledge, whether it be mathematical techniques or principles of economics or psychology. Such an approach is less concerned to make direct connections to the particularities of the 'real world' of management and business, although some connections will be more or less overtly assumed. This mode, which reflects the historical recruitment of discipline specialists into management and business departments, is perhaps more prevalent in undergraduate teaching than on postgraduate courses.

In disciplines where conventional epistemological and methodological assumptions are critically scrutinized, such teaching may constitute an alternative to positivistic orthodoxy. However, this scrutiny still relies on teachers' privileged access to the 'facts of the matter', albeit facts about bodies of disciplinary knowledge rather than about the 'real world'. Thus the disciplinary approach to teaching is dependent on a notion of the authority and expertise of the teacher, or established texts, as the arbiter of what is right and what is wrong. At the same time, the conditions which render knowledge of these 'facts' possible normally remain unexplored. Nevertheless, a disciplinary orientation is valuable in so far as it mitigates against descriptivism and managerialism.

The Critical Approach

There is, however, a third approach which we call critical. Here the frustration, instrumentalism and indifference that are commonplace in the context of conventional teaching, and the alternatives so far discussed, are used as a point of entry. They are treated as topics for exploring management that is sensitive to everyday experience and forms of 'knowledge' other than the purely disciplinary. This point of departure allows students to relate knowledge to their own experience of 'being in the world'. By this we mean not the discussion of experiences in terms of how they fit into textbook management theory, or how they might be mobilized to advance either variant of the staff development approach discussed earlier. Rather, we refer to students' work or non-work experiences of managing and being managed; of consuming; of being privileged or underprivileged within situations of inequality; and so on. Of course, there is considerable work to do here for, in the general run of things, students as well as academics tend to take for granted, confirm and legitimize conventional wisdom rather than subject it to critical scrutiny. In focusing on students' experience, we have in mind something quite different from the 'soft' techniques we considered earlier. For although such techniques take the form of experiential learning, and pay attention to students' experience, they do so in limited and limiting ways. Our focus on students' experience is a way of problematizing rather than validating that experience. Moreover, it is not a technique to sweeten the otherwise indigestible corpus of management knowledge. Rather it provides a basis for a critical reflection on experience as a means of subverting such knowledge. In other words, and in contrast to the first two alternative teaching approaches identified above, a critical pedagogy of management is not simply a new way of teaching existing management knowledge: its concern is to reflect critically on such knowledge as part of a more general development of critical management studies (Alvesson and Willmott, 1992; Knights, 1992).

On the basis of critical reflections on students' experience, it is possible to develop discourses which apprehend management as a social, political, economic and moral practice (Alvesson and Willmott, 1996; Anthony, 1977, 1986; MacIntyre, 1981). Teaching then becomes an activity that points to continuities and discontinuities between students' experience and bodies of literature. Such literature includes not only the literature of management, but also those of social science, philosophy and, indeed, fictional literature (Grey, 1996; Knights and Willmott, 1995). The latter can help students to identify the experiences of others in seeking to understand the nature of management. To illustrate more clearly how this third mode can operate, we now turn to our own attempts to put it into practice.

Teaching Management Critically

Our commitment to a critical approach to management informed the creation and development of an option for final-year undergraduate students. In this section we indicate our initial pedagogical 'moves' during the first few weeks of the option. These moves are significant because the course is found to differ from students' prior experience: it is therefore vital to foster interest and commitment from the outset.

While we would not claim that our approach is free of problems, it may well be a useful point of reference when developing a similar pedagogic approach in other institutions. It is important to realize that the use of this approach requires that teachers adapt themselves to a more open stance to their students than is commonly the case in institutions of higher education. In particular, we have consistently attempted to extend intellectual contact beyond the formal hours of teaching to informal times and venues. Our approach relies in part on developing relations of trust and honesty with our students, and for this reason we lay considerable stress on small seminar groups. We also make use of lectures, but depart from the conventional monologue where the teacher 'lectures at' the students by transforming them into participative events.

We seek to involve students fully in the course by asking them to reflect continuously and critically on the relevance of the topic under discussion, and on their own everyday lives as students, casual employees, family members, gendered subjects and so on. So, for example, the authority of the manager can be compared and contrasted with that of the father or mother, and rebellion against parents examined as a form of resistance to subordination which also occurs in employment relations. This readily leads to a reflection on processes of identity formation and the problems of reconciling dignity (closely associated with autonomy in Western cultures) with a subordinate identity. In this way we attempt to relate the content of lectures to students' experiences as well as seeking to involve them directly in the construction, or at least modification, of the content of the lectures.

We believe that to teach a critical management studies course in a conventional mode of pedagogy is a contradiction in terms. Just as conventional pedagogies arise from the epistemology of positivistic management research, so an attempt to teach material which is critical in character requires a critical pedagogy. On the other hand, our course exists in a context set by conventional pedagogies in accompanying courses. In these courses students find few opportunities to develop imaginative or creative insights about their work, and are more likely to seek out the 'least effort path' to attaining a degree. Our attempts to transform the process from one of learning by rote to one which involves student participation is threatening on two counts. First, both for students and for us as teachers, it removes the 'comfort blanket' of well-tried routines that have delivered students successfully through the education system so far; and second, it demands a higher level of commitment and effort. Despite the obstacles, however, most students on the course do, we believe, develop a greater degree of critical (self-)reflection with respect to the subjects and objects of knowledge and education.

The starting point in the course revolves around an exploration of the significance of Freire's critique of the 'banking concept of knowledge' (see Vince, this volume). Although many of the assumptions informing this work are problematized as the course develops, the idea of banking knowledge as an account of conventional education is one with which students readily identify. Indeed, our preliminary move does not make direct reference to Freire's work. Instead, students are encouraged to articulate and reflect on their own experiences of education. In particular, they work on preparing a list of the 'good' and 'bad' aspects of the degree programme in which they are currently engaged. This normally yields some quite heated discussion and debate.

In this way, it is established, right from that start, that discussion and debate are integral to the course. Moreover, apart from any pedagogical considerations, students' experience is one of the most legitimate forms of 'data' about the current state of management education. Students have much more immediate knowledge of the contemporary education process than most of their teachers. By inviting frank comments and criticisms of this process, students come to realize that our course and we, its teachers, entertain an open, if not directly oppositional, stance to the conventions of prevailing management education arrangements. Finally, and perhaps most significantly, we are able to 'come to' theory (in this case Freire's work on education) in a meaningful way.

In working with theory, we are not merely concerned to show its relevance to students' experience, although this is of value. Instead, what we try to convey is that reading the course literature can be exciting and enjoyable, and illuminate their everyday experiences, rather than a burdensome and painful obligation to be cleared out of the way with a minimum of time and effort. This both facilitates discussion and critique of the commonsense dualism of theory and practice, and paves the way for developing new orientations towards knowledge, which will be crucial for students' ability to engage with the subsequent development of the course. For example, students are enabled to move beyond some of their superficial criticisms of the teaching they receive as merely 'bad' or 'boring'. Although expressive of their lived experience, such blanket terms tend to obscure rather than enlighten, often by reducing the issues to the personality or indifference of the lecturer. By working from the start in the way described above, students are in a position, often for the first time, to depersonalize their criticisms and to recognize the link between the nature of the teaching, the conditions of its delivery and the types of knowledge which teaching seeks to reproduce.

At this juncture, it becomes possible for students to articulate a distinction between 'possessive' and 'relational' concepts of knowledge. Assisted by the discussion of Freire, students recognize that subjects are habitually taught as if knowledge were a 'fixed' entity that can become the property of an individual – a 'possession' that can be traded like a commodity in exchange for other goods. Of course, the examination system and the creditation economy give support to this view of knowledge, thus making it difficult for students to understand how the (mis)use of knowledge allows this edifice of power and status to reflect and reproduce structures of inequality. Nonetheless, because much of the experience of learning and memorizing 'facts' is comparatively boring as well as stressful (as is the accumulation and retention of property in general), students are partially amenable to an alternative, even though they are frequently confused and anxious about its content and consequences. In so far as their educational experience to date is almost entirely one of commodified knowledge which, once internalized, offers the security of dependency, this alternative can appear precarious and threatening as it cannot be managed through their routine coping mechanisms. It also demands considerable intellectual and emotional effort in rethinking what has for so long been taken for granted.

At this stage (which may only be two or three sessions into the course), student anxiety usually takes the form of questioning us about what they have actually learned. Unlike other courses, there is little evident structure, no textbook and no logical (and apparently rational) accumulated set of lecture notes that can provide them with a sense of security, however illusory. All students have are some readings, discussions in the seminars and a lecturer who is more intent on raising questions than supplying information or answers. How can we be examined, they ask, when you are continually suggesting that knowledge resides in social relationships and is not a concrete representation of the world itself?

At this point (and it generally requires frequent reiterations over the year), we point to the huge 'stocks' of knowledge that students routinely articulate and draw on in everyday life but which do not require any note taking or revision sessions. Whether this knowledge is general, as with

Table 6.1

Having	Being
Divided	Unity of 'being'
Passive	Active
Frustrated	Creative
Separation/isolation	Human solidarity
Following prescriptions	Taking choices
Denial of responsibility	Responsibility
Internalizing oppression	Overcoming oppression
Objectified being	Subjectified being

language for example, or specific to an activity such as fashion, music or sport, it is possible to show that in relating to this knowledge, students are familiar with aspects of education, management and organization, and have mastered huge amounts of material which it would be extremely onerous to learn through conventional lectures, textbooks and revision. Inevitably this leads to protracted debates about the alleged differences between such relational knowledge and the nature of a degree course: students will typically hold that their 'interests' and their 'studies' are quite divergent and separate. In this way, we are able to move from questions of knowledge to more general, but related, issues of 'being in the world'.

At the same time we constantly reassure students that they need not fear the absence of a list of 'facts' to memorize, as the exam and course work will seek to test the quality of thinking, not the quantity of what is thought. Relating to, and thereby understanding, knowledge as a dynamic process eradicates the necessity to memorize it, since like language such knowledge will have become part of everyday usage. In short, we invite students to reduce the distance between themselves and their studies, and give them confidence that this will not mitigate against their achieving 'good' results.

A consideration of being, once it has become established as a pertinent issue, can be approached in terms of Fromm's (1980) distinction of 'having' and 'being' (Table 6.1). This framework, introduced in response to students' own demands for an alternative to possessive notions of knowledge (which obviously relate to the 'having' mode), provides the basis for further reflections on students' lives:[3] such issues as motivations for taking the degree course, or relationships with friends, parents and partners all become relevant. In this way it becomes justifiable to the students that we subtitle this first section of the course 'Learning to Live'.[4]

An exploration of students' lives in these more personal ways requires careful handling. In seminar teaching, we seek to provide a comparatively relaxed and friendly environment which allows but does not force personal revelations, and in which teachers as well as students are 'open' about their experiences. But to repeat, critical pedagogy differs from traditional humanistic approaches in that students' experiences are not the focus for individualized 'self-awareness', but rather provide a starting point for subsequent work which repeatedly calls their knowledge and experiences into question in a variety of ways. As the course develops we pursue this questioning through a number of key concepts, particularly those of freedom, insecurity, power, inequality and identity (see Knights and Willmott, 1995). To this end, we use students' experiences to disclose and explore the socially constructed nature of reality (Berger and Luckmann, 1967) and of the self (Henriques, 1984) and how these constructions involve exercises of power which produce and reproduce inequality. Later in the course, we connect these insights more directly to students' past or potential future experience of work and organizational life.

From a comparatively inward-looking consideration of students' experience, we gradually move 'outwards' to connect this with broader issues, and to appreciate the relevance of 'critical' literatures, particularly those of Marxism and post-structuralism, to assist understanding. For many students, an acquaintance with work that departs from management orthodoxy is a refreshing, even exhilarating, experience. Although it may create short-term tensions in relation to the requirements put on them in other options, the course allows them to develop a critical consciousness which, we hope and believe, endures long after the regurgitated 'facts' of marketing, accounting and production, or the positivist theories of economics and psychology have been dispossessed.

Problems and Limitations

Although we have argued for a critical pedagogy of management, we are only too well aware of the difficulties and limitations such an approach entails. Some of these are inherent in this method of teaching, such as the problems of conforming to an examination system more suited to testing memory of concrete 'facts' rather than encouraging an active relationship with their precarious and problematic status. Other problems reside in the contradictory relationship to the institutionalized hierarchical structure which teacher and student typically inhabit. As we have hinted, the examination can be adapted to a concern with thinking, and hierarchy is not in itself an insurmountable obstacle to creative and critical discourse. It is not hierarchy itself, but the tendency for lecturers to hide behind it to avoid the threat of a student challenge to their ideas, that is the central problem in radical pedagogical reform. But there are other difficulties involved in such reform, to which we now turn.

The first set of difficulties relates to current developments within higher education in the UK and elsewhere. Increasingly, universities suffer from the twin constraints of resource shortage and the managerial recipes for remedying the problems that this shortage creates (Willmott, 1996). The most obvious effect of these developments is on class sizes which, as most readers of this volume will be aware, have increased dramatically in recent years as students numbers have risen, unmatched by an equivalent increase in teaching resources. The critical pedagogy we have advocated requires that lecturing and seminar teaching occur within reasonably small groups (say, 10 to 12 students) and, where these conditions cannot be met, its effectiveness is compromised. Additionally, because critical pedagogy involves teachers in particularly attenuated forms of intellectual and emotional labour, the increasing workload and demoralization experienced by many in higher education mitigate against the successful implementation of our approach.[5]

No less disheartening is the increasing pressure from institutions and government to conceptualize teaching (and research) in terms of criteria of 'relevance', defined in strictly managerialist terms (Grey and Mitev, 1995a; Willmott, 1994a). Such a conceptualization recasts education as training, and sets a premium on the acquisition of technical competences (see Thomas and Anthony, this volume). Although in many university management and business schools there exists, almost by default, a 'space' for critical and subversive teaching (Willmott, 1994a), the extent of this space is continuously, though often indirectly, subject to erosion. In particular, attempts to incorporate management teaching under the rubric of 'core competences' within an NVQ framework will, if successful, almost certainly pose a threat to critical pedagogies.

On a more positive note, the possibilities for critical teaching may in certain respects increase. Understandings of the changing nature of work in conditions of rapid economic and technological change may yet yield a greater legitimacy to pedagogies which develop analytical and conceptual abilities, as against strictly vocational and technical skills. At all events, it is incumbent on those who would seek to extend the scope for critical teaching to advance this argument. In many respects established management education is in crisis, and although this does not imply that changes will be desirable from a critical point of view, it opens up debate and at least the possibility for such radical changes (see Grey and French, this volume).

Yet another impetus which is generally seen as negative (because it is a further encroachment on academic freedom and a pressure to intensify even further the labour of academics) is the constant, and increasing, measurement of research output and teaching quality. Such scrutiny may be seen as an example of the disciplinary gazes to which the (management) academy is exposed (see Boje, this volume). Again though, it may offer unexpected possibilities. While we would not wish to deny that our labour is both devolved and intensified by these control mechanisms, those sympathetic to a critical approach tend, as a consequence of their intellectual and moral commitments, to be prolific in research output and comparatively student oriented. The 'added value' produced by such staff is of considerable benefit to their departments under current assessment regimes. Critical approaches are thus accommodated if not wholly endorsed. A more critical approach to teaching can also be turned to advantage when quality is at issue. Both in terms of meaningful relevance and active student involvement and participation, critical pedagogies are currently more likely to enjoy a favourable reception and, thereby, gain legitimacy. What at first sight may be regarded as a further constraint on critical pedagogical developments may, perversely, turn out to be an opportunity.

However, there is a second set of problems with the case we are putting forward for critical pedagogy, which is more difficult to understand and address than the pressure for managerialist relevance and the external demands for research productivity and teaching quality. This difficulty resides in the nature of the emancipatory claim of critical pedagogy. It is a claim that makes sense within humanistic discourses (Fox and Hodgson, 1995), where education is envisaged as maximizing the opportunity for self-expression and/or undermining ideological mystifications (Freire, 1972). But equally, Freire has articulated some potential contradictions in such emancipatory claims:

> We have very different ways of being authoritarian, no?, including a very false and very hypocritical way in which you make a manipulative appeal . . . [w]e can be authoritarian in sweet, manipulating and even sentimental ways, cajoling students with walks through flowery roads, and already you know what points you picked for the students to know. But, you don't want them to know your plans, your map. (Freire and Shor, 1987: 91)

In terms of the critical pedagogy we have outlined, it is clear that a potential criticism is that we encourage students to engage with ideas which *we* have identified, in advance, as important. At the strongest, we may stand accused of seeking to manipulate them into accepting, or at least mouthing, those ideas. To some extent this difficulty can be openly recognized, and thus obviated by explaining clearly from the outset that we, as teachers, necessarily have a certain set of commitments and interests. And, again to an extent, we can be seen to be learning from, as well as teaching, our students. But despite this, being placed in the role of teacher mitigates against the possibility of entirely suspending authoritarian relations. One way to address these difficulties could be by seeking to instigate a Habermasian 'ideal speech situation' in the classroom. But it is unclear how such a situation is to be reached in the absence of wider social transformations.

There are more profound developments of this argument. In engaging in critical pedagogies, and in encouraging students to be critical in relation to management knowledge, we are self-evidently promoting a certain conception of 'criticality' which might be regarded as no less disciplinary than what it stands against (see Foucault, 1980). Post-modern conceptions of truth and subjectivity render the emancipatory premise of even radical humanism problematic: the self is constructed and truth is constructed. We can no longer claim to be doing anything other than seeking to substitute one construction for another. And although we might argue that the substitution we propound is a desirable one in various ways, from other perspectives our aims might be seen as less laudable than we imagine. In particular, Ellsworth (1992) has argued that the notion of 'critical' routinely deployed in pedagogies such as ours is in fact a reaffirmation of a *logos* which is both ethnocentric and gendered. On this view, the supposed radicalism of critical approaches in fact disempowers students excluded or marginalized by this *logos* because it celebrates certain notions of argumentation, rationality and critique, while disqualifying and de-privileging other modes of apprehension within marginalized discourses, for it is no less involved than conventional pedagogies in constructing particular subjectivities and truths.

In response to such charges, it may be comforting to claim that an awareness of the problem is the beginning of a solution. But this in itself is scarcely an adequate counter. Certainly we can work to recognize, challenge, and have challenged for us, the nature and limitations of our authority. But we would be naive to believe that such sensitivity can enable us fully to transcend it. Nevertheless, we can claim that such issues would not even be thinkable were it not for the challenges to orthodoxy which critical pedagogy articulates and encourages. We recognize critical pedagogy to be provisional, ambiguous and contradictory. But we also believe that pride can be taken both in its practice *and* in attempts to transcend it. Moreover, while we cannot avoid exercising power over our students in such a way as to constitute truth for them, it is a power and truth that we would expect to be equally as subversive of itself should it no longer remain marginal (see, for example, Grey, 1995). For surely the whole point of a critical pedagogy is criticism of that which is taken for granted?

Conclusion

In this chapter we have attempted to explain the rationale for, and practice of, a critical pedagogy of management. Critical pedagogy, as we have described it, is a minority and marginalized activity within management education that deserves to be more widely recognized and adopted. Although there has been a proliferation of literature on management learning, especially in terms of techniques of teaching, the efforts of critical pedagogues in management education have rarely been articulated and consequently, we suspect, their practice probably occurs in a fragmented and *ad hoc* manner. The course we have described has been exceptional in the length of time it has been running and developing. Its 20-year history therefore provides an extended case study of the nature and limitations of critical pedagogy.

Conventional pedagogies are inextricably bound up with conventional, and problematic, conceptions of knowledge within the management disciplines. Increasingly, the critique of positivism has been taken seriously in the domain of research. The challenge for management teachers is to translate this into reconceptualizations of pedagogy. This requires more than refinements in the presentation of material or the recognition of the psychological and emotional processes of learning. For critical pedagogy involves a redefinition both of what is to be learned and how learning is to proceed. A critical pedagogy, we have argued, not only offers a challenging view of management as a social, political and economic practice, but does so in a way that stimulates student involvement of a kind that is rare in other forms of management education.

We have sought to be candid about some of the practical difficulties involved in critical pedagogy. We have also gestured towards the extremely difficult issue of what constitutes 'criticality'. An appreciation of these difficulties should enhance, rather than detract from, the value of critical pedagogy: a willingness to recognize and address these difficulties is a source of strength and renewal. Despite all of the difficulties, critical pedagogy has much to commend it. At the very least, it challenges positivist knowledge within management and, in so doing, it opens up debate about the social and moral implications of management practice. While it is far from providing Dr M with a technique for 'fixing' his problems, we believe that critical pedagogy offers students and staff the possibility of escape from the comforting yet dispiriting drudgery of more conventional approaches to management education.

Notes

An earlier version of this chapter was presented at the *Management Education in an Academic Context* Conference, University of Uppsala, Sweden, April 1991. We are grateful for comments made by delegates at that conference and by Robert French. Earlier discussions and the conference draft of this chapter involved a fourth author, Michael Shaoul, to whom we here give special acknowledgement.

1 Our teaching colleagues on the course in the period we refer to, Theo Vurdubakis, Michael Shaoul and Deborah Kerfoot, were similarly involved in the experience we describe. We should also make it clear that, although CG is no longer involved in its teaching, the course still runs in something like the form described here and is still taught by two of us (DK and HW), supported by other staff and researchers.

2 By management education, we refer to provision made by higher education institutions, and not to management training through, for example, government enterprise initiatives or particular organizations' in-house provision. Although demand for postgraduate management courses (especially MBA) was somewhat eroded during the early 1990s by economic recession, the popularity of undergraduate courses and options in management remains undiminished.

3 The morality of this approach can be challenged by those wedded to more conventional approaches who argue that our pedagogy is intrusive and makes unreasonable personal (psychological) demands on students. Our response to this is that we regard more 'normal' approaches as no less, and indeed more, demanding in so far as they widen (or alienate) the subject (students) from the object (knowledge) by treating both in an impersonal and instrumental manner.

4 Indeed, it is not uncommon to overhear our students on the campus using the terms 'having' and 'being' in their conversations with each other.

5 We were fortunate in the period of teaching on which this chapter is based to be working in a team of six which allowed us to maintain a reasonable staff–student ratio, in an atmosphere of mutual respect and commitment which did much to maintain morale.

References

Alvesson, M. (1987) *Organization Theory and Technocratic Consciousness.* Berlin: de Gruyter.
Alvesson, M. and Willmott, H. (eds) (1992) *Critical Management Studies.* London: Sage.
Alvesson, M. and Willmott, H. (1996) *Making Sense of Management.* London: Sage.
Anthony, P. (1977) *The Ideology of Work.* London: Tavistock.
Anthony, P. (1986) *The Foundations of Management.* London: Tavistock.
Berger, P. and Luckmann, T. (1967) *The Social Construction of Reality.* Harmondsworth: Penguin.
Bernstein, R. (1976) *The Restructuring of Social and Political Theory.* Oxford: Blackwell.
de Castell, S., Luke, A. and Luke, C. (1989) *Language, Authority and Criticism.* New York: Farmer Press.
Ellsworth, E. (1992) 'Why doesn't this feel empowering? Working through the repressive myths of critical pedagogy', in C. Luke and J. Gore (eds), *Feminisms and Critical Pedagogy.* London: Routledge. pp. 90–119.
Engwall, L. (1992) *Mercury Meets Minerva.* Oxford: Pergamon Press.
Feyerabend, P. (1988) *Against Method.* London: Verso.
Foucault, M. (1970) *The Order of Things.* London: Tavistock.
Foucault, M. (1979) *Discipline and Punish.* Harmondsworth: Penguin.
Foucault, M. (1980) *Power/Knowledge.* Brighton: Harvester.
Fox, S. and Hodgson, V. (1995) 'Studying management and management studies', paper presented at the *New Perspectives on Management Education* Conference, Leeds University.
Freire, P. (1972) *Pedagogy of the Oppressed.* Harmondsworth: Penguin.
Freire, P. and Shor, I. (1987) *A Pedagogy for Liberation.* London: Macmillan.
Fromm, E. (1980) *To Have or To Be.* Harmondsworth: Penguin.
Giddens, A. (1974) *Positivism and Sociology.* London: Heinemann.
Giroux, H. (1983) *Theory and Resistance in Education.* London: Heinemann.
Grey, C. (1995) 'Gender as a grid of intelligibility', *Gender, Work and Organization*, 2 (1): 46–50.
Grey, C. (1996) 'C.P. Snow's fictional sociology of management and organisations', *Organization*, 3 (1), in press.
Grey, C. and Mitev, N. (1995a) 'Management education: a polemic', *Management Learning*, 26 (1): 73–90.
Grey, C. and Mitev, N. (1995b) 'Business process reengineering: a critical appraisal', *Personnel Review*, 24 (1): 6–18.
Habermas, J. (1970) *Knowledge and Human Interests.* London: Heinemann.
Henriques, J. (ed.) (1984) *Changing the Subject: Psychology, Social Regulation and Subjectivity.* London: Methuen.
Knights, D. (1992) 'Changing spaces: the disruptive impact of a new epistemological location for the study of management', *Academy of Management Review*, 17 (3): 514–36.
Knights, D. and Murray, F. (1994) *Managers Divided.* London: Wiley.
Knights, D. and Willmott, H. (1995) 'Management as lived experience, management as text', paper presented at the *New Perspectives on Management Education* Conference, Leeds University.
Luke, C. and Gore, J. (eds) (1992) *Feminisms and Critical Pedagogy.* London: Routledge.
MacIntyre, A. (1981) *After Virtue.* London: Duckworth.
Wilkinson, A. and Willmott, H. (eds) (1994) *Making Quality Critical.* London: Routledge.
Willmott, H. (1994a) 'Management education: provocations to a debate', *Management Learning*, 25 (1): 105–36.
Willmott, H. (1994b) 'Business process re-engineering and human resources management', *Personnel Review*, 23 (3): 34–46.
Willmott, H. (1996) 'Managing the academics: commodification and control in the development of university education in the UK', *Human Relations*.
Winch, P. (1958) *The Idea of a Social Science.* Oxford: Blackwell.

7

Experiential Management Education as the Practice of Change

Russ Vince

In this chapter I am concerned with the possibilities for developing the practice of *experiential* management education. I focus on the experiential because the notion that managers learn best from reflection on their own experience has provided a very powerful underlying model for management education in practice, particularly through the work of writers like Revans (1971, 1983) and Kolb (1984). I reflect on and rethink how these approaches have been used in practice, thereby identifying a number of problems. First, I believe there has been an overemphasis on individual experience and this has led to an insufficient analysis of the social and political context of that experience. Second, there has been an overemphasis on the rational and intellectual aspects of learning from experience, emerging from the difficulty of managing and working with the emotions involved in learning and change. Third, existing models are inadequate for engaging with the social power relations present in management education, and the ways in which power relations within and outside learning groups contribute to the social construction of individual and group identity.

I therefore highlight some of the political and emotional issues that are often omitted in approaches to experiential learning. I propose an approach for management education, which is intended to increase opportunities for both individual and organizational change. My rethinking of the underlying models has implications for changes in the practice of experiential management education, and seeks to establish management education as a practice for change. My definition of experiential management education covers any process of management education, management development or management learning that is seeking to work explicitly with the lived experience of students or participants as a way of reviewing and developing their learning.

Learning and Change

The starting point of my analysis is an acknowledgement of the relationship between learning and change, whichever way round you look at them:

1 'The word learning undoubtedly denotes change of some kind' (Bateson, 1973).

2   'The factor most likely to influence our capacity to change is our capacity to learn' (Plant, 1987).

My own conceptual framework for experiential management education as the practice of learning and change is particularly influenced by three approaches. First, the work of Gregory Bateson (1973), which provides a general framework for understanding different 'levels' of learning. Second, the work of Paulo Freire, who offers a perspective on the relationship between learning and power. Third, a range of literature which explores the psychodynamics of organization (Hirschhorn, 1988; Hoggett, 1992; Jaques, 1990; Kets de Vries, 1991; Menzies-Lyth, 1990).

Bateson (1973) identifies four levels of human learning and looks at their implications for change (Table 7.1). Bateson's categories provide a framework that can be applied to an understanding of management education, particularly in the tension between methods that encourage *Reinforcement* (LI) and methods that encourage *Change* (LII). Learning II is the theoretical site of experiential management education since it is here that experience and the development of knowledge meet. Management education that promotes learning and change may take place where it becomes possible for the learning to break free from the constraints of habit, and to develop new ways to apply experience in the context of management.

Management education is potentially at its most useful when it promotes learning how to learn, when it challenges processes of habituation. Change

Table 7.1   *Bateson's levels of learning*

Levels	Implications
Zero Learning	Zero learning is based on predictable or specific responses which are not subject to trial and error. Zero learning does not signify the capacity to reflect in any way to enable change, it is simply about response. Even the recognition of a wrong response would not contribute to any future skill.
Learning I	Learning I implies a change as a result of trial and error, within a set of alternatives. Correction does therefore have an implication for future action. In other words, this level has moved from stimulus/response to stimulus/ response/reinforcement. Learning I is, therefore, about a process of habituation.
Learning II	Learning II implies some flexibility in the potential to act as opposed to reinforcement of action. It is therefore a change in the set of alternatives from which choice is made. Learning II implies a capacity to 'learn how to learn', in other words, a shift of the frameworks from which choices are made.
Learning III	Learning III is a shift in the underlying premises and belief systems that form frameworks. Level III learning involves a capacity to 'make a corrective change in the system of sets of alternatives from which choice is made'; in other words, the capacity to examine the paradigm or regime within which action is based.

occurs through an acknowledgement of, and an interaction with, current habits and 'attachments' (Marris, 1986) as an integral aspect of the learning process. It is the result of the implementation of actions that emerge from the acknowledgement of being caught in some form of dependency. Change is not a potential outcome of learning, but integral to it. If it is possible to learn how to learn by questioning our habits and attachments, then it is also possible to envisage that to learn this as a skill would have significant implications, not just for our understanding of change but also for our ability to change. This raises questions about how our habits in relation to learning are formed.

How we Learn to Limit Learning

Our education system defines for us, as well as with us, what is 'useful' knowledge. The initial process of schooling implies, for example, that it is more useful to acquire the technical skills necessary for our role within various industries and professions than it is to acquire the political skills that allow us to assert our perceptions of what we want from such a role (Illich, 1971). As the subjects of the schooling process we are mainly required to be actively unquestioning. We are encouraged to be the recipients of knowledge defined predominantly for us rather than with us. The consequence of this is that:

> Many people learn not to think their own thoughts, to speak their own language i.e. to unlearn their own culture. People are, in a sense, being forced not to see the truth of their reality any longer. (Fritz, 1982: 5)

Our schooling into society affects us as learners by promoting a dependency on other people's knowledge, and providing little support for the evolution of either political or emotional skills.

The legacy of schooling and the consequent dependency we develop on particular learning processes, affect our adult understanding of how to learn. We can become defensive about ways of learning if they challenge what we are used to. Our familiarity with some forms of learning can act as a block against the exploration of other forms. Claxton (1984) describes such blocks in relation to the individual adult learner and characterizes them as personal defence systems against non-familiar or threatening forms of learning, that is:

1   I must be *Competent*;
2   I must be *Consistent*;
3   I must be *In control*;
4   I must be *Comfortable*.

The need to feel competent, consistent, in control and comfortable for ourselves and with others sets a boundary around our capacity to learn and change. This boundary is built as a protection against anxiety and uncertainty, a protection against the unfamiliar. Claxton's analysis is useful in explaining the ease with which individuals create learning environments as places for the reinforcement of existing knowledge and experience (LI) rather than as opportunities for change (LII).

At every opportunity for learning there are powerful emotions (such as fear and anxiety) that can either promote or discourage change:

> Change is an excursion into the unknown. It implies a commitment to future events that are not entirely predictable as to their consequences, and inevitably provokes doubt and anxiety. (Menzies-Lyth, 1990: 451)

Anxiety can be seen as a starting point of individual and group defences against learning and change. Individual 'defensive techniques', like depersonalization and denial of feelings, easily become institutionalized within a group and become characteristic of its resistance to change (Jaques, 1955). Menzies-Lyth (1990) and Jaques (1990) have both undertaken studies which discuss how the social structure of organizations is built and maintained as a result of anxiety, and how this creates social defences against change. Jaques' work suggests that individual responses to a shared social situation combine, producing a common psychological response to organizational history and restraints, and that these interact with conscious goals. He sees this as an 'unconscious use of institutions', to be conceived of dynamically:

> There is therefore a constant movement between shared social experiences of the institution, the meshing of individual responses into a common psychological response, and the dynamic and evolving unconscious of the institution. (Samuels, 1993: 281)

Any initiative where there is an intention to produce organizational learning and change must therefore work with the largely unconscious needs of individuals to manage anxiety. I will be returning to and developing this theme in greater detail later in the chapter.

The struggle to learn and to change can be both complex and uncomfortable, involving strong feelings and prolonged uncertainty. Paradoxically, individual and group defences are both helpful, because they contribute to the manageability of learning and change, and unhelpful, because they place restrictions on them. Such defences create an outline within which change can be managed, but they also create a boundary within which change can be avoided. Management education, if it is to provide opportunities for learning about change and for changing the way we learn, will need to acknowledge and work with those educational and organizational boundaries that are perpetually and unconsciously created as an integral part of individual or organizational avoidance of change.

In addition to psychological issues, there are also political issues that need to be worked with in the development of experiential management education. One of the most fundamental propositions informing experiential learning is the notion that the review and development of individual experience forms the basic resource for learning (Smith, 1980). It often seems that such learning, because it focuses on the individual, is somehow detached from the social and political context of experience. Both individual and collective experience are invariably products of a social system, and in turn contribute to the capacity of that system to resist change. In other words, our experience is conditioned by, and an exercise of, power.

Learning and Power

In order to explore the political context of experiential learning I shall discuss aspects of the work of the Brazilian educationalist, Paulo Freire. The importance of Freire's work is that it takes into account the issue of power on two levels. First, it acknowledges the power of personal motivation towards change, activated and perpetuated through a process of experiential education. I would say that this is one part of the system of management education we are familiar with in the UK. Secondly it acknowledges the educational importance of confronting oppressive and/or paternalistic societal values and norms as an integral aspect of the educational process. This aspect is almost wholly ignored by the system of management education we are familiar with in the UK.

Freire's work highlights a dual relationship between the learner and power. He explores how powerful it is for individuals to reflect on their own experiences in such a way that new perceptions about themselves and their world can be formulated. He also explores the tools that people need to interact within the society that exploits them. The forms of learning that we are primarily familiar with, in the many different scenarios of management education, consistently ignore this second, more political aspect of the learning process.

To expand on this I will look more closely at some of the issues Freire raises about learning and power (see also Grey et al., this volume). In *Pedagogy of the Oppressed* he describes two types of learning. The first is 'the banking concept of education':

> in which the students are the depositories and the teacher is the depositor. Instead of communicating, the teacher issues communiques and makes deposits which the students patiently receive, memorise and repeat. (Freire, 1972: 45)

Freire's concern in describing this 'banking' model is to demonstrate that such learning is an 'exercise in domination'. He proposes instead a 'problem-posing' approach to learning, a balance of action and reflection by people on their world, explicitly in order to change it. Such a shift is a step towards confronting one aspect of the hegemony of the banking model. Learning requires engagement with the educational process (in addition to content) as a fundamental part of the evolution and development of contextually relevant knowledge. Such action struggles with the boundary of the educational process, seeking to redefine it as a clarification

Table 7.2 *Freire's banking and problem-posing models*

The 'banking' model	The 'problem-posing' model
1 The teacher knows The student doesn't know	1 Student and teacher exchange knowledge through 'dialogue'
2 The teacher talks The student listens	2 A process of reflection and action for both: 'a process of becoming'
3 The teacher chooses The student complies	3 'Critical intervention', i.e. consciousness of and within the learning environment
4 The teacher's experience is primary, the student's is secondary	4 Begins from the student's experience/expertise
Therefore the student is: Passive An 'empty cup' A spectator not a participant	*Therefore the student is:* Active A 'full cup' A participant not a spectator

not only of available knowledge, but also of its oppressive and/or liberatory nature. Therefore:

> Whereas banking education anaesthetizes and inhibits creative power, problem-posing education involves a constant unveiling of reality. The former attempts to maintain the submersion of consciousness; the latter strives for the emergence of consciousness and critical intervention in reality. (Freire, 1972: 54)

Table 7.2 explains the relationship between the 'banking' and the 'problem-posing' models in more detail. In the banking model, the relatedness between teacher and taught is not constrained by a desire to generate, develop or change knowledge, merely to exchange it through deposits and withdrawals. The teacher's role can be defined in simple terms: 'I know and you don't; I speak and you listen; I choose what and how you learn, and you comply' – because the idea of *praxis* (Freire, 1972: 60) is anathema. In the problem-posing model teacher and taught are both in a 'process of becoming', a process whose success depends on the 'dialogue' between us. Thus, the teacher's consciousness of the role of teacher, and the student's consciousness of the role of student, are constructed and enacted through a dialogue, in other words as a result of the relatedness between these two roles, in terms of both the content and the process of learning. Such a model opens up the politics of learning, by recognizing the social and contextual construction of consciousness.

The banking model relies on the individual authority of the teacher and the individual passivity of the student. To maintain this relationship, power must be excluded as an issue within learning. In the problem-posing model, experiential learning is not about an individualized experience. Rather, it concerns related experience, involving the individual, the group and the system. Power is thereby acknowledged as an ever-present and dynamic force, helping to define and redefine the experience of learning.

The main concept used by Freire to propose a way forward is that of 'dialogue'. The word dialogue signifies that the relationship of power between learners in a learning process (whether they are the teachers or the taught) is not an individualistic one: 'knowing is a social event with nevertheless an individual dimension' (Freire and Shor, 1987: 99). The 'educator' enters into dialogue with the social reality of the student as well as with their individual reality. In this way the problem-posing model is a challenge to those who dominate the individual as much as to the individual themselves. Therefore:

> the teacher has the right but also the duty to challenge the status quo, especially in the question of the domination by sex, race or class. What the dialogical educator does not have the right to impose is his or her position. But the liberating teacher can never stay silent on social questions, can never wash his or her hands of them. (1987: 174)

Freire's work provides an approach to understanding the nature of management education not simply in terms of the experiential reality of the individual, but in relation to the social reality in which the learning process is itself situated.

In experiential management education it is possible to work explicitly with the social and political nature of learning. Such a perspective involves working with various issues. First, it is necessary to acknowledge socially constructed and reinforced differences (with regard to race, gender and disability). Active engagement with the consequences of such differences has to be an integral rather than suppressed aspect of educational process. The suppression of this social reality in much experiential learning contributes to the alienation of individual and group identities from the learning process.

Secondly, there are complex processes of power at work in management education. To an extent these can be explained as processes of 'structuration' (Giddens, 1984, 1993; Roberts, this volume). Giddens' theory of structuration asserts the 'duality of structure': structures are both produced by human action and are the medium of human action. People draw on various material and authoritative resources in the course of their interactions, and in doing so maintain 'regularised relations of autonomy and dependence' (Giddens, 1984: 16). Giddens depicts power as bound up in relations of reciprocal autonomy and dependence, which he terms 'the dialectic of control'. A learning environment is a powerful and contained arena for viewing negotiations on autonomy and dependence. This is particularly focused on expectations and feelings about the respective roles of tutor and student.

Finally, a political perspective on experiential learning provides the connection between management education as a here and now experience, and the experienced reality of politics or power in organizational life. Therefore, the boundary or the 'margin' between what is happening in an experiential group now, and its mirror image in experience of organization, becomes the focal point for both learning and change. It is the learner's capacity to work with marginality as the site of experiential learning that will create real possibilities for learning and change:

I am located in the margin. I make a definite distinction between the marginality which is imposed by oppressive structures and that marginality one chooses as a site of resistance – as location of radical openness and possibility. This site of resistance is continually formed in that segregated culture of opposition that is our critical response to domination. We come to this space through suffering and pain, through struggle. We know struggle to be that which pleasures, delights and fulfils desire. We are transformed, individually, collectively, as we make radical creative space which affirms and sustains our subjectivity which gives us a new location from which to articulate our sense of the world. (hooks, 1991: 153)

At this point I want to review and bring together the perspectives I have mentioned. Initially, I discussed Bateson's distinction between different 'levels' of learning in order to establish that experiential management education aims to encourage change through processes of reflecting and acting on meta-levels of experience, what Bateson refers to as learning how to learn (and therefore, learning how to change). From here I introduce the idea of learning and change as emotional as well as rational experiences, influenced and blocked by individual and collective anxiety. According to writers like Elliott Jaques and Isobel Menzies-Lyth, a powerful and dynamic organizational unconscious is created through the interplay of individual anxiety that can structure an organization, and the structure of an organization that can promote anxiety. This psychological dynamic is also attached in organizations to a political dynamic, a dialectic of control. I use the work of Paulo Freire to explore the impact of social power relations in educational processes and to explain the social reality within which learning processes are situated. Finally, I refer to the importance of the boundary or margin as a place where individual identity meets the experienced reality of power in organizations. These perspectives provide a picture of what I feel experiential management education involves.

In the next section of the chapter I look in more detail at some of the dominant theoretical models underpinning current approaches to experiential management education. Rethinking these in the light of the above discussion enables the development of a practice which supports both learning and change.

Learning and Management Education

Many of the approaches which provide the theoretical basis for management education are firmly rooted in the experiential reality of the individual in the context of the group. 'Learning from experience' has been a strong theme in management education since the 1950s and 1960s, through such mechanisms as 'T-groups' or 'sensitivity training'. Although T-groups arise from the work of Kurt Lewin (1951), the term became a generic one for a range of development methods which sought to enhance individual and group learning (Handy, 1985). The methods used might vary considerably, but the aim in relation to individuals within groups can be generally expressed as:

> An approach ... which, broadly speaking, provides participants with an opportunity to learn more about themselves and their impact on others, and in particular to learn how to function more effectively in face to face situations. (Cooper and Mangham, 1971)

The primary mechanism for such learning is feedback from other members of a group, prompting individual self-examination, the consideration of new values, attitudes and behaviour. Such approaches emphasize that issues like disclosure, which have an emotional content or 'risk factor' are often subverted or avoided in management and organization. Since much of management is undertaken within groups or teams, these and other interpersonal skills enhance (or at least clarify) the relationships between people engaged in management tasks. The idea of learning as a process integral to everyday management experience is a strong theme in the literature which underpins management education. Revans' (1971, 1983) 'action learning' process and Kolb's (1984) work on 'learning cycles' are influential models.

Although both of these models have arisen as a challenge to rationalistic approaches to management and organization, I want to argue that they both fall short of providing a way of integrating the emotional and political into experiential management education. I have explained elsewhere (Vince and Martin, 1993; Vince, 1995) that the application of these models has often tended to encourage the rational/intellectual skills of managers in interpreting and working with their experience. This has led in some cases to reflection on experience being constructed or interpreted as managers 'thinking about their experience' (Mifsud, 1990), emphasizing the rational nature of the reflective process. If, as I outlined earlier, part of learning from experience is about working with the emotional and power dynamics generated in learning processes, then the reflective process also needs to occur through a combination of the rational, the emotional and the political.

Models like those of Revans and Kolb can only be helpful if there is an explicit recognition of the relationship between an individual's capacity to integrate rational, emotional and political experience. Our tendency as learners to avoid and deny the emotional and political aspects of management learning means that thinking about experience tends to dominate. In this chapter I offer a perspective on ways of communicating both models in order to encourage and extend the possibilities for exploring emotionally based experience and for representing the politics of experiential learning. Such an exercise is important in rethinking management education, because the overemphasis on rational/intellectual aspects of learning from experience has led to a difficulty for management educators in fully representing the change process within our work.

To explore in detail the implications of combining the rational, emotional and political dimensions of experiential management education, I shall analyse and expand Revans' 'action learning cycle'. Action learning was developed as an approach for encouraging managers to work on real

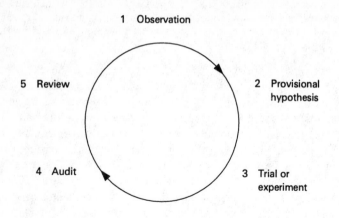

Figure 7.1   *The action learning cycle*

work tasks as learning experiences (Revans, 1971, 1983). It is constructed as an approach to individual development, but important also in the strategic task of integrating learning into the everyday working lives of managers, thereby helping to create organizations where learning, and therefore change, are taken seriously. The original features of action learning have been summarized by Mumford (1992) and developed in a variety of ways by others (McGill and Beaty, 1992; Pedler and Boutall, 1992).

Within the action learning process Revans perceived learning to be based on the interaction between two kinds of learning, programmed knowledge (P) which is the introduction of knowledge or skills, and questioning (Q) which is the process of exploring such knowledge in practice. This allowed him to formulate the equation 'L = P + Q', or learning occurs when programmed knowledge meets questioning insight. Revans (1983) emphasizes that behaviour change is more likely to occur as a result of reflection on experience (questioning insight) than on the acquisition of programmed knowledge. Reflection with other managers, who may well be engaged in similar issues of management practice, therefore affords the most practical and effective learning. Management learning is achieved both through focusing on real work problems, and as a result of managers learning from and with each other.

The structure of the action learning approach to reflection on experience has five successive stages: observation, provisional hypothesis, trial, audit and review. This can be represented as a 'cycle' or developmental loop, returning again and again to different situations and phenomena (see Figure 7.1). Revans (1983: 17) describes these five stages as 'the intellectual structuring of experience to achieve a command over the world', in essence then an intellectual process of reflection and action which affects everyday practice.

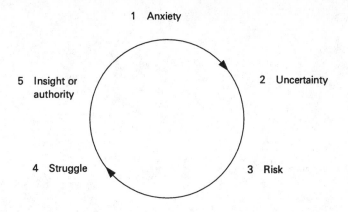

Figure 7.2   *Cycle of emotions promoting learning*

The emphasis of Revans' model is on the use of intellectual processes to review experience. He uses the phrase 'the scientific method' to describe action learning. The model concentrates on the rational aspects of learning, providing a map of the intellectual processes involved. However, it does not, I feel, explore or offer models for the understanding of the emotional or political processes described above, that also underpin learning. In his writing on action learning, Revans does discuss the emotional or psychological implications of the approach, but in general and rather dismissive terms: 'exercises such as sensitivity training, non-directive counselling and other excursions into group psychotherapy are but rarely anchored to the here and now demands of business' (1983: 64).

His views seem to create two problems. First, the model or method does not openly consider the effects of emotional resistance to, or avoidance of, learning. Implicit in the model is an assumption that such experiences as fear and anxiety are managed separately from the issue of addressing the work task. This exclusion effectively dismisses the process of individual and group defensiveness against learning which is always present within learning and working groups. Secondly, the rationality of the model does not make an analysis of power and oppression possible within learning. The bias present in learning groups shapes the language and the interaction used to address a work task.

In order to develop the action learning method so that the underlying approach recognizes emotional and political as well as rational processes, two additional five-stage developmental processes have been produced. These are represented in Figures 7.2 and 7.3.

The starting point for both cycles is anxiety. Approaches to learning that break free of dependency on the teacher, and place emphasis on the responsibilities of the learner, always create anxiety (Claxton, 1984). It is anxiety provoking not to be taught or told because it means that the

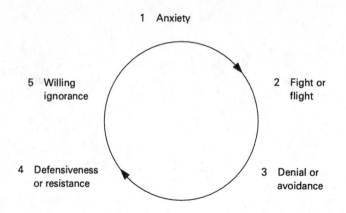

Figure 7.3   *Cycle of emotions discouraging learning*

learner is confronted with responsibility for what and how he or she needs
to learn. Such responsibility has both psychological and political implications: psychological because the individual may need to overcome fears,
for example 'getting it wrong' or 'taking a lead'; and political because
getting it wrong or taking a lead always has an impact on the social system
within which the learning is taking place.

The emphasis of Revans' original model leans strongly towards what
managers *perceive* about their experience, rather than what they *feel* about
their experience. Such an emphasis allows anxiety to be denied and
discarded. The consequence of a dependency on the rational aspects of the
model is the denial of an emotional reality that is constantly present in
learning groups.

If the starting point in the rational cycle (Figure 7.1) is what we observe,
then in the underlying cycles it is what we fear, those things that inspire
defensiveness and resistance. In Figure 7.2 (the cycle of emotions
promoting learning) the anxiety created from fear gives rise to uncertainty.
Some participants in experiential groups are more ready or able than others
to be challenged, or to move themselves towards some new or revised
knowledge. Their uncertainty, that feeling of being on the edge of change,
does not get the better of them; rather it has created the conditions for risk.
Risks are many and varied in learning groups: the expression of powerful
feelings like anger; the risk of speaking or not speaking; the risk of leading
or of staying out. Individuals struggle with the consequences of their risk
within a group. They may have to struggle through other people's reaction,
or their own emotion at having aired something long suppressed. The result
of this cycle of uncertainty, risk and struggle is a feeling of empowerment
involving either an insight or increased authority.

There are times in learning groups when the risk seems too great and our
intuition towards defensiveness and resistance wins through. In Figure 7.3

(the cycle of emotions discouraging learning) anxiety leads not to a form of uncertainty that can be held, rather to feelings that set in motion reactions of either fight or flight. What an individual receives within a learning group can easily feel unwanted. There will be times when people in groups are not ready or able to be challenged or to attempt to question existing knowledge. Invariably, such feelings are supported by denials and avoidance strategies and, if these do not work, with open resistance and defensiveness either towards the group itself or individuals within it. It seems common in learning groups, for example, that individuals attempt to create a scapegoat in order to avoid and defend against their own need to change. As an individual sets up denials, defences and avoidances so he or she creates the right conditions for her or his own willing ignorance.

The following examples help to explain these models further:

An individual manager is working on her problem, the difficulty of relating to a member of her staff. One of her colleagues in the learning set, notices that the manager seems to be avoiding her competitiveness with her subordinate, and questions her on it. Our manager's immediate feeling is to deny the competition, yet something in what her colleague has said rings true. She feels suddenly on the spot, uncertain, as if she would rather be elsewhere. However, because she feels some truth had been acknowledged, she talks about envying her staff member's ability to be liked by the rest of the team. Through their questioning, the set help her to struggle through her own feelings of difficulty in being in the managerial role. The experience in the set eventually provides her with the insight that her envy is a block to her effectiveness, both with the specific individual and with her team. She resolves to undertake some practical actions which she imagines will overcome this particular problem.

A senior administrative manager is working on his difficulty with delegating to his staff. He manages a team mostly of women, and some set members have begun to question him about his difficulty passing his work on to his women staff. The things he is saying about the women who work for him seem to be both controlling and rather paternalistic. When challenged, he insists that this is not the issue, and resists this 'irrelevant' questioning, emphasizing that he always treats everybody equally in his team. He feels as though he has to fight off this line of questioning by the set in order to get to the 'real' issue. Some set members see this as an avoidance of issues that would make a difference if he could take them on board. Our manager becomes more and more defensive about the problem he is addressing, he feels that the women in his set are being 'bloody feminists'. The experience in the set convinces him that he doesn't have a problem and is a much misunderstood person. To shut the group up he says he will talk to his staff and see what they say.

The two cycles of emotion are an attempt to describe that point in a learning group where an individual, a part of the group, or the group as a whole has the (largely unconscious) option to move either in the direction of self-empowerment or self-limitation, change or non-change. An awareness of separate emotional forces that promote or discourage learning will provide improved opportunities for experiential groups to manage and make sense of processes of change, both personal and organizational.

The application of experiential models in isolation from emotions that either promote or discourage learning supports and perpetuates two complimentary difficulties for managers: their over-reliance on the intellectual experience of their work, and their fears about emotions at work. Thus, managers can quickly come to value the task-oriented or problem-solving aspects of models such as those of Revans or Kolb, without addressing their own emotional experience of work. The feelings generated, which might produce learning and change if they were acknowledged and worked with, instead become detached or 'split' from the objectives of the group. The same process that banishes emotion from work organizations affects the learning group. In other words, the learning group begins to mirror constraints on knowledge and understanding present in the manager's work.

It is possible, therefore, that the models which commonly underpin experiential management learning, which are explicitly designed to work with managerial experience, can also help an individual deny what such experience means, especially the significance of its emotional dimension. The danger is that an experiential group can develop the same self-limiting structure characteristic of the organization it comes from, where emotional meanings are suppressed as a result of managerial fears about their consequences. The potential for understanding and working with change in such circumstances is considerably lessened. To accept the notion that emotional meanings are suppressed allows for a clearer understanding of the politics of experiential learning. In order to highlight this, the two cycles of emotion promoting or discouraging learning (Figures 7.2 and 7.3) have been combined to create Figure 7.4.

The meeting of people in experiential groups brings together in one place differing emotional realities, different systems of meaning, different types of bias. The encounter between people in a learning environment is therefore necessarily a political process. The word 'political' signifies social power relations, both at the institutional and interpersonal levels, and their effects on the individual and the group. People are positioned unequally in and by organizations and groups as a consequence of social constructions of their identity. Consequently, women and men, black and white, disabled and able-bodied, gay and straight people have to address differential experiences of power and powerlessness as aspects both of their organizational practice and of management education.

The power and powerlessness of individuals within learning groups is an integral aspect of the group process. Both power and powerlessness can be avoided or denied, they can become fixed, or they can change and evolve. The impact of the relationships between power and process constantly shapes the agendas and the practice of experiential management education. Consequently, it is important to consider how power relations are acknowledged and worked with. All educational contexts represent and replicate, within their own internal processes, external social power relations. Transactions between individuals in learning groups can also serve to act out or restimulate power struggles, and the intense emotions associated with power and difference: fear, hatred, rage, contempt. The

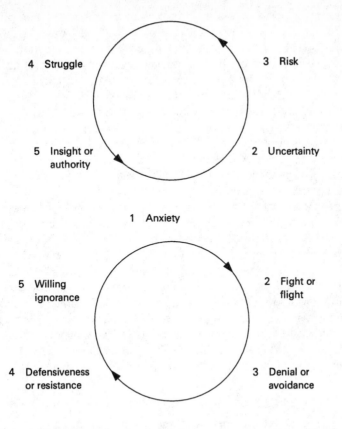

Figure 7.4 *The politics of action learning*

intensity of these emotions, and anxiety about how to deal effectively with power relations in groups and organizations, means that educational or learning groups have a high investment in defending against and avoiding these issues. Group members, at various stages in their interactions within learning groups, move backwards and forwards between positions or roles as the powerful and the powerless. Such positions are a reflection of the politics of learning in groups.

Emotions promoting or discouraging learning are affected by the internal politics of a learning group, and the struggle between these two emotional states underpins and explains the nature of political struggles within a learning group (see Figure 7.4). The political nature of experiential management education is expressed through the strategic choice available to learning group members to move in a direction that promotes learning, or a direction that discourages learning. In other words, movement towards either risk or denial/avoidance is often a political, as well as an emotional act on the part of the individual.

The examples already used to clarify both cycles can be referred to again.

In the example of the 'senior administrative manager', the political motivation for his behaviour is clearly to defend his power against the assumed or actual threat posed to him by either his women staff, women colleagues, the notion of equality in practice, or a combination of all three. The manager's defensiveness or silence is strategic, it is a political mechanism employed to defend authority. In the example of the 'team leader' there is an advantage to this manager in accepting herself as a block to her own effectiveness. Her choice to risk working through this emotional material can also be seen as strategic, as it may increase both her standing in the team (because she can admit to being human) and the general effectiveness of the team. This manager takes such a risk because there is a good chance it will strengthen her authority.

Thus an individual's or a group's risks and struggles, defences and avoidance strategies are political acts as well as emotional responses. They are the product of different levels of power and powerlessness within organizations and groups. If the model of management education being used denies such forces then it cannot be an adequate model for learning, because it contributes to the reinforcement of managerial experience that is willingly ignorant of power issues. It is important to have a political perspective on management education so that managers can reflect on the personal and institutional significance of different managerial experience (black/white, female/male, disabled/able-bodied, gay/straight) for the practice of change within their work.

A Revised Practice for Experiential Management Education

So far in this chapter I have suggested that the practice of experiential management education might be enhanced if practitioners addressed, with equal importance, the rational, emotional and political levels inherent in both learning and change. At present, experiential management education seems either excessively rational, in the sense that it focuses on managerial 'problem solving' or strategic development, and/or excessively humanistic, in its reliance on the 'person-centred' form of 'openness' in groups. The tendency in both of these approaches is to avoid a range of highly significant psychological and political dynamics, thereby mirroring and reinforcing the avoidance of the same dynamics in organizations.

This 'management by avoidance' (Vince, 1991) is shaped both by internal responses to learning and change and by external, socially constructed processes of interaction, particularly around power and powerlessness. In this final section of the chapter therefore, I want to propose three particular areas for the development of a revised practice in experiential management education. These are: working with the emotions of avoidance; working through the avoidance of power issues; and working through the avoidance of underlying dynamic processes.

Working with the Emotions of Avoidance

Fineman suggests that: 'We could regard all organizations as having zones of expressive tolerance which are likely to vary according to organizational type and part' (1993: 218). Similarly, I think that specific organizational contexts of experiential management education (for example groups of managers from the same organization; organizationally tailored management competences) have characteristic and largely hidden 'zones of expressive tolerance' that signify boundaries of individual and group learning and change. The challenge for educative programmes is therefore to identify and work with the student and tutor roles on the emotional boundaries of learning, and within their organizational context. This means working in ways that clarify what these unspoken, unseen, yet powerfully present boundaries are.

One boundary I have already identified is that anxious place within a learning group where it is possible to move in a direction that promotes, or one that discourages learning. The ways in which anxiety affects the learning process are seldom acknowledged as an overt issue in management education. Anxiety can promote learning through risk and it can discourage learning through defensiveness, avoidance and denial. The effectiveness of experiential management education will be enhanced where work is done overtly with these and other key emotional processes. Such work requires management educators to be highly sensitive to their own emotional states, and to hold and work effectively with those feelings that are projected onto them in their role as staff in the learning environment.

Working through the Avoidance of Power Issues

Power and powerlessness in organizations are shaped and practised through the interplay of interconnecting and significant 'transactions' (Martin, 1994) between individuals, groups and systems. There are many ways to describe the exercise of power (Vince, 1991) and these combined descriptions testify to the complexity of the issue. It would be insufficient to say that power can be expressed solely as the hierarchical authority one manager has over another; or as the legitimacy given to particular groups; or as the mobilization of bias; or as a self-perpetuating phenomenon created from the interface between structure and action. Power is all of these and more.

In experiential management education, the ways in which power affects the learning process are often avoided. The primary mechanism of this avoidance is an unhelpful but pervasive humanistic myth that different individuals come as equals into experiential groups. As a result, despite the clear differences between people, it is held to be possible to work together, without needing to work on the impact of difference. A revised practice for experiential management education involves the acknowledgement of this avoidance of different positions of power between individuals and groups in the learning environment. This means that management educators will need to address the interpersonal and inter-group politics involved in the processes of learning, which reflect socially constructed power differences.

Power and powerlessness find expression in two particular areas: first, in the many avoidance strategies and habits which encourage educators to ignore socially and politically constructed inequalities; secondly, through the difficulties educators have in working with challenges to the power of their own role. In the first instance, avoidance may be promoted by fear, hatred or guilt; in the second, through the anxiety that surrounds the possibility of losing face and/or control.

It is possible for the practice of experiential management education to be enhanced where work is done explicitly on different expressions of power in the learning context. This will involve educators in developing their abilities to hold and explore differential positions of power and equality as an integral aspect of understanding their subject. The content of all programmes of management education is affected by power and equality, since all management is undertaken within the context of organizations that replicate the social systems around them.

Working through the Avoidance of Underlying Dynamic Processes

Another way of seeing avoidance in managers and organizations is as 'defence mechanisms', processes through which resistance to change is brought into being. Kets de Vries and Miller (1985) offer six types of defence mechanisms which they consider 'play a major role in obstructing or inhibiting organizational change'. These are as follows.

Repression Certain memories, desires, emotions, thoughts and wishes are made unconscious and thereby divorced from awareness.

Regression Attempts to revert to earlier ways or to actions that have previously provided some security.

Projection Ascribing to another person or group an attitude or quality that one possesses but rejects in oneself. An attempt 'to keep the self conflict free'.

Identification Thinking, feeling, acting as one conceives another person to think, feel, act. Adopting the behaviour, values, attitudes of a significant individual.

Reaction Formation One of a pair of contradictory attitudes or traits is kept unconscious and hidden by emphasizing the opposite. Hate is replaced by love, selfishness by overgenerosity, etc. The opposite, non-observable attitude persists unconsciously.

Denial Attempting to exclude the existence of an unpleasant or unwanted piece of external reality, the truth being too anxiety provoking. The individual creates a delusion that nothing has changed.

The decision to work with and through the defence mechanisms that promote avoidance opens the door to a significantly different level of engagement with change. Psychodynamic insights provide the context for a reframing of traditionally humanistic words like 'participate' and 'collaborate'. Such concepts no longer have to contain a denial of the regressive and defensive characteristics that underlie all group and organizational dynamics. Psychodynamic theories are crucial to the development of experiential management education, because they extend the definition of 'learning from experience' away from both the problem-oriented rationality of many change initiatives, and from the 'sharing-our-feelings' oriented humanism of traditional experiential learning approaches.

Experiential management education as the practice of change, shifts emphasis from the 'sharing' of experience to 'working through' experience. This requires the educator to develop particular abilities. First, the ability when working with organizations, with groups and with individuals, to focus on what is being avoided. Second, the courage to engage with the underlying dynamics through interpretative interventions (see Pines, 1993). This involves interpreting transference and counter-transference, individual defences and avoidances, and those forces that have shaped individual and group identity. An interpretive stance also brings into the open the key dynamic of role differences between tutor and student.

In the same way that managers in their organizations consciously and unconsciously block the working-through process, so managers in educational settings use various specific mechanisms to block processes of working through experience. These include:

1   the tendency to blame others or to redirect anger;
2   the inclination to escape into rationality or to deny emotion;
3   the capacity for self-blame or positioning the self as a victim;
4   the desire to take control, to take responsibility for providing solutions.

The practice of experiential management education can be enhanced where educators take seriously that aspect of their role which demands that they are responsible for identifying and working with the underlying organizational dynamics reflected in student groups. As Clayton Alderfer points out, this is by no means an easy task:

> The requirements for people who accept staff roles for experiential group dynamics learning events are substantial. They call for extensively developed emotional and intellectual capabilities . . . for the flexibility to adapt to changing circumstances while attempting to remain whole as human beings and realistically responsive to the events that occur. (1990: 275)

If experientially based forms of management education and management development are to continue to be employed as a method for approaching individual, group and organizational change, then practitioners will also need to change. I am suggesting that the starting point for such change, and for a rethought practice of experiential management education, emerges from a deeper exploration of the three areas discussed in this chapter, that are currently replete with avoidance strategies; work with emotions that are avoided; the avoidance of power and equality as ever present process issues; and the avoidance of the complex underlying dynamics of working groups.

References

Alderfer, C.P. (1990) 'Staff authority and leadership in experiential groups', in J. Gillette and M. McCollam (eds), *Groups in Context.* Reading, MA: Addison-Wesley.

Bateson, G. (1973) *Steps to an Ecology of Mind.* St Albans: Paladin.

Claxton, G. (1984) *Live and Learn.* London: Harper and Row.

Cooper, C.L. and Mangham, I.L. (eds) (1971) *T Groups: a Survey of Research.* Chichester: John Wiley.

Fineman, S. (ed.) (1993) *Emotion in Organizations.* London: Sage.

Freire, P. (1972) *Pedagogy of the Oppressed.* Harmondsworth: Penguin.

Freire, P. and Shor, I. (1987) *A Pedagogy for Liberation: Dialogues on Transforming Education.* London: Macmillan.

Fritz, K. (1982) 'Because I speak Cockney they think I'm stupid: an application of Paulo Freire's concepts to community work with women'. Newcastle: Association of Community Workers.

Giddens, A. (1984) *The Constitution of Society.* Cambridge: Polity Press.

Giddens, A. (1993) *New Rules of Sociological Method*, 2nd edn. Cambridge: Polity Press.

Handy, C. (1985) *Understanding Organisations*, 3rd edn. Harmondsworth: Penguin.

Hirschhorn, L. (1988) *The Workplace Within: Psychodynamics of Organisational Life.* Cambridge: The MIT Press.

Hoggett, P. (1992) *Partisans in an Uncertain World: the Psychoanalysis of Engagement.* London: Free Association Books.

hooks, b. (1991) *Yearning: Race, Gender and Cultural Politics.* London: Turnaround Books.

Illich, I. (1971) *Deschooling Society.* London: Calder and Boyars.

Jaques, E. (1955) 'Social systems as a defence against persecutory and depressive anxiety', in M. Klein, P. Heimann and R. Money-Kyrle (eds), *New Directions in Psychoanalysis.* London: Tavistock.

Jaques, E. (1990) 'On the dynamics of social structure', in E. Trist and H. Murray (eds), *The Social Engagement of Social Science, Vol. 1.* London: Free Association Books.

Kets de Vries, M.F.R. and Associates (1991) *Organisations on the Couch.* San Francisco: Jossey-Bass.

Kets de Vries, M.F.R. and Miller, D. (1985) *The Neurotic Organisation.* London: Jossey-Bass.

Kolb, D.A. (1984) *Experiential Learning.* Englewood Cliffs: Prentice-Hall.

Lewin, K. (1951) *Field Theory in Social Science.* London: Harper and Row.

McGill, I. and Beaty, L. (1992) *Action Learning: a Practitioner's Guide.* London: Kogan Page.

Marris, P. (1986) *Loss and Change.* London: Routledge and Kegan Paul.

Martin, L. (1994) 'Power, continuity and change: women managers' experience in local government', in M. Tanton (ed.), *Women Managers' Learning.* London: Routledge.

Menzies-Lyth, I. (1990) 'Social systems as a defence against anxiety' (revised), in E. Trist and H. Murray, *The Social Engagement of Social Science, Vol. 1.* London: Free Association Books.

Mifsud, A. (1990) 'Guidelines for trainers: a trainers' manual'. Malta: Staff Development Organisation, Office of the Prime Minister.

Mumford, A. (1992) 'New ideas on action learning', in *Approaches to Action Learning.* Keele: Mercia Publications, University of Keele.

Pedler, M. and Boutall, J. (1992) *Action Learning for Change.* Gloucester: National Health Service Training Department Publications.

Pines, M. (1993) 'Interpretation: why, for whom and when', in David Kennard, J. Roberts and D.A. Winter (eds), *A Workbook of Group Analytic Interventions*. London: Routledge.

Plant, R. (1987) *Managing Change and Making it Stick*. London: Fontana.

Revans, R. (1971) *Developing Effective Managers*. London: Longman.

Revans, R. (1983) *The ABC of Action Learning*. Bromley, Kent: Chartwell, Bratt.

Samuels, A. (1993) *The Political Psyche*. London: Routledge.

Smith, P.B. (1980) *Group Process and Personal Change*. London: Harper and Row.

Vince, R. (1991) 'Management by avoidance: male power in local government', *Management Education and Development*, 22 (1): 50–9.

Vince, R. (1995) 'Behind and beyond Kolb's learning cycle', paper presented at *New Perspectives on Management Education* Conference, University of Leeds, January.

Vince, R. and Martin, L. (1993) 'Inside action learning: the psychology and the politics of the action learning model', *Management Education and Development*, 24 (3): 205–15.

8

The MBA: The Potential for Students to Find their Voice in Babel

Audrey Collin

It is commonly believed that management is a 'socially valuable technical function' working in the best interests of all (Alvesson and Willmott, 1992: 1). Like the chair and CEO of General Motors, many value its role in 'the evolution of an ethical and humanistic capitalism' that 'stimulates innovation, fosters excellence, enriches society, and dignifies work' (Johnston et al., 1986: 33). The education of managers, therefore, must be of significance not only for them as individuals but also for society.

The Master's degree in Business Administration (MBA), according to Cameron (1991: 16), 'has been traditionally aimed at increasing a manager's ability to take good strategic decisions'. It covers the analysis of problems and appreciation of their context; the use of 'appropriate conceptual tools and analytical and evaluative techniques'; and often the development of consultancy skills. A similar view is seen in Beard (1992) and the *Harvard Business Review*'s debate (1992) on the relevance of the MBA today, and is well expressed by two graduates of the archetypical MBA at Harvard Business School:

> What do they really teach you at the Harvard Business School? A method. A method of looking at the world, for taking a problem and searching your vast mental file drawer of examples to see which ways this problem is similar to any of them. A method of using examples that are similar, yet by no means the same, to extrapolate what a solution might be to the problem at hand. What they teach you at the Harvard Business School is to deal with that problem today, not tomorrow; to deal with it as best you can and not to dwell on it. Because tomorrow there will be another problem, equally baffling, equally challenging, equally possible to solve. (Kelly and Kelly, 1987: 260)

This traditional model of management education is, however, being called into question in a whole series of ways, as discussed by Grey and French (this volume) and by Thomas and Anthony (this volume). In place of what, rightly or wrongly, seemed like the old consensus, management educators and students are now faced with a bewildering array of discourses – a tower of Babel. The task of this chapter is to explore how students may 'find their own voice' within or among these multiple discourses.

The Multiple Discourses of Management Theory and Practice

The discourses of both practitioners and theorists of management intersect, interpenetrate and influence one another. Many of the various interpretations of management made by its stakeholders are filtered through the discourses current in the relevant academic disciplines (sociology, psychology, economics, etc.), with their subgroups and schools of thought and underpinning epistemologies, philosophies and ideologies. The wide variety in focus and range can be seen in any management textbook. Morgan (1986) covers both mainstream and alternative discourses, while the epistemological and (positivist) philosophical assumptions and the socially constructed nature and technocratic focus of orthodox approaches to management become visible through the exposition of more recent critical discourses (for example Alvesson and Willmott, 1992; Fineman, 1993; Frost et al., 1991; Hassard and Parker, 1993; Hearn et al., 1989; Hosking and Fineman, 1990; Reed and Hughes, 1992).

Management is, in part, a technical activity, 'the instrumental activities that transform nature and deliver goods and services' (Alvesson and Willmott, 1992: 18). However, it is on this one element that mainstream discourses focus, attributing technical or professional expertise to managers, so that other significant elements of management and managing become submerged. Such discourses ignore, and perhaps have no means of acknowledging, the significance of (*inter alia*) the social and political values underpinning the particular division of labour selected to undertake the technical function (Alvesson and Willmott, 1992; Braverman, 1974; Whitaker, 1992); the manager's practical intelligence (Sternberg, 1985) and tacit knowledge (Cooper and Fox, 1990; Polanyi, 1968); and the manager's identity, emotions and morality (Fineman, 1993; Hearn et al., 1989; Hochschild, 1983; Watson, 1994).

The iconoclastic writer Mant (1979) (aware in the 1970s of the significance of language in this field) asserts that emphasis on the professional rather than the practical aspect of managing can be attributed to 'subconscious perceptions of cleanliness and dirtiness' (1979: 18–19) and the deep split between clean/dirty, brains/hands, the professions/industry, managers/workers. He sees this as a British characteristic, and British management education as a preparation 'to be' (as in social status) rather than 'to do'. He comments that management is frequently seen as 'a series of disembodied skills or techniques' (1979: 162) and, in a passage echoed in the quotation from Butler cited below, suggests that 'in the management school, you hang up your guts at the door and bring in just the brain' (Mant, 1979: 150). He continues:

> Until management education . . . deals with the whole man or woman instead of, in fantasy, the spiritless, intellectual, split-off bit that goes to the office, or the works, then it is simply toying with the problems that face us. (1979: 171)

Watson (1994) pays attention to some of these submerged aspects of managing, seeing this as 'a very practical, down-to-earth activity', which 'seems complex because it involves *people*' (1994: 215). It is thus 'a social and moral activity . . . a human social craft' (1994: 223). Watson describes the managers he had studied as 'practical theorists' (1994: 164). He suggests (1994: 211) that they appeared to have placed so little store by 'managerial techniques or textbook theories' because, for them, managing was not 'a morally neutral activity which involves applying control techniques to achieve effective performance'. Rather, he argues, quoting Roberts (1984), effective managing is 'a form of *practice* in which there is a mutual recognition of one another as interdependent subjects'. Hence, in recognition of 'the necessity of negotiating trusting and consistent relations with others' (Watson, 1994: 211), Watson's managers mixed 'the principled and the pragmatic' in their personal 'theories'. Watson's thesis challenges management education to address the nature of managers' discourse of practice and to articulate it with those of 'textbook theories'.

The interactions and inter-relationships of these various discourses create (to change the metaphor) a kaleidoscopic pattern, making this field so fascinating although often confusing. This could be illustrated by tracing how a particular set of ideas is worked and reworked in various arenas and generations. For example, the technical, social, ethical, practical and ideological aspects of management identified by Child (1969: 23) are reworked by Mant (1979: 56) and reappear in various combinations in today's various discourses. Here the relationship between information technology and human potential is cast in a positive light in the mainstream 'learning organization' discourse (Senge, 1990), but viewed negatively in Willmott's (1994) critical interpretation of business process re-engineering.

It will be apparent from the above that many of the differences between these discourses, which are confusing for those trying to understand the field, stem from the significant differences in their underlying assumptions. However, as exponents of critical theory point out, mainstream management theory and practice lack critical self-awareness and pay little attention to their underlying assumptions, many of which are shared. Alvesson and Willmott (1992: 1) identify these as 'a narrow, instrumental form of rationality'. They note (1992: 1) that 'the neutrality or virtue of management' is considered 'self-evident or unproblematical'. Grey and Mitev (1995) refer to the reproduction of 'knowledge which is at best problematic and at worst discredited'. Such criticism is not peculiar to this field. For example, Giroux and Freire (1990: vii), writing of the 'dominant discourses' in educational psychology, discuss their 'appeal to science, objectivity, prediction, and control'. Educational psychology constitutes 'a hegemonic discourse' which uses 'its power to discipline, test, sort, and label' in order to adapt students to 'existing relations of power'. This view could equally be applied to accepted management practices such as, for example, the use of psychometric testing for selection, or the adoption of competences as a response to the national need for management training.

Asserting that 'positivism is still the dominant ideology of academia', Mitroff and Churchman make the connection between this and attitudes to management practice. Academia 'regards application and implementation as dirty and beneath the concerns of the scholar' (1992: 134), whereas they believe that:

> 'truth' is only discovered through the process of implementing ethical ideas that make a difference. Implementation is perhaps the most critical component in the production of knowledge. (1992: 136)

While theorists attempt to interpret and explain the world of practice, practitioners themselves, as Watson (1994) shows, are influenced by the language and concepts of theorists. Management discourses, therefore, run across both practice and theory, feeding on both, although the subtle relationship between them has not necessarily been reciprocal or comfortable. Child (1969: 237), for example, noted that managers openly criticized academia's 'system of knowledge superficially so attractive ideologically and technically', while academics 'expressed their exasperation at managers' lack of concern for their ideas'. Fox (1994: 580) suggests that academics take managerial goals on themselves, valuing their own work according to its contribution to managers' operational goals, 'uncritically defined in pervasive and taken-for-granted ways'. This makes academics' enquiry 'technical in orientation', and 'prevents them from taking a *critical* perspective on management itself'.

It may be concluded that students of management need to understand the complexity of this field:

> It is critical to the success of managers that they understand how we know what we claim to know about management, that they comprehend what the eclectic array of disciplines that make up their subject can or cannot tell them about the shifting realities with which they deal. Students should understand with some sophistication both what is surrendered and what is gained as a result of the heavy dependence of management study on research in the social and behavioural sciences. They should understand what sorts of knowledge it is possible to attain through objective analysis of empirical data and what must come through the combined efforts of reason, emotion, and intuition – head, heart, and gut. (Butler, 1986: 159)

It should not be assumed that, when in the role of student, managers will necessarily be deterred by an approach which examines their discourses and introduces them to others. It can, after all, be inferred from the distinction between their 'espoused theory' and 'theory-in-use' (Argyris and Schon, 1978) and from Watson's study (1994) that many are already aware of the co-existence of various discourses of practice and theory. If a course such as the MBA neglects the 'resources' they 'deploy' 'to make sense of events' (Watson, 1994: 173), they are more likely to be frustrated than if it attempts to help articulate them, understand the relationships between them and identify their underlying assumptions. A key task of management education must, therefore, be to attend to these multiple perspectives (Fox, 1994) and to question the assumptions and values underlying them, and so begin the process of critical self-awareness. This provides a clear agenda for the MBA.

Learning Opportunities Presented by the Awareness of Multiple Discourses

The theories of learning commonly referred to in management education concern, in particular, different and preferred learning styles (Honey and Mumford, 1982; Mumford, 1988) and the processes by which managers learn, as seen in the Lancaster and Kolb models (Binsted, 1980; Kolb, 1983). (Vince, this volume, argues that the underpinning assumptions of such models also need critical examination.) The Lancaster model represents learning as a cycle with three phases: the reception of an input of knowledge, a discovery loop of action and feedback and a reflection loop of hypothesizing and conceptualizing through which an individual incorporates the significance of new knowledge and understanding in a meaningful way. The literature from the wider educational field, particularly that concerning adults (see Jarvis, 1988), offers further views of learning as a process of personal change, which are relevant to the MBA, as I shall note below.

Perry (in Daloz, 1986) sees learning as 'intellectual and ethical development'. Starting from a dualistic view of the world ('good' or 'bad'), individuals can come to recognize the existence of diversity, accept the legitimate uncertainty implied in this, begin to perceive that all knowledge and values are context bound and so relativistic and arrive at a personal commitment to a particular viewpoint in full realization of this contextual relativism. Not all will complete this process. Mezirow (1977, 1981) also views learning in terms of personal change and transformation. It is a developmental process 'towards meaning perspectives that are progressively more inclusive, discriminating, and more integrative of experience' (Mezirow, 1977: 159). For him, learning takes place as the individual reflects on disjunctions between assumptions and experience, leading to:

> a sequential restructuring of one's frame of reference for making and under-standing meanings . . . successive transformations towards analyzing things from a perspective increasingly removed from one's personal or local perspective. (1977: 157)

Mezirow (1981) regards this transformation as an emancipatory process: critical awareness of constraining assumptions, revision of those assumptions and erosion of the perceptions of the constraints and action in the light of this. This could be particularly significant for managers who, according to Alvesson and Willmott, 'are "victims" as well as perpetrators of discourses and practices that unnecessarily constrain their ways of thinking and acting' (1992: 7).

Exponents of critical theory (such as Grey et al., this volume) find support in Freire's (1972) radical approach to education. His literacy programme tackled the oppressive 'culture of silence' in Brazil in which the ruling, colonizing classes had been able to impose their construction of reality on the indigenous people:

> the oppressed are imprisoned in a cultural construction of reality that is false to them but one from which it is difficult to escape, since even the language used by them transmits the values that imprison them. (Jarvis, 1988: 91)

Literacy gave the oppressed the means to 'name' their own world and hence a voice in a new and potentially emancipatory dialogue. The critical theorist might suggest that MBA students need to learn how to 'name' the experiences of managers: awareness of the multiple discourses would improve their 'literacy'.

These theories suggest that the need to recognize, orientate and respond, both conceptually and in practice, to the multiple discourses of management would be a significant opportunity for intellectual and personal development. It would constitute a stimulus for students to become aware of their own assumptions, experience transformation (in Mezirow's term) and develop towards a mature position of contextual relativism (in Perry's term). By making these competing perspectives explicit, the MBA would be encouraging its students' fluency of thinking, and hence meeting mainstream needs while also setting in process both a critical awareness and personal development.

The rest of this chapter describes a study which explored whether the various elements of learning described above were experienced by a group of former students on their MBA courses.

The Study of Former MBA Students

I interviewed seven colleagues, men and women, awarded an MBA between 1987 and 1993 via full-time, part-time and distance learning modes at different institutions. Six had been working in managerial or professional jobs when they started on the course, but later became management teachers themselves. The tape-recorded interviews lasted between 1 and 2 hours and, although unstructured, explored the experiences of learning on the MBA and whether it had discussed the existence and nature of an orthodoxy in management thinking or had challenged assumptions, and briefly touched on the relationship between theory and practice. The study adopted a critical interpretive methodology (Sullivan, 1990).

Because of the number and nature of the respondents, they cannot be treated as representative of MBA students in general. Indeed, some of them clearly saw themselves as different from their peers on the course. Moreover, the interpretations of their student experiences that they now, as university teachers themselves chose to convey to me, their colleague, will almost certainly be different from those they would have made when they were living through them. Nevertheless, my colleagues treat their student experiences as authentic and valid, and reported that they had drawn on them for their own teaching practice. In interpreting their accounts, I am also able to draw on my own experiences of teaching over 10 cohorts of MBA students. These interviews, therefore, illustrate something of the specific learning experiences on MBAs, and raise issues of more general concern to management educators. (To safeguard anonymity, I have given the students pseudonyms – Bosworth, Clephan, Fletcher, Gateway, Hawthorn, Kimberlin and Portland – and omitted details of gender and university attended.)

The initial motivation for undertaking an MBA varied, of course, between the individuals involved and included concern for career prospects, for a move into management, promotion, or improved job performance; the desire for stimulus, challenge and job satisfaction and, on the part of one individual who was already a management lecturer, the strengthening of the existing 'academic base'; the wish to 'break the mould' set early in life by low school expectations and social class; the rerouting of the career, thwarted by family circumstances that had necessitated leaving school early, back into academia.

Outcomes also varied, although almost all emphasized their increased self-confidence and self-esteem, both as persons and as managers. As Hawthorn expressed it:

> If I can go through a Master's programme, the pinnacle of business education, *the* MBA . . . then there is no limit to what I can do . . . For me it was the best two years in my life.

There was a sense of increased enthusiasm and a greater ability and readiness to challenge others. Most described themselves as having learned a great deal in terms of knowledge, understanding and the ability to use a broader conceptual framework as the basis for questioning individual perceptions and organizational patterns. For some, this development did not, however, enhance their work or prospects in their current employment. They mentioned the lack of opportunity for putting their new learning into operation there, or the lack of fit with the organization that they began to experience. This mismatch contributed to their reasons for moving into management teaching during or after completing the MBA.

Experiences of the MBA

Although, as I shall show, my colleagues' MBAs appear to have been largely lacking a critical perspective, they evidently had the potential to develop varying degrees of independent thinking and personal development. However, these accounts raise doubts about their value in preparing and developing students as managers.

Experiences of Challenge on the MBA

I shall examine my colleagues' experiences of being challenged on the course in terms of their awareness of the multiple discourses and underlying assumptions of the mainstream approaches, and the stance of their tutors.

Awareness of Multiple Discourses and Underlying Assumptions   Although several colleagues mentioned that there had been reference to different schools of management thought, they did not allude to such alternative perspectives as social constructionism or critical theory. To prompt them to consider whether their MBAs had identified the assumptions of the mainstream managerial approach, I asked, *inter alia*, whether the historical, social and ideological context of management had been formally discussed. Although, in the main, it had not, their replies indicate that their awareness may have been raised in other ways.

Kimberlin's MBA encouraged a 'healthy scepticism'. Different modules used the same case study to show that 'there are other ways of looking at this': the HRM module was 'reasonably explicit' in exposing students to several viewpoints and 'invited' them 'to deal with this'. This course was not 'intellectually naive', and recognized 'that we lived in a capitalist society'. Of the students there, 'a surprisingly large number were political dissenters': 'some of the most intelligent critiques of the Thatcher view of capitalism as well as of capitalism itself that I've ever *heard* I encountered there [from students]'.

The greatest questioning of orthodoxy had taken place in the organizational behaviour, strategy and business ethics modules. The result of this was that: 'People who were stunted in thinking about the philosophical implications of what they did started to grow in that way.' Kimberlin also noted that the mix of private and public sector employees had presented challenges. The former 'believed that the public sector were not good managers, living in a cosy, cushioned world'; it was 'quite a shock' to work alongside people who had 'very sharp minds and could often out-think them'. However, Kimberlin reflected that this course may not have been questioning at the level of epistemology, that 'some things could have been intellectually beefed up'. Attention to these issues, however, would have been at the expense of others.

Fletcher had been aware of two approaches to learning on the MBA: a sterile, 'tablets-of-stone', knowledge-not-understanding kind, and a rich, fulfilling, 'very philosophical, questioning, double-loop' kind, calling for reflection and experienced particularly in the OB teaching. Here the tutor had challenged the class to recognize that 'a way of seeing is also a way of not seeing'. The course considered various perspectives (such as economics, accounting or marketing) on a given problem, so that several solutions could be identified. It also raised questions about 'the status quo, power, politics', but not the '*wider* underpinnings – is that a good system or not?'

Asked whether the course acknowledged orthodoxy in management, Hawthorn replied that, formally, there was 'not a forum for that', it was 'fairly straight down the line'. The only discussions took place in informal talks in the bar. Since courses in business ethics or corporate responsibility did not then exist, moral and political issues were not discussed either. However, the class exercised independent thinking, and on one occasion attracted the tutor's disapproval for 'something that the students were constructing for themselves rather than being *taught* about'. Hawthorn also glimpsed the existence of different assumptions through the experiences and responses of the overseas students in the class: 'the *perspectives* they gave me rather than the actual facts'.

Although Clephan's MBA put human resource management and operations management in their historical context, it nevertheless assumed 'a certain economic order and a certain political order, and there was no challenging of that, not that I picked up anyway'. Clephan did become aware of alternative approaches, but 'in ragbag sort of way'. Because there was 'no sort of coherence', this awareness depended on the 'values you initially come with'.

In Bosworth's experience, such issues were raised only during debates in the full-time periods, but 'more as an entertainment or side issue'. This MBA was 'pragmatic, not perfect but it worked'. It 'did not deal with the social consequences of capitalism'; it was assumed, though never discussed, that 'the MBA tag has "capitalist" in small type underneath it'. Some lecturers 'were perhaps more to the left than a lot of the students'. 'It was assumed, rightly or wrongly, explicitly or implicitly, that we were all there to want to make money . . . all of the capitalist bent, and it was probably also assumed that we were all of the capital "C" Conservative type.'

Gateway contrasted the relative sterility and blandness of learning on the MBA with the impact of learning in another setting, which 'really knocked me about a bit . . . profoundly altered my way of looking at the world'. Gateway commented that learning occurs when a new idea 'suddenly *links*, clicks in one's mind with other things that you've been working on'. This suggests that this MBA may not have been grappling with the urgent or emerging issues of the day.

Portland gives an instructive account of how prior experience was activated to overcome the absence of challenge on the MBA. Whereas Portland's first degree in the humanities had encouraged 'exploration', the MBA was 'geared toward success, to passing, getting a qualification' and 'conformed to a free market approach to business'. The students appeared to want a hard-nosed business approach presented in a schoolroom style, where 'the lecturer knows best', and at times they acted like 'schoolboys' (there was only one woman in the class). After initial surprise, Portland went along with this, but wonders: 'Maybe the environment I worked in determined that [the "hard" approaches to management] were the only things that were taken seriously.'

Thus for Portland the first two years of the MBA provided only instrumental experiences. Its approach was to 'apply tools rather than thinking about it', with 'no questioning of prevailing beliefs'. Portland contrasted this with the experience of the first degree, where:

> there'd been a *wealth* of things, a wealth of avenues to explore. And I felt that ... from that very open subject I was going to this fairly narrow, 'you don't think outside here, no, we're just here for profit' ... very narrow business – it seemed to me quite depressing ... [In the first degree] I came across ideas, philosophies, *basic* ways of looking at the world that made sense to *me*, and I was able to explore them ... Whereas the MBA I never felt *touched* upon that at all ... never challenged my world view ... an MBA should provide the individual with some insight into where they do maybe stand in the scheme of things and what they can base their later judgements on.

It was while researching for the Year III thesis that Portland began to see 'that what goes on in business is a reflection of what goes on outside', and began to draw on the work done in the first degree, where Marxist models had offered 'a way of looking at society and interpreting it – *that* was real learning'. Portland now began to be able 'to see how other people might be able to interpret things in a certain way':

> I suppose that was the real break-through, because I began to see how the Porter model wasn't just – 'here's a model you can apply to the environment' – there were actually values behind it, there were assumptions behind it – and [in class] we'd never challenged those, we'd never explored those ... nobody ever said 'But Porter believes in ... Porter's got these assumptions'. And it was then that I thought, 'Just a minute, I've been going around with my eyes closed for the last couple of years' ... And once I reached that, it almost exploded back into a reevaluation of the things that I'd been taught ... And I suppose once I started thinking of those almost off my own back, rather than just accepting what had been given, it began to snowball into the other parts.

Portland reflected on the implications of these experiences for teaching and management practice:

> And we almost encourage people, we make it easy for them to leave their values at the door, because we say 'Here are some objective models that you can apply, and the decisions are almost value-free, so you don't need to worry about it.'

Because of its significance:

> The critical perspective needs to be embedded like a stick of rock, be there throughout the whole of the course, otherwise it will get lost.

The Stance of MBA Tutors The MBA has a vocational purpose; students are generally expected to join it for instrumental purposes and with instrumental expectations (see Beard, 1992). They may, therefore, find it uncomfortable to have their often pragmatic world views questioned. Although critical of this, Portland acknowledged that such expectations may have influenced what was actually experienced in the class. This, however, makes a considerable challenge to tutors who may wish to introduce a critical perspective to the MBA.

Although Kimberlin experienced a respect for alternative views on the course, several other accounts suggest that tutors may have found difficulties, even risk. I have already noted how Portland saw the class as instrumental in purpose and acting like 'schoolboys': 'teacher knows best'. One can interpret that this may have been part of a vicious circle because at the same time, according to Portland, the tutors seemed to believe that 'students know more'. Gateway recalled the class's reaction when a lecturer drew an earthworm to illustrate a point. Although this was 'a superb analogy', the group was not prepared to enter into his mindset: 'as far as they were concerned it was useless information, and he got a real hammering'.

Hawthorn also reported disagreement between the class and the tutor: 'I could see him going red because he was getting angry to some extent, [it] didn't fit in with his preconceived models.' This report, however, emphasized the class's independent rather than dependent mode of thinking.

These comments suggest that the expectations that students bring to the MBA not only frame their learning but, conveyed to tutors and, in some groups, perhaps even imposed on tutors through group norms, also frame what tutors attempt and therefore influence what other class members experience. My colleagues' reports suggest that in some instances the tutor does not necessarily fully control the class; control may have to be achieved by negotiation with the class. As I have felt in my own experience, this may at times call for risk taking and moral courage on the part of the tutor.

The Value of the MBA in Preparing and Developing Managers

My colleagues' MBAs may not have raised critical awareness, but they could have been expected to address the needs of managers as defined by mainstream management thought. However, many of their experiences suggest that this was not unequivocally so. Six of my colleagues, it will be recalled, left the world of the manager for academia: the MBA had clearly not made that world more acceptable or desirable to them but had, indeed, become a vehicle by which they left it.

There are several instances in these accounts which throw some doubt on the value of the MBA to practising managers. Clephan, for example, indicated that little attention had been paid to practical applications on the course, except when 'largely self-driven'. Moreover, Clephan's company did not encourage the application of learning to the workplace, although one of the strengths of part-time MBAs is generally assumed to be that students will engage in discovery/feedback in everyday practice. Bosworth's learning uncovered the unacceptable realities of the company. Members of Portland's class apparently found little to benefit their practice and did not seek to be challenged, although by the third year some had begun to recognize the value of the course in personal development, if not in their development as managers.

These experiences raise questions about the purpose of the MBA. They may be hinting that the MBA primarily addresses not the general population of managers, wishing to progress or become more effective as managers, but those who wish to progress in the wider management 'industry' – as experts about management, whether academics or consultants. They may also be a recognition that the practice of managers is not easily amenable to the scientific analysis and training espoused by the MBA, but is a form of *bricolage*, or 'science of the concrete' (Hebdige, 1979). Hence, as Mant (1979) observed, it is regarded as an inferior activity. On the other hand, they may be an acknowledgement that management practice is a far more complex, subtle and moral activity than at first appears, so that learning has to take place through practice, observation, imitation and reflection rather than through the ingestion of management theory and techniques. If so, the role of the MBA must be to encourage reflection and to challenge taken-for-granted approaches.

The Design of Learning on the MBA

My colleagues' experiences also raise issues relating to the design of learning on the MBA. Although it is common to refer to the theories of managers' learning in, for example, MBA full-time periods, the following suggests that this may often be done more as ritual than realistic commitment.

I had asked my colleagues whether their course had encouraged them to complete the Lancaster 'cycle' of learning (referred to earlier). Several of their responses suggest that these MBAs may not have been designed in terms of a holistic approach to learning, although some of my colleagues had experiences in which both cognitive and affective aspects of learning had been integrated (see Collin and Cumberpatch, 1995).

Earlier in this chapter I pointed to the significance that different theories of learning attribute to reflection. It did not feature strongly in my colleagues' accounts of their courses, although it can be inferred, especially in the experiences recounted by Hawthorn, Kimberlin and Portland. In response to my question, Clephan replied: 'input of knowledge strong, reflection weak, practical application somewhere between the two and largely self-driven'. By contrast, Fletcher was aware that opportunities for reflection were built into the course, and found this 'refreshing'.

Writing of the development of 'general management skills', Burnett (1992: 33) suggests that there are three 'ingredients' which 'blend to create a powerful reaction'. These are organizational experience, the intellectual curiosity to want to learn from experience, and:

> The last ingredient – and this is where management schools enter the stew – is a medium that allows and stimulates mangers to reflect on their experiences and compare them with the experiences of others. (1992: 33)

It is not clear that all three ingredients were present in my colleagues' experiences. Not all, as already noted, had appropriate learning opportunities at work; not all will have been able to compare their experiences with others in the classroom. Full-time, part-time and distance learning courses will have had very different outcomes. One colleague noted the importance of relationships within the class and suggested that on a full-time MBA there was time to spend with people 'in same boat'. This promotes bonding and:

> tends to make you think a certain way, and because of the class of people there it can only be advantageous. It's up to you what you pick up and what you refuse to take on board, but the total thing just gives you something you can't experience if you've only got it in spots here and there [as in a part-time course].

Overall, much of my colleagues' learning may have been achieved through informal rather formally designed means.

The Beneficial Outcomes of the MBA

Given the aims of this chapter, I have largely concentrated on what, from the perspective of this book, would be seen as the shortcomings of MBAs. Yet it will be apparent that my colleagues viewed some of the outcomes of their courses very positively. (Again, some of these issues are discussed more fully in Collin and Cumberpatch, 1995.)

Intellectual Development

Almost all my colleagues referred to their enjoyment of their course and to their intellectual development because of it. For example, 'everything' on the MBA had challenged Bosworth's thinking who, without a first degree, responded 'like a sponge . . . give me more, give me more'. Clephan found 'the intellectual process exciting'. Some of the topics 'really fired me up', although Clephan was frustrated in attempts to apply these new ideas in the company. Fletcher's 'frames of reference' had been 'modified, broadened, added to', although never ultimately 'up for grabs'.

Kimberlin's account of this development set me off on a new tack in my interpretation of what an MBA achieves. Citing the view of the novelist Barbara Pym (1990) that good writing was 'finding your own voice', Kimberlin applied this first to good teaching and then to being a student:

> I did find my voice at the end as a student – I could jump through hoops – and then bring it all into question again . . . when I was doing my last assignment – I thought 'I could *not* have written this two and a half years ago – I haven't said the last word on this, but I now have something to say . . . I'm pleased with this – it's not a seminal contribution to the world of learning, but I have found a voice.' The programme was well designed and enabled you to end with an assignment like that, that gave you an opportunity to say something.

Personal Development

My colleagues believed that their courses had not only had a positive effect, whether directly or indirectly, on their careers but, more significantly, on their confidence and sense of self. According to Mant (1979), this outcome is characteristic of management education:

> Management students rarely apply anything of substantive usefulness but they almost invariably return more *confident* from the experience. What that confidence is a function *of* is difficult to determine, but its importance ought not to be underestimated. (1979: 165)

Bosworth and Hawthorn emphasized the considerable personal development they had experienced through the MBA, Bosworth in particular acknowledged an increase in social status as part of this. Mant (1979: 161), too, has recognized this. Referring to the 'Palladian splendour' of London Business School, he writes:

> The sensation is more than symbolic; if you happen to work in despised industry and, worse, if you missed university of any kind, not to mention Oxbridge, then to pass through this building is to press a little closer to the extreme centre of concentric British society. It is not a process to be despised; it is a matter of no little import to British businessmen to be made whole again, to re-enter society more fully from the social outskirts of trade and commerce. (1979: 161).

It may have been these changes in self or social status, rather than any specific learning from the course itself, that made possible the career changes.

From a critical perspective, this development could be interpreted as further adaptations within the process of socialization, the reconstitution of the person to the needs of new roles. However, from the perspective of Mezirow's (1977) developmental view of learning, the 'transformation' achieved through the MBA can lead on to further 'transformations'. Indeed, there are echoes in the words of Bosworth and Hawthorn of Mezirow's view of learning, transformation and emancipation, outlined earlier in this chapter: the awareness of constraining assumptions, the revision of these assumptions and gradual emancipation from the perceived constraints. The MBA changed their perception of themselves and their world, and they then changed part of that world in ways that they could not have done without the confidence and status they derived from it. Moreover, the way in which they now teach flows from these experiences, which are now influencing another generation of students. Portland believed that:

> maybe 10, 20, 30 [years] – as they progress through organizations, if they realise the value of it, they send their subordinates on an MBA course . . . you could over a period of time effect some sort of change . . . it might be very difficult for people to put ideas into practice immediately, but it would influence the way they made decisions.

The Sources of Beneficial Outcomes

The Design of the Course

Reviewing my colleagues' experiences, it is difficult to attribute these positive outcomes to the intentional design of their MBAs as they portrayed them. With the exception of Fletcher and Kimberlin, none indicated that their course had deliberately or extensively incorporated the significant elements of learning picked out earlier from the educational literature. These were the need for reflection, the significance of context and of contextual relativism, the recognition of the learner as a person and the personal effects of learning, and the recognition of the possibility of effecting social change through learning.

What is clear, however, is that these elements could be created coincidentally, as by-products of other processes and interactions. Often not designed by tutors, such learning opportunities existed for those students who were hungry enough (like Bosworth), had the appropriate academic background (like Portland), organizational experience (like Clephan), the percipience (like Gateway), the class mix (like Hawthorn). It is therefore, perhaps, to the considerable diversity on these MBAs that we can look for the generation of much of their students' development.

The Experience of Diversity

The accounts of my colleagues point to the considerable diversity on MBA programmes. There is a wide range in the backgrounds, expectations, aspirations, attitudes and values among and between students and lecturers, as well as different modes of delivery of these courses.

This diversity was highlighted in the emphasis several of my colleagues gave to how they had differed from their peers on the course, being less instrumental and more questioning. Perhaps they had by now overlaid their learning experiences with those of teaching; or were responding to being interviewed by a colleague. Whatever the reason, they made several references to their peers' instrumental approach to the MBA. Bosworth saw them as using it as a passport to greater earnings and as a means of putting them 'on the winning side', and believed that this was a common assumption. As already noted, Portland's class at times acted like 'schoolboys':

> the attitude of the group was to get through the MBA . . . and, if I'm honest (and I still keep in contact with a few of the people) a lot of them have stayed at that level . . . they've never wanted to go beyond that.

Portland also recalled a 'Theory X and Y competition' for who had the 'hardest' set of attitudes. Gateway's report of the class's intolerance when a lecturer used an unconventional example has already been noted. Gateway saw the MBA as a 'game' and believed that those students who 'latched on to it being a game seem to do *better*': by making as much contact as possible with tutors, they 'flush out . . . these covert rules'. Another colleague described the tactic of ensuring that lecturers knew 'who I was' in the large class.

This experience of diversity in which multiple demands meet and interact with multiple messages makes the MBA a complex, creative and dynamic matrix of learning opportunities, pregnant with many possibilities although not easily amenable to control and direction. In terms of the initial theme of this chapter, the MBA is a site of intersecting and interacting discourses. Viewed from mainstream or critical perspectives, it is an arena in which many and diverse actors generate, discuss, dissect and negotiate multiple, shifting, diverse and sometimes conflicting meanings. This makes it a field of rich and random heterogeneity, multivocal and multivalent, a veritable Babel.

How Can we Help Students Find their Own Voice in this Babel?

I shall now conclude by discussing how management teachers may more effectively develop their students' critical awareness. I should first like to suggest that what we are aiming at is to help our students become independent thinkers, to find their own voices in this Babel, not to parrot ours. Using the words of Habermas (in Alvesson and Willmott, 1992: 4) to different effect, we should be aware that 'demythification which does not break the mythic spell but merely seeks to evade it will only bring forth new witch doctors'.

My colleagues' experiences have shown something of the intellectual and personal development that takes place even when a critical perspective is minimal or absent. We need not suppose that our intervention is essential to this: the process of learning itself will develop people over time. Moreover, they will learn from the experience of being on an MBA, whatever they learn from its teaching. Its very diversity and the numerous discourses of management to which they will be exposed will constitute a Babel, or a polyphonic text, which expresses 'heteroglossia' (Bakhtin, 1981):

> an orchestration of diverse discourses culled from heterogeneous sources, oral and written, conveying different ideological positions which are put in play without ever being subjected to totalising judgement or interpretation. (in Jeffcutt, 1993: 39)

Engagement in the heteroglossia of the MBA Babel by students with searching minds, differing needs and career trajectories will generate unimaginable possibilities for individual learning. However, as Butler recognizes, 'If the purpose of the course is to be realized, it must also include devices designed to force students to engage their own intellects and intuitions in the disciplinary interplay' (1986: 167).

We can prepare ourselves by learning how to harness the process of learning and the role of education in it. The theories of Freire (1972), Mezirow (1977), Perry (in Daloz, 1986), noted earlier in this chapter, will augment those of managers' learning with which we are already familiar. We need our colleagues' support to give us confidence and courage and help in identifying appropriate 'devices'. We can call on them to join us, in Portland's metaphor, in embedding a critical perspective through the MBA 'stick of rock' rather than marginalizing it in, say, business ethics. Even though they may not share our own critical perspective, we can solicit their support by arguing the need to develop students' intellectual fluency and quoting, for example, Perry and Mezirow, on the potential role of the recognition of diversity in this. We can use this same argument with our students and, as Grey et al. (this volume) advocate, make them aware of the learning process in general and their own in particular. We must be aware of the emotional and interpersonal implications of their 'journey' (to use Daloz's (1986: 24–6) metaphor), reinforce our students' confidence and – a point Hawthorn also made – give them support as well as challenge.

Overall, we should be looking for some chink through which they can glimpse an alternative to their taken-for-granted world. However, as Bhavnani (1990), writing in a somewhat different field, recognizes, the giving of a 'voice' is a necessary but not a sufficient condition for empowerment; the framework of power relationships that creates silence must also be exposed. Our students are managers, or aspire to be. We can, therefore, count on their interest in management when inviting them to examine its nature. From their own experience, they will recognize the existence of many and often conflicting interpretations. Disclaiming expert status ourselves, with its power to silence them (Power and Laughlin, 1992: 130), we can draw on their perspectives and encourage them to 'name' their experiences. We can challenge them to consider what the purpose of the MBA is – whether to make effective managers, to carry out an academic study of management, or to make more marketable graduates – and recognize the interactions between these different goals.

Clearly, we need to introduce our students to a wide range of discourses – through 'dialectical pluralism', as Grey and French (this volume) put it – making the critical perspective explicit by our attention to their epistemological and ideological assumptions and to the socially constructed nature of management. There are various 'devices' we could use for this: contrasting several perspectives on a given situation; encouraging them to identify and compare the perspectives of different subjects and lecturers; contextualizing situations and experiences; putting ideas and situations into historical perspective; comparing public and private sector values and experiences; drawing on the diversity of culture, race, gender, social class present in an MBA class; using the class as a forum to exchange and debate organizational experiences. We need to keep a focus on the pressing and emerging issues of the day, but could, for example, set a class the task of identifying the various strands interwoven in today's discourses. In those MBAs which are examined by thesis, we should make effective use of the inherent ambiguity in the initial phases of research to encourage our students to explore widely and confront the new perspectives they encounter.

Importantly, we must find ways to ensure that our students reflect on their learning and their practice, encouraging them to be aware of this reflection and its significance. For part-time students, it might be appropriate to initiate a greater interest in this in their workplace by, for example, fostering an interest there in reflective practice (Schon, 1987) or

9

Plato on the Education of Managers

Jonathan Gosling

Why, one might ask, should anyone concerned with the education and development of managers in the late twentieth century be in the least interested in what Plato had to say? Was he not, after all, the apologist of totalitarianism (surely our organizations are not totalitarian) and the progenitor of a discredited absolutism (surely no one these days is interested in absolute truth)?

Well, first, his central assertion is startling: that the people most suited to lead are those who persistently show the least inclination to do so, and who are most convinced that the material conditions over which they preside are unreal and ultimately unimportant. Secondly, many of the issues that were problematic in state administration in classical Greece are problematic today: the criteria for selecting management trainees; how to develop their thinking, judgemental and creative abilities; the relationship between private gain, the good of an enterprise and that of the state. Thirdly, debates about the proper stance to take in relation to thinking and knowledge continue to be couched in dichotomous terms that would have been familiar to Plato: idealism/materialism, individualism/collectivism, induction/deduction and so forth. Fourthly, Plato is compelling, humorous and witty and more than most gives a fair hearing to his opponents – so much so that many of the arguments in the dialogues end without a conclusion, but leave the reader with the sense of having been exposed to some profound and stimulating approaches to important questions such as the rewards of justice, the nature of love and the criteria of virtue. For these reasons, this chapter will offer a reading of Plato as a theorist, educator and thinker on management, and will draw out the significance of that reading for contemporary management education.

Plato was born into the upper classes of Athenian society in 428 BC and was clearly marked out for a career in politics and public administration. He received some training for this, but in the event spent most of his mature years (from the age of 40 onwards) in setting up and running what I shall take to be equivalent to a leading international management school: the Athenian Academy. In his *Seventh Letter*[1] he explains how his earlier experience of the corruption and ineffectiveness of political leaders and policy makers had led him to become an educationalist.

action learning (Revans, 1983). This could begin to overcome some of the barriers between management education and practice.

In conclusion, I shall repeat the view of Alvesson and Willmott that management is 'too potent in its effects upon the lives of employees, consumers and citizens to be guided by a narrow, instrumental form of rationality . . . too important . . . to be left to the mainstream thinking of management departments and business schools' (1992: 1–3). Just as we have, we believe, found our voices, so we must work to help our students find theirs in this Babel. We shall perhaps help them best by demonstrating our respect for the 'social and moral activity' (Watson, 1994: 223) in which they are engaged.

Notes

The study to which this chapter refers is based on ideas originally conceived with Zena Cumberpatch. Although she was unable to continue to be involved in the study, we have explored some of the issues further (Collin and Cumberpatch, 1995), and she has given me her support and helpful comments on this chapter. I thank her and my other colleagues who played a part in the study by being interviewed, commenting on my interpretations and this chapter. I hope that we shall use this as the basis for future shared action.

References

Alvesson, M. and Willmott, H. (eds) (1992) *Critical Management Studies*. London: Sage.

Argyris, C. and Schon, D. (1978) *Organizational Learning: a Theory of Action Perspective*. Reading, MA: Addison-Wesley.

Bakhtin, M.M. (1981) *The Dialogic Imagination: Four Essays*. Austin, Texas: University of Texas Press.

Beard, P.R.J. (1992) *The MBA Experience: the Reality Behind the Myth*. London: Association of MBAs.

Bhavnani, K.-K. (1990) 'What's power got to do with it? Empowerment and social research', in I. Parker and J. Shotter (eds), *Deconstructing Social Psychology*. London: Routledge. pp. 141–52.

Binsted, D.S. (1980) 'Design for learning in management training and development', *Journal of European Industrial Training*, 4 (8): whole issue.

Braverman, H. (1974) *Labor and Monopoly Capital: the Degradation of Work in the Twentieth Century*. New York: Monthly Review Press.

Burnett, S. (1992) 'HBR case study', *Harvard Business Review*, September–October: 32–3.

Butler, D.W. (1986) 'The humanities and the MBA', in J.S. Johnston Jr et al. (eds), *Educating Managers: Executive Effectiveness Through Liberal Learning*. San Francisco: Jossey-Bass. pp. 143–69.

Cameron, S. (1991) *The MBA Handbook: an Essential Guide to Effective Study*. London: Pitman.

Child, J. (1969) *British Management Thought*. London: George Allen and Unwin.

Collin, A. and Cumberpatch, Z. (1995) 'Closing the loop, opening the mind: a challenge to orthodoxy in management education', paper presented at the *New Perspectives on Management Education* Conference, Leeds.

Cooper, R. and Fox, S. (1990) 'The "texture" of organizing', *Journal of Management Studies*, 27 (6): 575–82.

Daloz, L.A. (1986) *Effective Teaching and Mentoring: Realizing the Transformational Power of Adult Learning Experiences*. San Francisco: Jossey-Bass.

Fineman, S. (ed.) (1993) *Emotion in Organizations*. London: Sage.

Fox, S. (1994) 'Debating management learning I and II', *Management Learning*, 25 (1): 83–94; 25 (4): 579–97.

Freire, P. (1972) *Pedagogy of the Oppressed*. Harmondsworth: Penguin.

Frost, P.J., Moore, L.F., Louis, M.R., Lundberg, C.C. and Martin, J. (eds) (1991) *Reframing Organizational Culture*. Newbury Park: Sage.

Giroux, H.A. and Freire, P. (1990) 'Introduction: towards a critical psychology of schooling', in E. Sullivan (ed.), *Critical Psychology and Pedagogy: Interpretation of the Personal World*. New York: Bergin and Garvey.

Grey, C. and Mitev, N. (1995) 'Management education: a polemic', *Management Learning*, 26 (1): 73–90.

Harvard Business Review (1992) 'Case study', September–October: 16–33; 'Debate', November–December: 128–40.

Hassard, J. and Parker, M. (eds) (1993) *Postmodernism and Organizations*. London: Sage.

Hearn, J., Sheppard, D.L., Tancred-Sheriff, P. and Burrell, G. (eds) (1989) *The Sexuality of Organization*. London: Sage.

Hebdige, D. (1979) *Subculture: the Meaning of Style*. London: Methuen.

Hochschild, A.R. (1983) *The Managed Heart*. Berkeley: University of California Press.

Honey, P. and Mumford, A. (1982) *Manual of Learning Styles*. London: Peter Honey.

Hosking, D. and Fineman, S. (1990) 'Organizing processes', *Journal of Management Studies*, 27 (6): 583–604.

Jarvis, P. (1988) *Adult and Continuing Education: Theory and Practice*. London: Routledge.

Jeffcutt, P. (1993) 'From interpretation to representation', in J. Hassard and M. Parker (eds), *Postmodernism and Organizations*. London: Sage. pp. 25–48.

Johnston, J.S. Jr et al. (1986) *Educating Managers: Executive Effectiveness through Liberal Learning*. San Francisco: Jossey-Bass.

Kelly, F.J. and Kelly, H.M. (1987) *What They Really Teach at the Harvard Business School*. London: Piatkus.

Kolb, D.A. (1983) *Experiential Learning*. New York: Prentice-Hall.

Mant, A. (1979) *The Rise and Fall of the British Manager*. London: Pan.

Mezirow, J. (1977) 'Perspective transformation', *Studies in Adult Education* (Leicester: National Institute of Adult Education), 9 (2): 153–64.

Mezirow, J. (1981) 'A critical theory of adult learning and education', *Adult Education*, 32 (1): 3–24.

Mitroff, I.I. and Churchman, C.W. (1992) 'Debate', *Harvard Business Review*, November–December: 134–6.

Morgan, G. (1986) *Images of Organization*. Beverly Hills, CA: Sage.

Mumford, A. (1988) 'Learning to learn and management self-development', in M. Pedler, J. Burgoyne and T. Boydell (eds), *Applying Self-Development in Organizations*. New York: Prentice-Hall. pp. 23–37.

Polanyi, M. (1968) *Personal Knowledge*. Chicago: University of Chicago Press.

Power, M. and Laughlin, R. (1992) 'Critical theory and accounting', in M. Alvesson and H. Willmott (eds), *Critical Management Studies*. London: Sage. pp. 113–35.

Pym, B. (1990) 'Finding a voice: a radio talk' (BBC, 1978), in B. Pym, *Civil to Strangers and Other Writings*. London: Grafton. pp. 408–16.

Reed, M. and Hughes, M. (eds) (1992) *Rethinking Organization: New Directions in Organization Theory and Analysis*. London: Sage.

Revans, R. (1983) *ABC of Action Learning*. Bromley: Chartwell-Bratt.

Roberts, J. (1984) 'The moral character of management practice', *Journal of Management Studies*, 21 (3): 287–302.

Schon, D. (1987) *Educating the Reflective Practitioner*. San Francisco: Jossey-Bass.

Senge, P. (1990) *The Fifth Discipline: the Art and Practice of the Learning Organization*. London: Century.

Sternberg, R.J. (1985) *Beyond IQ: a Triarchic Theory of Human Intelligence*. Cambrid Cambridge University Press.

Sullivan, E. (ed.) (1990) *Critical Psychology and Pedagogy: Interpretation of the Perso World*. New York: Bergin and Garvey.

Watson, T.J. (1994) *In Search of Management: Culture, Chaos and Control in Manager Work*. London: Routledge.

Whitaker, A. (1992) 'The transformation in work: post-fordism revisited', in M. Reed and I Hughes (eds), *Rethinking Organization: New Directions in Organization Theory a Analysis*. London: Sage. pp. 184–206.

Willmott, H. (1994) 'Business process re-engineering and human resource managemen *Personnel Review*, 23 (3): 34–46.

When I considered all this, the type of men who are administering affairs, and the condition of the Law and of public morality – the more I considered it and the older I grew, the more difficult appeared to me the task of decent government . . . And so I was forced to extol true philosophy and to declare that through it alone can real justice both for the State and for the individual be discovered and enforced. Mankind (I said) will find no cessation from evil until either the real philosophers gain political control or else the politicians become by some miracle real philosophers. (1973: 326d)

The Republic, one of the longer Socratic Dialogues, is largely a justification of this view; central to his thesis is the importance of education – both of intellectual ability and of the whole character. In an attempt to apply his ideas Plato did in fact undertake what we might think of as two significant overseas consultancy contracts in Syracuse, in both cases as advisor to the Tyrant. Neither of these was particularly successful in practice, which is probably not far from the experience of most consultants trying to introduce innovative new ideas ever since.[2] However, from the point of view of management education there are two aspects of Plato's writings that are of particular interest: the curriculum and the pedagogic method. As we shall see, it is by no means clear that these two are properly distinguishable, and it is in these considerations that the contemporary significance for management education of Plato's thought can be found.

So what did Plato have to say about how to improve the quality of management? In none of the principal texts on the subject does Plato specifically address the management of limited companies, privatized utilities or welfare agencies: but although some might consider the analogy between city-state and contemporary management overstretched, I hope to show that it is justified. The reader will, I hope, excuse and enjoy the anachronisms. My scheme is as follows:

1 list briefly the main problems that Plato identified in the management of the state and its affairs;
2 explain why he saw the underlying cause of these problems to be derived from a lack of education – particularly his own branch of philosophical education;
3 describe the educational method, scheme of study and curriculum he recommended;
4 comment on some implications for the subject matter of management education today.

The Failings of Management

In *The Republic* Plato identifies the main causes of the problems facing Athens as conflict between the rulers and the ruled; bad government; and bad education.

Conflict between the classes seemed to Plato to arise because of the tendency of political theorists and activists to hold to one of two extreme views: either that power belonged to a particular social class by hereditary right, or that it belonged to all people equally. Against this Plato argued for the early selection of people who showed signs of being intellectually, morally and emotionally capable of leadership, and providing them with an appropriate education, including character-building experiences and the opportunity to serve in junior or 'auxiliary' positions.

Bad government seemed to be due primarily to the tendency of the predominant political systems to put forward into leadership positions those whose principal qualifications were ambition, avarice and a scheming self-interest; and even those who were generally of upright character would have spent their formative years struggling for political power rather than studying the nature of the 'good' for which they were supposedly legislating. The cause of this tendency was private property, which focuses the attention on personal gain rather than the good of the state, and thus contributes to the construction of a self-image that is overly material and carnal. Philosophers who might be expected to know something of the best purposes of government and the nature of the soul, on the other hand, were either put off political activity by its general corruption, or incapable of leading owing to their long retirement from the world of affairs.

> The uneducated have no single aim in life to which all their actions, public and private, are to be directed; the intellectuals will take no practical actions of their own accord, fancying themselves to be out of this world in some kind of earthly paradise. (*The Republic*: 519c)

Bad education was, likewise, due to teachers who were ready to expound theories that conformed to the prejudice of their wealthy pupils without consideration of the public good or even the long-term benefit of the souls of their charges; or who were simply ignorant of the purposes of what they were teaching.

The Cause of the Problem is a Lack of Philosophical Education

At the root of all three failures lies a misconception of what constitutes a good life. Managers need therefore to correct this misconception in themselves and to help others do likewise; practical affairs of state and commerce can only be judiciously managed in the light of this knowledge, and so the education of managers is crucial. The problem then is to decide what they need to learn, and how. In pursuing this course one has to address questions about the objects of knowledge, different kinds of knowledge, the capacities of individuals to learn and understand. And so in order to decide how to improve the quality of management Plato argues that we need first to clarify the nature and the getting of knowledge.

The 'line' and 'cave' metaphors in *The Republic* famously describe the difference between the knowledge of phenomena and of principles, associated with which are grades of certainty. At the bottom of the line (and deep in the cave) one is in a state of illusion (*eikasia*), perceiving only the shadows of objects; next one is in a state of belief (*pistis*) or 'commonsense assurance', seeing physical things and representations of them, and also recognizing patterns that, for example, one might take to represent 'justice' or 'fairness'. But all this is perceived without a knowledge of the underlying rules, knowledge of which involves reason (*dianoia*). With reason one can take a general postulate and apply it to various figures and illustrations; in this way the truth of the postulate can be tested and refined – it is an experimental, provisional sort of truth that one is dealing with, a kind of knowledge that comes to life as one applies ideas of justice, beauty, goodness, and so forth. Intelligence (*noesis, nous*), on the other hand, is the upward movement to these ideas themselves.

It is clear that to design and manage a system of any sort one needs to be able at least to perceive the overall pattern, and ideally to understand the principles on which it is working. Methods of enquiry, from traditional operational research techniques to soft systems methodology (Checkland, 1981), are means for making precisely these kinds of progressive discoveries. But it is in this process that Plato identifies one of the causes of bad management: in fact the danger is double edged. There is, on the one hand, the failure to distinguish between image and object, between specific and general or systemic problems (this was the insight picked up by Deming, 1986); and on the other hand, there is the tendency to mistake any cognition as a thing in itself.

Perhaps the most useful description of the problems of knowledge of this sort is contained in the *Seventh Letter*, in which the 'instruments' of knowing are described as follows (1973: 342):

1   the name of a thing or process (*onoma*);
2   its logic or reasoning (*logos*);
3   examples or illustrations (*eidôlon*);
4   a knowledge or understanding of or insight into a thing (*nous*).

Added to these four 'instruments' is a fifth: the thing itself. Each of the preceding four refer to the thing, but each is conditioned by the medium of the instrument itself: names are specific to languages and to context, deriving their import from what they are not rather than what they are (Saussure (1974) makes the same point); definitions refer to classificatory structures that are themselves contingent, continuously deferring to others; illustrations exist in certain conditions and are 'true' only in those specific circumstances; while knowledge itself is always 'known' by a particular subject ('it resides not in sounds or in physical shapes, but in souls'), and thus is a personal *eidôlon* or image. Although all these 'instruments' are necessary in getting to know something, the thing itself somehow remains distinct:

unless a man somehow grasps the first four, he will never attain perfect knowledge of the fifth. Moreover, owing to the inadequacy of language, these four are as much concerned to demonstrate what any particular thing is like as reveal its essential being . . . it is not the soul of the writer or speaker which is at fault, but the four instruments . . . each of which is by its very nature defective. (1973: 343)

It is only when all these things, names and definitions, visual and other sensations, are rubbed together and subjected to tests in which questions and answers are exchanged in good faith and without malice that finally, when human capacity is stretched to its limit, a spark of understanding and intelligence flashes out and illuminates the subject at issue. (1973: 344)

What we know is always an approximation, a reference to things, and not the thing itself; and understanding comes from talking and debating, reasoning about examples and definitions, holding in view the object we are trying to get to know – 'lingering', as Gadamer calls it (1980: 111).

Because understanding can only be found in this way, one of the greatest hindrances to learning is the tendency to write things down. Written words, 'if you ask them what they mean by anything . . . simply return the same answer over and over again' (*Phaedrus*: 275).

Written works contribute to bad management in another way: they are available to everyone, including those who might misunderstand the ideas and apply them unwisely or even maliciously. Good management is not simply the clever application of techniques and skill; it makes a distinction between good and evil. *The Republic* presents an argument that it is in the best interest of individuals and collectivities to act with justice. I shall not go over that argument here: what is important is the assertion that not everyone can or will comprehend the argument itself. In the course of presenting the case Socrates has to abandon Thrasymachus and Callicles, who have argued that justice is the 'interest of the powerful', because they are unable to follow him. Socrates demonstrates to them that their own case is contradictory and self-defeating, and goes on to talk with Glaucon about a state that would instantiate justice; but the others cannot really participate. What this points to is not merely the intellectual inadequacy of Thrasymachus, for:

not only is it possible for him to point to what 'everybody' says or does in order to evade unpleasant obligations. He can justify his evasion theoretically by placing moral obligation as a whole in question . . . he who has no sense of propriety and obligation, he from whom no response is drawn when recourse is had to these concepts, will never understand what they are about. (Gadamer, 1980: 116)

Plato says that the educator 'cannot put into mind knowledge that was not there before' (*The Republic*: 518c), but must turn the mind to reality, 'and at the brightest of all realities which is what we call the good' (518d). Effecting this turning is, Plato grants, a matter of professional skill. This he distinguishes from the training needed to implant the 'excellences of the mind', by pointing out how some people are clever but evil – and the cleverer they are, the greater the capacity for evil.

Combining these two points – the elusiveness of knowledge and the need for the student to be tuned in to moral virtue – we arrive at the basis of the educational programme that Plato lays out in *The Republic* and elsewhere. Its key purpose is the orientation of the will towards goodness, and the training of the mind to use the four 'instruments' of knowledge. The main characteristic is conversation; I shall return to this shortly.

The third case of bad management is attention to the wrong things. Socrates advocates self-awareness, a concern echoed in modern exhortations to self-assessment and self-development.

> he who takes care of his money takes care neither of himself nor of what is his, but of things still further removed from what is his . . . Then the businessman is not minding his own business. (*Alcibiades*: 96)

By arguing that 'the soul is the man' (*Alcibiades*: 95ff), Socrates can define the body as a possession of the soul, and assert that 'he who has some knowledge of his bodily nature has gained a knowledge of that which is his, but not of himself':

> Then the husbandman and the other craftsmen are very far from knowing themselves; for they, it seems, do not even know that which is theirs, but things still further removed from it, according to the trades which they follow. For they only know that which is the body's, and by which it is served . . . If, then, wisdom is knowledge of oneself, none of these is wise owing to his craft . . . And for this reason such crafts seem to be vulgar, and not such as a good man would learn.

As it is unlikely that someone can know what is theirs if they don't know who they are, it is improbable that craftsmen, for example, can really know their craft – that which belongs to that which is theirs – if they do not know themselves: they must instead be working on some sort of estimative basis (*pistis*). Furthermore, if a person is ignorant of that which is theirs, how much more so must they be of that which belongs to others, and of the affairs of businesses and cities? Such a one, Socrates claims, could not be entrusted with the management of a household, let alone a state; he or she is bound to make mistakes, and thus be miserable. It is impossible for anyone to be happy who is not wise and good: happiness is the reward of wisdom (the virtue of the soul), not of wealth.

> And if you are to manage the affairs of the city rightly and well, you must impart virtue to the citizens – which you cannot do unless you possess this virtue yourself.

> You yourself, then, should first acquire virtue, and so should any other who means to govern and manage not only himself and his own private affairs, but the state and the affairs of the state. (*Alcibiades*: 105)

The conclusion of this argument is that the proper concern of anyone is, in the words of the Delphic Oracle inscribed on the Temple of Apollo at Delphi, 'know thyself'.[3]

The Educational Method, Scheme of Study and Curriculum

Socrates described himself as a midwife, helping people to give birth to their ideas (*Thaetetus*, Burnyeat: 210); Plato was an educator, and had a lot to say about it. Here I will concentrate on his views on management education, and draw mainly on *The Republic* and the *First Alcibiades*.

A key construct in *The Republic* is that of the 'ideal state', a fictional scenario specifically invented to explore the notion of 'justice' as it emerges in the course of the dialogue. It is tempting to take the particular structure and ordering of the elements of this 'ideal state' as a kind of blueprint or manifesto. Taken as such one is struck by the impracticality of many of the recommendations – a fact which was pointed out in or shortly after Plato's lifetime by Aristotle (see his *Politics* and *Ethics*, for example), among others. But as with all scenarios, the implicit 'if' is fundamental. In this case, the question is: if our principal concern was a state that was itself just and which fostered and rewarded just people, what issues would we address and how would we consider them? It is in this heuristic context that the importance of leaders arises; and this also explains why the selection and education of leaders are so central to the dialogue. These people are considered responsible for the just state being just. Equally importantly they are considered here as being leaders by virtue of their own justice – justice is in fact the precise nature of and reason for their leadership. To the question 'in what sense do they lead?', one would answer 'in their knowledge and administration of justice'.

It is not therefore Plato's concern to take leaders who have become so by virtue of other qualities, and then to see how they might be made to exercise their authority more fairly, ethically or prudently. That is, he does not define leaders in terms of their ability to motivate others, organize a production or service delivery operation, extract efficiency savings from resources or to do deals, and then seek to make them 'good' and 'just' in the way they do these things or in terms of their social and environmental responsibility. In this sense his project is not to contribute to a debate about 'ethical management' or 'socially responsible business'. Instead it is to start from a quite distinct interest in what it means to lead a life that is 'good'; in pursuit of this interest Plato takes 'doing justice' to be the activity of leadership.

It should perhaps be said that the conception of justice (*dikaiosynë*) developed in *The Republic* and elsewhere is not a narrow legalistic term, nor a more commonsense notion of fairness; it has in it more a sense of balance, of civic virtue, personal integrity and beauty. I hope this will become clear, and meanwhile propose to begin with an outline of the principal elements of the educational programme in the ideal state.

Plato's management education curriculum is more concerned with ways of thinking and acting than with knowledge of specific processes or technical skill. Subjects were chosen for study for both their practical value and for the intellectual training they offered. Nevertheless he did advocate a 'core curriculum', although not of the type that is now common to almost all MBA programmes in Europe and the USA.

The essential task in educating the broad mass of managers was the following: because they will often have to take decisions which affect the well-being of the whole, managers need judgement and skill in handling a wide variety of unpredictable problems in a manner which will accord with the ethos of the whole enterprise. At the same time they will be confronted with an almost infinite variety of events which are open to all manner of interpretation. Their upbringing and education are thus crucial in instilling three main characteristics: a dedication to the benefit of the state over and above any personal or selfish gain; physical fitness; and the intellectual ability to discriminate between adventitious events and underlying principles. They should not own wealth themselves; but as their main motivation is to govern they will find adequate reward in their growing status and authority. They should also be physically fit, as they must serve as soldiers, be inured to discipline and untiring in the public service.

So the early training of young people destined for managerial positions consisted mainly of gymnastics and *musike*. In this context music included rhetoric, literary composition and appreciation as well as rhythm and harmony. The purpose was to 'impart . . . a kind of harmoniousness by means of harmony, and a kind of measuredness by means of measure' (*The Republic*: 522a)[4]. This elementary education continued until about the age of 20, when some would be selected for the next stage, consisting of the following six disciplines: arithmetic, plane geometry, solid geometry, astronomy, harmonics and dialectic.

As the aim of this education was to develop knowledge of underlying principles, and as this knowledge cannot be gained simply by reciting them, understanding must emerge from reflection on all that is experienced. Learning how to reflect or to think was thus the core aim of education, over and above its practical utility. More recent work on 'the reflective practitioner' (Schon, 1983) has made the same point, and models such as 'the learning cycle' (Kolb et al., 1974; see also Vince, this volume) have inspired many educationalists to seek ways of encouraging this reflective capacity. For example, it is now common for executive education pro- grammes to include a demand for 'critical reflections on the learning process' in reports of work-based projects (Gosling and Ashton, 1994). The experience of many in this field is that it is not easy to develop the ability to reflect beyond a descriptive account of events and experiences or the cursory reference to descriptive models. Action learning and group relations approaches have been used to help people articulate aspects of their experience that are not immediately obvious (Revans, 1971; Miller, 1990). These may indeed be a useful form of training for reflection, specifically because the process of interpretation draws attention to what is denied in the obvious and desired in the ignored. They are in this sense method- ologies of critical thought, and it is this that is central to Plato's method. For him the ability of any subject to stimulate abstract thought is the main criterion for its inclusion in the curriculum: I regard as non-stimulants all the objects which do not end by giving us at the same moment two contradictory perceptions' (*The Republic*: 523).

The example given for the arithmetic course is one that should be familiar on accounting and finance courses. To count a series of objects – say three fingers – does not stimulate much thought. But reflection on the manner in which these are three fingers, but yet are not three of the same (that is are different relative sizes) prompts contradictory assessments: the rather simple example Socrates gives is that of three fingers the middle-sized one is both bigger and smaller than others. An appreciation of relative dimensions and numbers is important, because in the first place the utility of counting depends on being able to assess the relative size of armies or the cost of goods; and more crucially because it compels the mind 'to call the aid of reasoning and reflection' (*The Republic*: 524). The outcome is that, whereas sight or simple perception of objects makes no distinction between small or large, reflection seeks to clarify sensible perceptions by seeing small things and large things distinct in relation to each other. It is thus this kind of contradiction which causes us to ask 'what then, after all, is greatness, and what smallness . . . and to distinguish between objects of sight and objects of reflection' (*The Republic*: 524).

Geometry is included in the curriculum for much the same reasons as arithmetic: it is indispensable in war and navigation, and it also refers to 'a knowledge of what eternally exists' (*The Republic*: 527). By this is meant the most abstract of ideas which, although never observable in fact, are fundamental to our ability to think about existence: in this case, the relations between points conceived as existing in a plane. For example, there may be no such thing as a perfectly straight line, but it is impossible to consider any kind of line without the idea of a direct relationship between points. The benefit of studying geometry, apart from its practical uses, is therefore because it habituates the mind to thinking in the abstract, and to excluding non-essential attributes of phenomena in an attempt to clarify what they are in themselves. Examples in modern management studies would be the notion of a 'role' or 'job' which exists independently of the particular person filling it. The contrast between the virtual (that which *ought*, in principle, to be) and the actual is an important stimulus to thought and enquiry. (See also the comment above about the difference between an idea (*eidôs*) and its representation or image (*eidôlon*).)

The third field of study – really an extension of the second – is the science of solid bodies, as a natural progression from planar geometry. The principal reason for this seems to be both to develop the thinking abilities mentioned above, and to lay the ground for the consideration of bodies in motion.

Astronomy is the fourth field of study, useful in agriculture (to determine the seasons) and navigation; but it is recommended in *The Republic* because it leads one to consider the dynamic relations between things; more precisely, it engenders the ability to think dynamically; to conceive of

Table 9.1

Sight perceives the visible	Dialectic perceives the intelligible
The Sun = the source of light, which gives visibility to objects and the power of seeing to the eye	The Good = the source of truth, which gives intelligibility to objects of knowledge and the power of knowing to the mind

Source: Adapted from Lee, in Plato, 1987.

'things' such as planets, stars, orbits, seasons, months and days as temporary and contingent appearances indicative of 'those true revolutions, which real velocity, and real slowness, existing in true number, and in all true forms, accomplish relatively to each other, carrying with them all they contain: which are verily apprehensible by reason and thought, but not by sight' (*The Republic*: 529e). It is a much debated matter whether Plato here refers to a set of immutable and fixed laws to which material existences adhere (and which it is the function of science to discover); or whether he is talking of an awareness of existence as 'flux', and therefore an ability to see reality in terms of activity rather than fixed states. The debate itself, of course, continues in other fields too, notably in physics and the philosophy of science.

The fifth mathematical discipline is harmonics, or the special quality of beauty and 'rightness' that pertains to some combinations and ordering of motions, sounds, and especially ideas. In modern terms it might correspond to a sense of 'fit' between organizational structure, environment, resources and strategy. But, of course, Plato is adamant that the study of harmonics is above all a mental training, preparatory to the study of dialectic. He explicitly ridicules the interpretation of harmonics as the measurement of the distance between notes, but supports it as a refinement of perception.

Having mastered the five mathematical disciplines (*mathesis* means discipline) in both theory and application, students concentrate increasingly on dialectic. Socrates' interlocutor in this section of *The Republic* is Glaucon, who asks for an exposition of dialectic. Socrates refuses on the grounds that Glaucon would not understand without the use of metaphors and similes which would be counter to the purely abstract nature of the objects of dialectical reason. However Socrates does in fact refer back to the metaphors of the sun, line and cave which he has used earlier in the dialogue. The nature, object and process of dialectic can be apprehended by comparing it to sight (see Table 9.1).

Dialectic, then, is the noetic intelligence in which the distinction between the subject and the object is resolved. As a form of 'direct knowledge' it is clearly related to what is often called intuition; however, Plato quite explicitly refers to it in *The Republic* as a science and art to be studied. The ability to become a dialectician can be determined by the students' ability to bring together the various aspects of any subject and to consider it as a whole, with all the parts in their co-relations, these considered as dynamic processes and their harmonic qualities related to their extant phenomena.

The specific educational experiences Plato recommends are in the context of a long-term programme. Studies should first of all be voluntary, as 'no study pursued under compulsion remains rooted in the memory' (*The Republic*: 536). Up to the age of 20 the programme consists of gymnastics and *musike*, with various experiences to build and test the moral fibre, such as work placements (observing a battle from horseback). At 20 those selected for management training begin work on the five mathematical disciplines. This might take about 10 years in total – presumably while undertaking various junior administrative roles.

Socrates recognizes some dangers arising from the educational environment at this stage, dangers familiar to anyone in executive education who has sought to stretch the boundaries a little. People who have grown up valuing and respecting certain norms of behaviour and standards of beauty will begin, in the dialectical process, to question the meaning of goodness, beauty, truth, virtue and so forth. As they perceive that their received opinions were merely vestiges of tradition and cultural ethnocentricity, they might let themselves go to all manner of debauchery, as it may seem that any action can be justified as well as any other. Young people who develop a taste for dialectic 'delight like puppies in pulling and tearing to pieces with logic any one who comes near them . . . and when they have suffered many triumphs and many defeats they fall quickly and vehemently into an utter disbelief of their former sentiments' (*The Republic*: 539). In order, therefore, that educators 'may not have to feel pity for those men of thirty, must [they] not use every precaution in introducing them to dialectic?' (*The Republic*: 539).

The study of dialectic, then, is to be taken while apart from other pursuits, and should take about five years. Following that, Socrates prescribes 15 years in various managerial jobs (such as taking command in war) and living as a member of the public. At the age of 50 those who are considered worthy of further promotion may devote themselves to philosophy and the contemplation of the Good, returning from time to time, in rotation with their philosopher colleagues, to lead the state in applying their arcane knowledge of the ends to which policy should be applied.

Another slightly different account of the educational programme is given in *The First Alcibiades*. This can also be read as a management development text, and Socrates is in fact quite explicit about this (Plato, 1931: 105). First, a distinction is made between the particular skills and techniques associated with specific jobs, and more general competences, closer perhaps to notions of 'meta-competencies' (Burgoyne and Stewart, 1976) than the Management Charter Initiative's 'standards of competence'.

The equivalent to 'meta-competencies' were the 'virtues', listed by Plato (*The Republic*: Bk. 3; *Laws*; *First Alcibiades*: 68) as Wisdom, Courage, Prudence and Justice. Here Socrates is particularly concerned to ensure that

Alcibiades, a wealthy and precocious young man, should be properly prepared for a managerial role in the state apparatus. In a lengthy admonition of Alcibiades, who has claimed his right to be a manager on the basis of his 'natural abilities', Socrates describes the education of the kings and rulers of Persia, then the wealthiest and most successful state in the region (the equivalent perhaps of Peters and Waterman's 'excellent companies').

> When the child is fourteen those whom they call the royal tutors take charge of him. These are picked men in the prime of life, reputed to be the cream of the Persians. They are four in number: The wisest of them, the most just, the most temperate, and the bravest. The first of these teaches him the secret wisdom of Zoroaster the son of Oromades – this is the worship of the Gods – and also the art of kingship; the most just teaches him to speak the truth throughout his whole life; the most temperate teaches him not to be ruled by any kind of pleasure, so that he may become accustomed to be free and a king in reality by first governing his own appetites and not being a slave to them; while the fourth, the bravest, makes him bold and fearless, since if he feared he would be a slave. (Plato, 1931: 68)

If this expects a lot of top management, it also sets some exacting standards for management educators and business schools! On the other hand, Alcibiades seems to have completed his education with Socrates with some qualities similar to those of modern MBA graduates: he deserted the 'firm' (Athens) and joined its rival, Sparta; and ended up with the old enemy, Persia. This sort of behaviour brought as much opprobrium on Socrates as it does on business schools today.

Some Implications for the Subject Matter of Management Education Today

In the ideal state described in *The Republic* one can identify many features and problems that are pertinent to managerial work today. Although not directly related to the education of managers, many of these issues contribute to current debates. I have selected those that seem to me to be interesting.

The division of labour in relation to managerial authority and responsibility was to be threefold. The mass of the population ('craftsmen' in direct translation, sometimes termed 'civilians' (Crossman, 1959)) were to play no significant part in management, but were to be free (slaves excepted)[5] to engage in trade, commerce, crafts or agriculture in their own right or employed by others. They could amass wealth, and conduct themselves more or less as they wished within the law, but must pay taxes to support the activities of the other two classes. The 'auxiliaries' were to be concerned with executive management and public service. They would be responsible for the day-to-day running of the enterprise (the state), for its internal harmony and also for its defence and trading relations with other states. The third division is that of the 'philosophers' – similar in some senses to the board of modern corporations in terms of their responsibility for policy and strategy, but with no remuneration save the satisfaction of doing good – although they would of course rather spend their time as scholars. In effect, the two managerial castes are one in relation to the non-managerial 'civilians'. Most auxiliaries would spend their working lives in junior and middle management, with some rising to senior executive positions. Very few would develop the capacity for true philosophical knowledge and the consequent qualification for top leadership.

Selection for these managerial roles was clearly understood to be problematic. The necessary abilities were not intrinsically hereditary, although some allowance was to be made for the likelihood of inherited characteristics. Candidates should have 'a piercing eye for their studies, and they must learn with ease . . . a good memory, a dauntless demeanour and a thorough love of work' (*The Republic*: 535). Upbringing was seen as the most important process, and Plato thought it likely that the children of 'auxiliaries' would be exposed to the proper sorts of experiences. Allowance was to be made, however, for movement between the classes in both directions by assessing people's 'temperance, fortitude, loftiness of mind, and all the separate virtues' (*The Republic*: 536a).

In spite of contemporary practice, Socrates comes out in favour of equal opportunities for men and women (but not for slaves). He advocates the recruitment of both according to merit to the ranks of 'auxiliaries' and thence to more senior positions. He goes somewhat further.

> 'you have already picked your men Guardians. You must now pick women of as nearly similar natural capacities as possible to go with them. They will live and feed together, and have no private home or property. They will mix freely in their physical exercises and the rest of their training, and their natural instincts will necessarily lead them to have sexual intercourse. Or do you think necessity is too strong a term?
> 'The necessity will be sexual and not mathematical' he [Glaucon] said; 'but sex is perhaps more effective than mathematics when it comes to persuading or driving the common man to do anything.' (*The Republic*: 458d)

In such circumstances it will be impossible for more senior management to control the amorous feelings of these younger aspirants, so rather than risk the indignity of unenforceable laws of celibacy or monogamy it would be wiser to legislate for common marriage within cohorts (*The Republic*: 457d). However, this sort of unregulated activity, subject to so base a necessity, is clearly antithetical to the rule of reason and especially to the great impetus to arrange the state around an organizing principle: management must, to put it bluntly, be crafty in order to regulate impulse and ensure that the outcome of sexuality is to produce tangible benefits for the organization as a whole. In effect, management must make sure that the right sort of babies are born and raised, while allowing adequate expression to everyone's sexual desires. The precise means of this regulation are important, because Plato uses for the third time (see also *The Republic*: 377b, 382b, 389b and 414d) the notion of telling a lie or creating a fiction (*pseudos*) as a form of medicine for the potentially troubled body politic. Socrates points out that there is a potential contradiction between the aim of equality on the one hand, and the responsibility to distinguish and select higher from lower quality people. His recourse is simple: he proposes that sexual intercourse should be allowed between couples for whom it has been sanctioned, and that, in the rhetoric of equality, the pairing should be accomplished by lottery. However the senior managers or guardians should take care to rig the lots so that mating might in fact be eugenically organized; he uses the example of breeding thoroughbred dogs, birds and horses (*The Republic*: 459). At the same time, Socrates recognizes that complete control will be impossible, and so recommends certain sanctions for transgression – and an end to all controls once people pass childbearing age.

This raises two important points for current debates:

1   the recognition of sexuality and the need for its regulation (but only when it has productive significance);
2   the conscious use of 'fiction' in constructing a rationale for regulation.

One can easily see parallels to both of these in modern organizations. The fantasies, day-dreams and less conscious *erotic* longings of people for each other are ubiquitous features of organizational life, even if seldom spoken of openly – still less written about in management textbooks. Yet these feelings and thoughts are important aspects of the desire to come together to work, to engage in productive activity.[6] Although they are generally experienced as private goings-on in the mind, many things in organizations simply would not be accomplished if it were not for the giving and receiving of favours, flirtation, and so forth. The term 'macho management' refers, of course, to a certain image of manliness, a stylized sexuality; and the maintenance of macho management – or any other style – is always in a large part the collusive result of the shared fantasies of organizational members. At the same time, any manager putting together a project team, or anyone working in a group, will be aware of the dynamics of desire, envy and pride, of the 'frisson' of competition and flirtation, and of the opportunity that work relations offer for liaisons involving more than collaboration around the stated primary task.

Yet in regulating these relationships all manner of rationales are brought to play: one cannot, as Socrates points out, be seen to be manipulating these things; on the other hand, it would be naive not to bear them in mind. And so managers make use of a panoply of devices: psychometric tests, personality types, team styles performance appraisals – even lotteries – to give the impression that the intimate, emotional and unconscious selves are controlled by rational and scientific mechanisms; that the personnel professionals are not interested in the persons (and their relationships) but only in the type, the category, the measurement.[7] And indeed the members of organizations seem to go along with these devices, in spite of the strength of their own feelings, or perhaps because they too need to be reassured that it will not get entirely out of hand. In this sense, of course, constructions of 'rational practices' serve to contain all sorts of anxieties other than sexual ones – mortality, for example (Lawrence, 1977). Foucault, on the other hand, points to the way in which a preoccupation with the control of sexuality – especially experienced as self-control – comes to represent other problems of control. Referring specifically to classical Greece he argues that:

> For them, reflection on sexual behaviour was not a means of internalising, justifying, or formalising general interdictions imposed on everyone; rather it was a means of developing – for the smallest minority of the population, made up of free, adult males – an aesthetics of existence, the purposeful art of a freedom perceived as a power game. (Foucault, 1984: 253)

The power game here is power exercised over oneself, in pursuit of an aesthetic ideal – *dikaiosynë* or justice – where happiness is a function of virtue. One should manage the ways in which sexual pleasure is pursued, such that it may contribute to the general good. It is not surprising that the problem of self-control – of how to exercise one's freedom – was an issue for free men, and it deserved attention for those in management and aspiring to leadership (especially when this leadership was defined as the aesthetic result of self-control, the consummation of virtue). In the same way, it is not surprising that managers in our own age are concerned with self-development, personal skills and time management. Managerial excellences stand in for sexual ones, to the extent that the terms used to describe one can be applied to the other. The experience of sexuality is compounded with that of managerial activity – and the focus on personal conduct in both serves to hide the relations of power in which both sex and management exist:

> [The Greeks'] sexual ethics, from which our own derives in part, rested on a very harsh system of inequalities and constraints (particularly in connection with women and slaves); but was problematized in thought as the relationship, for a free man, between the exercise of his freedom, the forms of his power, and his access to truth. (Foucault, 1984: 253)

It is indeed true that Plato was writing in a state in which women were hardly permitted out of the house, let alone into full participation in the affairs of state. It has been argued (Annas, 1981) that women were not even men's primary sex-objects: romantic and physical pairing was focused on young boys, who could share men's social and psychological life. Plato's comments, if taken as more than symbolic, may seem thus all the more revolutionary; but he is not advocating a free choice for either women or men as to their occupations. There should be, he holds, equality of opportunity to do what is best for the state. Neither men nor women are valued for their masculinity or femininity (except in the reproductive sense), but as citizens. His proposals are not therefore aimed at relieving the oppression of women, but at making them available as a 'human resource'.

> What Plato should be arguing for is what he once recognises at 540c: that sex is irrelevant to the highest intellectual and moral studies, and women can take their rightful place as equals with men in a society where virtue and all excellence is attained in challenging and co-operative study and there is no premium on aggression and pushiness . . . Plato forgets this, and spends his time claiming, irrelevantly and grotesquely, that women can engage in fighting and other 'macho' pursuits nearly as well as men. (Annas, 1981: 184)

It is, of course, arguable whether modern 'women in management' movements have enabled our organizations to take any more heed of the different contributions of masculinity and femininity.

On the use of fiction in organizations Socrates is similarly forthright: his managers would probably not pass a modern ethical audit, for all their concern with justice. There are several circumstances in which the use of fiction is countenanced, two of which employ the metaphor of a medicine administered for the benefit of individuals or the body politic: spoken falsehoods may 'on some occasions be useful . . . for example as a kind of preventive medicine against our enemies, or when anyone we call our friend tries to do something wrong from madness or folly' (*The Republic*: 382b), and it's clearly a kind of medicine that should be entrusted to doctors and not to laymen . . . it will be for the rulers of our city, then, if anyone, to use falsehood . . . and if any citizen lies to our rulers we shall regard it as a grave offence' (*The Republic*: 389b). The manipulation of the mating lottery is another example, and the fourth is the tale of the origin of inequality among people – that some are born gold, some silver, and others bronze; that each must go to their rightful place in the organization, and accept being moved if some higher or lower metal is discovered in their blood by the rulers.

Introducing this fiction (*The Republic*: 415a), Socrates is quite explicit about its use: to make people accept the authority of the rulers and the interest of the organization as a whole. It is a 'corporate culture' story, and the comments of Socrates and Glaucon are probably realistic as to its reception:

> 'That is the story. Do you know any way of making them believe it?'
> 'Not in the first generation, but you might succeed with the second and later generations.'
> 'Even so it should serve to increase their loyalty to the state and to each other.'
> (*The Republic*: 415d)

Finally, some mention should be made of private property: there should be none for managers and rulers, as it would tempt them to place personal interest before that of the state, and distract their attention from its proper object: the public good. Compared to their modern counterparts Plato expected his managers to live quite austerely, and without the security of civil service contracts. On the other hand, those appointed to the higher echelons would have been accorded considerable status, and as the only rewards they would value would be philosophical, the right people would be content to serve without pay – although they might rather remain at their studies.

Conclusions

My intention in this chapter has been to show that Plato's work raises some issues of interest to management educators. Yet for those wedded to a utilitarian conception of education (see Grey and French, this volume; Thomas and Anthony, this volume) the most pressing question might be how these insights can be put into performative use. For the Greeks this would itself have been a question open to critique, for the main concern of philosophy (as distinct from the crafts) and of theory in general was to determine how one's life should be led, what constitutes well-being (*eudaimon*). This chapter is written within that orientation; it is neither a manifesto nor a manual.

Certainly some students of management, and many management courses, are concerned primarily with performative questions. But some are interested in arguments about justice, and are willing to face the consequence that, as Gadamer (1980: 116, cited above) says, 'they place moral obligation as a whole in question'. A short insert on ethics hardly provides a forum for such considerations, and yet, as I hope I have indicated, they are central to leadership and authority. At Lancaster University Management School we have developed a new management education programme, the MPhil in Critical Management, explicitly for those who want to explore these issues. The participants are practising managers and entrepreneurs, many of whom have MBA or equivalent qualifications: they know something of the 'excellences' of management in the sense of the skills and indicators of success within the managerial craft. This programme is more concerned with what constitutes 'good' management, and with recognizing the responsibility of the Academy to provide a forum for such considerations.

To put the former point slightly differently, there are those whose turn of mind takes them to a critical stance in relation to their experience, a turn that departs from (but need not abandon) performativity, and no longer cedes to it such hegemonic centrality. However, the dilemma is then the relationship between the content of a 'critical management' curriculum and the 'turn of mind' we define as 'critical'. For example, people may come on such a course having identified a mismatch between the models in their mind and their experience. The exploration of the disjuncture can lead to the improvement of the models and of the way things are done. On the other hand, it can lead one to ask about fundamental distinctions between abstractions, and in this manner to train the mind and soul to distinguish, for example, between the *eidôs* (an idea) and *eidôlon* (its image) – a distinction that is, by the way, crucial in considering questions of authenticity in the study of corporate culture, of advertising imagery and so forth.

And the 'by the way' exposes my position. Let me try to reverse it: 'corporate strategy' on the critical management programme examines the presumed agency of the strategist, the networked nature of relationships that cannot be reduced to 'competition and co-operation', the aesthetic sensibility that characterizes strategy discourse. All of which incidentally refines the student's sensitivity to design, pattern, form, rhetoric. I cannot, I am afraid to say, demonstrate that this leads inexorably to higher profits for their organizations, so one must be content with the hope that there is some well-being to be found in the philosophical life itself.

More prosaically, several leading American management schools are currently publicizing changes to their established MBA programmes. In effect, they are putting greater emphasis on leadership, interpersonal relations and individual reflection. These changes may reflect a shift towards 'character building' and away from 'knowledge filling' – and a recognition that training for leadership requires a long-term rounded development. The same concerns are evident in some of the leading schools in the UK, and in many in-company programmes; indeed, whereas academics are wont to criticize company training courses for lack of intellectual rigour, it may be that they contribute to rounded development of the kind foreseen by Socrates.

Another new initiative is to do away entirely with the organization of management education around knowledge areas, and instead to encourage executives to consciously adopt 'mindsets' – reflective, analytical, co-operative, contextual and transformational – as appropriate. The relationship of these 'mindsets' to Plato's five mathematical disciplines is obvious. Interestingly, this initiative is being simultaneously developed in countries that have resisted – or not been excited by – previous attempts at general management education along with those where it is well established (Canada, Britain, France, India, Germany and Japan). Perhaps the very existence of this volume is indicative of this developing dissatisfaction with traditional management education and of attempts to transcend it.

Notes

1 This letter was written to the supporters of Dion, a Syracusan nobleman who brought Plato in as a consultant to the tyrant Dyonisius II. In effect it can be read as an explication of the ideas that lay beneath his advice. Although its authenticity is debated, the close correlation of its argument to that of *The Republic* lends it compelling authority. The central portion of the *Seventh Letter* deals with the problems posed by the media of knowledge, in parallel with the typology presented in the 'line' metaphor of *The Republic*. Four means of knowing a thing are described, each necessary but at the same time introducing a certain distortion derived from the medium itself. This demonstration is used to argue that 'knowing' is essentially discursive, and arises from 'lingering' in the proximity of that which is to be known. Of importance for the current argument is the thought that true knowledge can only be had by those with the character as well as the intellectual ability to do so: those with an 'eye for the *eidôs*' – and hence the importance of a rounded education (Gadamer, 1980: 93–123). The same point is made at *The Republic*: 486d.

2 One might think of total quality management (TQM), business process re-engineering (BPR) and so forth as recent examples. While the failure of such programmes to deliver the hoped-for benefits is often cited, the clarification of thinking that results is generally of long-lasting value. This clarification can be seen to involve the four means of communicating described by Plato in the *Seventh Letter*. The iterative repetition of these attempts at knowing is the core of the art of dialectic; yet as Plato says most forcefully, and Gadamer (1980) emphasizes, the danger lies in mistaking the knowledge gained at any point for the thing itself. In the same way, when quality is named, explained, illustrated or perceived, it is both known in particular and obscured in itself at the same time; and hence remains elusive. Nevertheless, the paraphernalia of TQM and BPR can be seen to aim at providing fora for dialectic discourse around the four means of communicating cited in the second section of the chapter.

3 To get some idea of what this might mean, Socrates employs the metaphor of sight. He asks, 'Suppose the Oracle had inscribed "See Thyself", how would we understand it?' His answer is, by looking in a reflective surface, such as a mirror or, better still, the eye itself. For if we look another in the eye, in that part by virtue of which it has sight and is thus an eye, we see ourselves. (This is why, apparently, we call this part of the eye the *pupil*, because in it is an image of the beholder (*Alcibiades*: 100).) 'And so an eye beholding an eye, and looking at its most perfect part and by which it sees, would see itself.' Thus to see itself an eye must use sight to look into the seeing part of another eye. This applies where sight is the virtue of the subject, the eye. By analogy, 'the Soul, to know herself, must look at soul, and especially that region of the soul in which wisdom, the virtue of the soul, resides'. Wisdom is knowledge of oneself. Thus the virtue of the soul is knowledge of herself, and to know herself we must look at knowledge and understanding, which in turn are what makes the soul what she is. (In the same way Proclus argues that number originates in the mind. 'If it be enquired how number subsists in the human soul, we must say, that the soul, by her self-moving energies, procreates number, while she numerates, and by this energy, causes the existence of quantity' (Taylor, *Commentaries of Proclus, I*, xiv, in Raine and Harper, 1969: 37).)

4 The notion that qualities derived from a 'form' of their type (red from redness, harmony from harmoniousness) is characteristic of Plato. It suggests that what one learns is important not just for the use-value of the knowledge, but also for the way of thinking and feeling that it imparts. This is not quite the same as saying that it is the way one learns that is important: our attention is directed rather to the effect of ideas themselves. One wonders what effect terms like 'competitive advantage' and 'strategic positioning' have on the character of aspiring managers these days.

5 The position of slaves in Plato's writing is interesting – both in terms of the inclusions and exclusions. In the *Meno* Socrates asks the untutored slave of Meno to describe and explain certain geometrical relationships. The ability of the slave to reason correctly and to provide definite answers is used as a part of a demonstration of the innateness of ideas in the human soul. The implication is clearly that in so far as the boy in question is enabled to reason, he is free; his slavery in a political sense is used in the dialogue as a metaphor for the lack of philosophical education. In the state as a whole slaves represent the non-intellectual functions of the state organism: they are so many units of labour, a 'human resource' rather than 'personnel' with whom rulers (management) might enter into 'industrial relations'. The parallels to our own organizations are obvious.

6 In the *Phaedrus* Socrates is fascinated by the bulge in Phaedrus' cloak, and asks 'dear heart, let me just see what it is you are holding in your left hand under your coat' (228). The erotic impulse to the discussion that follows is full of irony: they discuss a speech about the role of love in a love affair, and then go on to consider the relationship between writing, speech and knowledge. The implication of the argument is that writing may serve to tempt and seduce people into real thinking and knowledge, but that on its own it is a mere supplement, an unproductive act of self-gratification.

7 One is tempted here to point out that measurement is a sensitive and troublesome matter in sexual as well as other productive relations. Size (of profit) does make a difference; failure to live up to expectations, stay the course, meet targets, delight customers are proper things to worry about. The comparative assessment of performance is also problematic.

References

Annas, J. (1981) *An Introduction to Plato's Republic*. Oxford: Oxford University Press.

Aristotle (1953) *The Nicomachean Ethics*. Tr. J.A.K. Thomson. Harmondsworth: Penguin.

Aristotle (1962) *The Politics*. Tr. T.A. Sinclair. Harmondsworth: Penguin.

Burgoyne, J. and Stewart, R. (1976) 'The nature, use and acquisition of managerial skills and other attributes', *Personnel Review*, 5 (4): 19–29.

Burnyeat, M. (1990) *The Thaetetus of Plato*. Tr. M.J. Levett. Indianapolis and Cambridge: Hackett.

Checkland, P. (1981) *Systems Thinking, Systems Practice*. Chichester: Wiley.

Crossman, R.H. (1959) *Plato Today*. London: George Allen and Unwin.

Deming, W.E. (1986) *Out of the Crisis*. Massachusetts Institute of Technology, Center for Advanced Engineering Study.

Foucault, M. (1984) *The Use of Pleasure*. Harmondsworth: Penguin. (1992 edition.)

Gadamer, H.-G. (1980) *Dialogue and Dialectic*. Tr. P.C. Smith. New York: Yale University Press.

Gosling, J. and Ashton, D. (1994) 'Action learning and academic qualifications', *Management Learning*, 25 (2): 263–74.

Kolb, D., Rubin, I. and McIntyre, J. (1974) *Organisational Psychology: an Experiential Approach to Organizational Behaviour*. Englewood Cliffs, NJ: Prentice-Hall.

Lawrence, W.G. (1977) 'Management development: some ideals, images and realities', *Journal of European Industrial Training*, 1: 21–5.

Miller, E. (1990) *The Tavistock Method*. Occasional Paper No. 10, London: The Tavistock Institute of Human Relations.

Plato (1852) *The Republic*. Tr. J.L. Davies and D.J. Vaughan. London: Macmillan.

Plato (1931) *Two Dialogues of Plato: The First Alcibiades and The Meno*. Godalming, Surrey: The Shrine of Wisdom.

Plato (1970) *The Laws*. Tr. T.J. Saunders. London: Penguin.

Plato (1973) *Phaedrus and Letters VII and VIII*. Tr. W. Hamilton. Harmondsworth: Penguin.

Plato (1987) *The Republic*. Tr. H.D.P. Lee. Harmondsworth: Penguin.

Raine, K. and Harper, G. (1969) *Thomas Taylor the Platonist*. Princeton, NJ: Princeton University Press.

Revans, R.A. (1971) *Developing Effective Managers*. London: Longman.

Saussure, F. (1974) *Course in General Linguistics*. Tr. W. Baskin. London: Fontana.

Schon, D. (1983) *The Reflective Practitioner*. New York: Basic Books.

10

Management Education as a Panoptic Cage

David M. Boje

This is a Foucauldian analysis of management education. Like the prison, management education is a dense network of disciplining mechanisms. The university, AACSB (American Assembly of Collegiate Schools of Business, an association of deans that dictates standards for course content, college mission and professor evaluation) and professional practices of management each operate on business school deans, professors, and students as subtle, but very complete controls to make humans docile, and dominate them by a panoptic network of surveillance, examination and normaliz-ation. Thinking of the discipline of management in terms of its complex organization of disciplinary mechanisms which govern its various models of rationality, including management pedagogy, takes us further than earlier 'control', 'professional', or 'contingency' models of organizations. In the past, one reason we have not been able to change management education significantly is that we have not focused on the subtle and pervasive network of disciplinary machinery. The contribution to management edu-cation theory is to revise theory and to develop research interest in the phenomenon of panoptic discipline as a fundamental area of management and organizational behaviour.

The Textbook Salesman Story

I am holding office hours, when a salesman named Joe (not his real name) hands me a card from one of the major houses and initiates this discourse:

Joe: Can I have a few minutes of your time?
Dave: Sure.
Joe: What are you up to?
Dave: I have a book on postmodern management that is being published by a smaller house. Houses like yours won't touch it, why is that?
Joe: We have management – OB texts in seventh edition. Some houses have 11th edition texts. We'd be giving up a lot of investment to turn to something new.
Dave: These management books have not changed since 1950. I notice some are putting pictures of people of color in place of all the white male shots. Diversity shots are in. But, the books are . . .
Joe: These texts are instructor-proof!
Dave: What do you mean – instructor-proof?

Joe: Well, you do not need an instructor. The books are self-taught. Students get pre-tests, concept lists, vignettes, summary boxes, and the like. All the instructor is there for is to select items from the exam book, items from the exercise book, and items from the overhead kit.

Dave: I see. I hate textbooks. There is no more freedom to teach.

Later that same day, I was teaching Max Weber on bureaucracy and came across the passage in a speech which he made late in his life:

> each man becomes a little cog in the machine and aware of this, his one preoccupation is whether he can become a bigger cog . . . this passion for bureaucracy is enough to drive one to despair. (Weber, in Mayer 1956: 127)

The textbook salesman story illustrates a modernist facet with one centre, one logic of performance that is replete in the taken-for-granted fibre of academic life. It illustrates how complicit one has become in managing one's own 'docilization'. It is the story of our control by the textbook industry. This encounter also made me stop and think: Am I just a cog in the management education machine with no role in instruction other than choosing test bank items, exercises, cases and overheads from some toolkit of instructional apparatus? What happened to my academic freedom? Am I acting out very restricted, even pre-selected super-system options, in some grand disciplinary machine, a nightmarish Weberian iron cage of pseudo-rationality?

Dead authors have no academic freedom. The author is dead in both the modern and the post-modern project. First, the modernists kill the author as they celebrate positivism, accumulate dead metaphors, proliferate surveillance practices, herd us into academy disciplines and teach us to teach rationality. Modernist management texts have pretended to be scientific texts: progressive accumulations of theories, pedagogies, methodologies and taxonomies constructing singular and objective meaning that privilege the expertise and power of the author. I was taught to pretend to be clear in the classroom so that I could pretend to measure objectively the student's precise recitation of my communication, and then the dean could objectively pretend to measure the student's evaluations of structure and clarity of my classroom presentations. Another partner in modernism that affects my writing and teaching texts is the university. I am the dis-embodied product of tenure, promotion, and the power of the university, the college and the Academy of Management to administer peculiar rewards and punishment that silence my academic freedom. All of this kills individuality in management education.

Secondly, the post-modernists advocate the death of the author, a playful death in which readers are free to ignore my intent and creatively interpret and playfully reconstruct my text (all management education is oral or written text) into a variety of equally valid interpretations. Yet, I am a happy post-modern corpse – free to dance, sing and play because in death what I do in my writing and teaching has nothing to do with me (Derrida, 1976: 158). I am not responsible or accountable for how my management students turn out, 'I did not author their lives, author(ize) their efforts, have author(ity) over their choices' (Rosenau, 1992: 33). Management education practice (a text) is independent of this (dead) author. As a post-modernist, I teach students that our texts have no correct meaning; my author's voice is no more privileged than theirs; the text itself is a multiplicity of novel interpretations of other interpretations. In this post-modern world, I write a more open text, compose my pedagogy with ambiguity, equivocality and an infinity of interpretive possibilities. Therefore, in the death of the author, there is freedom.

The purpose of this chapter is to apply concepts of Michel Foucault's (1977) prison analysis to management education-as-text. I believe that academic freedom is dying. On all fronts there is a sharp increase in control over the student and faculty 'body'. The faculty and student 'body' in management education is responsively subject to rules, including the subdivision of academic disciplines, watchdog associations like AACSB, the Academy of Management with its journals and conferences, and within the university the bidding of presidents, trustees, deans and department heads (Hetrick and Boje, 1992: 52). Management education discourse, as a text, is backed up and guaranteed as objective by the AACSB, by the Academy and by the committees of the college and university (Rosenau, 1992: 28). Foucault suggests that the point of disciplining the body is to control the person's mind (Boyne, 1990). My body and mind are punished and rewarded for my 'objective' performance in the classroom (course evaluations and tenure review), in the journal writing (publish or perish), in the Academy conferences (invited to present or not) and in the college (given travel for one more conference or not). Hence, I agree with Clegg (1989a) in his contention that 'employers face at least two sources of resistance by virtue of their employees having both discursive and bodily capacities that require some disciplining if some control is to be achieved' (1989a: 102–3). My concern is that modernist control is usurping academic freedom for both student and professor. Despite the post-modern project, management education remains embedded in a modernist order (Boje and Dennehy, 1994).

My thesis is that the management discipline, taken to include the university, the AACSB, the Academy and the business institution, constitutes a panoptic machine, where probationary tenure functions as a period of disciplined obedience to the rules; where surveillance is everywhere; where academic freedom, transformed from the Middle Ages, now means intellectual subordination to the more or less plural professorial paradigms (Beale, 1936; Kibre, 1962; MacIver, 1955; Metzger, 1955). This 'total management education' machine makes both professors and students increasingly docile performers. There is talk of automating the professor role so that video performance of master teachers will facilitate downsizing of the numbers of professors currently employed. Management education superimposes models of organization, subordination and domination imported from various institutional arenas: the family (a family of brothers, sisters and elders); the army (commanded by a head and divided into colleges, and ranked from freshman to senior and from assistant professor to full professor, where people are numbers); a factory (with supervisors, foremen regulating the work, timing the movements, a brand of Taylorism); the judiciary (justice and reformation is meted out each day by minor officials judging the most minor offences); the monastery (where the voice of religion speaks about idle time, the path to enlightenment through discipline, the solitude of cellular life, the sanctity of work and a God who sees into your very soul, let alone your study, that modern monastic cell); science (technologies for measurement and normalization used to engineer conduct, monitor transformation and movement and accumulate knowledge through empirical observations, examinations and scientifically valid interrogations); the professions (external accreditation, monitoring and normalizing by AACSB); and, most of all, the prison (a system of penal disciplinary systems, regimentation of time, allocation of cellular occupations and dormitory housing). Of course, no one of these is institutionally pristine: monasteries, perhaps more than most, have the greatest claim to primacy (see Clegg, 1989b).

When I refer to management education as a panopticon (a reference to Foucault's analysis of prisons), I do not mean to suggest that our workplace has bars, wardens and cell blocks.[1] Rather, the panopticon, as we shall explore, is an ingenious cage of discursive control with a capillary network of mechanisms that erode academic freedom not to go along with the herd, to celebrate the death of objectivity, and to invite plurality into the management classroom. Neither the death of the author nor the panopticon collapses into structural contingency or other theories of power than centre on an elite or a dominant coalition administering control. Rather, Foucault's capillary mechanisms are part of the fabric of discursive practices, not contextualized in contingencies or human agency. Therefore, a study of the capillary control mechanisms rooted in management education discourse presents an alternative approach. Being aware of the control over our own freedom also allows us to resist the erosion of our freedom. In keeping with Burrell (1988: 233), one concurs that 'the reality of organizations is that they reflect and reproduce a disciplinary society'. Management education is reproduced within this disciplinary society and then produces the cadre to enact an even more disciplinary society.

What does a critique of management education as a panoptic prison contribute? If our academic freedom is eroding and if we are being disciplined to be docile in the classroom, then our texts take on a more conservative, bland and non-controversial tone. How can we critique newly emerging forms of capitalism if we cannot radically critique our own complicity? How can we teach discourses of social transformation and ecology, if our doctrinal premises, content and values have already been surrendered? I do not like to be thought of as a priest of the status quo. I think we can teach management as a critique of our industrial practices, as a dialogue among ethical positions and as self-criticism. Yet, I experience most management education as a denial of our socio-political-economic development and function in society. We do not teach the homeless to own and operate their own businesses. We do not teach employees to master the secrets of production and marketing, so they can construct their own companies. No, our stakeholder is the corporate manager, seeking to scale the pyramid and accumulate more corporate toys than anyone else on the horizon. The reason I think we do not do this is that our curriculum materials and practices are prepackaged and the pedagogical performance is thoroughly prescripted and Taylorized in ways that remove choice and de-skill our face-to-face dialogue.

This chapter begins with the modernist reformation of academic freedom as specialized 'time and space' disciplines, in which 'signalling' is used to reconstitute students and professors; defines three instruments of discipline: (1) the gaze, (2) recording, (3) penal mechanisms (exams, normalization, gratification–punishment, panopticism and auxiliary penal mechanisms); summarizes the five principles for disciplining professors: (1) isolation, (2) regulation, (3) transformation by tenure, (4) co-opting cycles of reform and (5) recidivism. The chapter concludes with an analysis of management education.

Methodologically, I will use stories to capture how in the modern university freedoms that were once conceived of as the *sine qua non* of the free scholar have eroded. I invite each reader to inject their own stories into this writing. Management education, as other organizational communities, has a rich oral tradition, an anthropologically profound repository of value and orientation to the cultural significations of everyday life (Boje, 1991a, 1991b; Boje and Dennehy, 1994). Just as we retrieve a historical sense of place through stories of the past, stories of the present can locate for us, not just the world we have lost, but also that which we have gained, perhaps without always recognizing it.

Management Education as an Iron Cage

Management education is a pedagogy of discipline with many parts and cogs moving in concert with one another to achieve a networked configuration that disciplines both the student and professor. Management education is disciplined by universities that have adopted a language of discipline: academic disciplines, controllers, evaluation, registrars, ranks, tenure and promotion, semesters, classes, units, upper divisions. Management education in the US is also disciplined by AACSB, the Academy, the Organizational Behavior Teaching Society, the programmes that train instructors and by the business culture that supplies both students and jobs.

In modern management education, exams have replaced leadership, apprenticeship and mastery of administrative practices. Many professors rely on multiple choice tests as a disciplinary technology. Apprenticeship pedagogy did not fit with mass production, semesters or quarters, AACSB evaluation studies and the needs of the curriculum committee. The modernist form also emphasizes surveillance of the professors. 'Surveillance thus becomes a decisive economic operator both as an internal part of the production machinery and as a specific mechanism in the disciplinary power' (Foucault, 1977: 175). Judgement, evaluation and ranking create distinctions and individualize faculty and students. Management education is a disciplinary regime: an activity where normalization is the dominant technique of control. Management education is part of a larger disciplinary machine: the modernist university which contains many juridical and penal apparatuses that pertain to a set of rules and offences against them that did not exist in pre-modern university life (four-years reviews, classroom visitations, merit pay, absences, lateness, inattention and lack of zeal, impoliteness or disobedience). The disciplinary mechanism also rewards and awards through its system of ranks, offices with or without windows, access to executive education and other means we shall explore.

In management education, the pressure of disciplinary power is to make every professor and student in one section of a course like every other professor and student in other sections. 'Please co-ordinate your book orders . . . watch your distribution of As, Bs, and Cs . . .' Examination, for example, is for Foucault (1977) a normalizing gaze to qualify, classify and punish. Exams, exercises and teaching notes are provided by most major textbook sellers. The exam, especially the PhD exam, is a highly ritualized ceremony of power to establish truth: one which 'manifests the subjection of those who are perceived as objects and the objectification of those who are subjected' (1977: 184–5). The oral and written examination is the root of the gaze of one in power upon the less powerful, who are subject to the gaze. In the classroom, students, through quizzes, presentations, mid-terms (sometimes there are two or three) and final examinations are placed under an almost perpetual gaze. This is good training for their graduation into the 'real world'. Management education is organized around the examination, as an 'examining apparatus'. Well-disciplined management education is the counterpart to the university and business community disciplines of knowledge. The discourse of management education is shaped by the political regime that supports the university, business college and management programme financially. 'The power of examination can eliminate or marginalize individuals and discourse even though these disciplines lack the most minimal theoretical consensus' (Shumway, 1989: 131).

For Foucault, there was no post-modern university, just a steep rise in the modernist mechanisms of normalization (particularly in colleges of business, one might add). We are increasingly dominated by a power that is not our own. It is not the power of a papal tyrant or a ruling class, it is the network of power of the institutional discourses that produce the disciplined student and professor bodies.

Secondly, for Foucault, resistance, like power, is not centred anywhere, it is spread over the surface of the capillary power network. Therefore, the

Marxist formulation of power, where an oppressed class of students or faculty seize control from a dominating class through revolution, is irrelevant. The cessation of lectures and the migration of masters with their loyal students died as resistance tactics, once medieval universities became endowed with foundations, permanent libraries and other properties (Hofstadter and Metzger, 1955: 41). The faculty that championed Aristotle and Copernicus in the face of the Inquisition, said 'no' to Henry VIII's divorce, and demanded the Pope respect the freedom of its liberal arts inquiry has become too timid and too immobile, and far too financially dependent on sovereigns, princes, parliaments, trustees and accrediting agencies to threaten the powerful with mass migrations and lecture cessations. There have been spurts of lecture cessations, such as the McCarthy inquisitions which saw scores of professors dismissed or denied tenure without much resistance (Summers, 1954; Califano, 1970; Cantelon, 1969). In the Vietnam years, a tactical naivety characterized the resistance movement. Strategic responses by administrators to student resistance have contributed to the diffusion of many of the panoptic mechanisms, such as student representation on admission committees, student letters for tenure files. In the 1990s, the university is such a dense network of power that there is only repetition of the same old reforms and no substantive or post-modern change at all. Any resistance appears feeble and local. Except for AACSB, and its rivals, there are few centres of power to focus our resistance.

The Disciplining of Time, Space and Signalling

Disciplining Time

The disciplinary time of a military organization has been imposed on pedagogy. In contemporary management education, everything is regulated by the clock. Time is broken down into 16-week intervals. Each discipline breaks its subject down into simple elements that can be arranged into interval steps to develop more difficult elements across the 16 weeks. Management education is meticulous in detail as complex disciplines become strings of simple elements like debit, valence, do loop, niche, tactic. Totalization of the functional elements is left to each student; they must recombine the fragmented elements of instruction after they leave the university. Management education pedagogy has fragmented knowledge to allow students to traverse the timetable easily in parallel paths called majors, as they move in one rhythmic march to graduation, employment in a *Fortune* 500 corporation, retirement and death. In the ancient university, the student's rhythmic march was into apprenticeship, able to become masters of their own small business, apprenticing others along their journey. It is ironic that management education is the puppet of big business, when most new jobs in many countries are coming from joining or starting a much smaller company.

Time Seriation Within the finely segmented time seriation, students are drilled in repetitive experiential skill exercises, cases, and then tested at the close of each segment. Discipline along the time path occurs by correction, punishment, elimination, reprimand and minor humiliation.

There is a military system of hierarchical ranks as students progress from freshman to senior rank, and then from entering MBA to graduating PhD. Rank has its own privileges. Recruit and alumni are also ranks. Students are permanently classified, documented, recorded and numerically summarized as objects in relation to other objects. These numbers are hand carried by professors to the registrar who acts as the accountant in the student disciplinary process. Students and professors of management are part of a clockwork that is unyielding.

Disciplining Space

Cellular Segmentation The disciplinary space of a military organization has been imposed on management pedagogy. Our students are spatially distributed and regimented into class programmes as they sit in rows and columns during 50-minute intervals. In each classroom cell, repetitive exercises are performed as the student body moves rhythmically in time and cellular-spatial segmentation. 'Count off by seven; each group take their assigned space; we will begin with the spokesperson for group one.' This is the ascetic life of management education.

The student is a mobile element repeating discipline programmes in time chronology and spatial intervals. It has been so since the classical age of Socratic apprenticeship gave way to the mechanical technology of knowledge production. But is it knowledge that universities produce, or do they merely extend a chain of regimented discipline to make adults docile that began in 'element-ary' school and is polished off at the university to produce the cogs for the military–industrial–bureaucratic complex? It was announced at Northwestern University that their MBA programme would offer a joint engineering–MBA track in which Northwestern, by one newscaster's account, would be 'manufacturing MBAs for the manufacturing industry'. In sum, the unstated objective of management education is to manufacture docile subjects for the business community.

Disciplining Signals

When the bell rings, the hour begins or ends. The students take their seats in their row and column. They posture their body to receive the lesson. At the signal bell, they immediately 'hear and obey'. The programme of the body is absolutely disciplined. Signals allow the repetitive positioning of students to one another in their ranks in relations to different ranks, in majors in relation to different majors and in college disciplines in relation to other college disciplines. This total machine controls the body movements through gentle coercions as bodies progress from hour to hour, class to class and rank to rank. The cogs appear meticulously subordinated as they are perfected along learning tracks advertised for their increasing difficulty, in a discourse that cloaks much that is less rational and more disorderly. For example, seven years ago, the management course absorbed all organizational behaviour (OB) topics, and the OB course was eliminated. It is a particular type of subordination: subordination to the discourse of the university machine.

The Instruments of Discipline

Management education is a network of many subtle mechanisms of discipline.

Gaze Mechanisms

Management education coerces discipline by observation. The gaze is a multiple, automatic, continuous, hierarchical and anonymous power functioning in a network of relations from top to bottom, from bottom to top, and laterally holding the whole university together, functioning like a piece of fine machinery, seeking to eliminate all recesses and shadows in which to hide (Foucault, 1977: 175–80). It seeks to be omnipresent. The eyes are everywhere in an encompassing network. In modern times, the gaze process runs parallel to the entire length of the production technology. In our new building, there will be windows designed into the hallway wall of each office to prevent management and other business faculty from being accused of sexual harassment. Our classrooms will have electronic surveillance linked to one of the dean's offices. Videos of our performance will be mailed to absent students and sent to the committee on instructional improvement. The committee on rank and tenure, the dean and my department head review each and every course evaluation. We are planning to add peer evaluators better to assess our instruction. Each year I turn in a report detail for all conferences, presentations, papers, grants and other activities I intend to pursue.

Hierarchical Surveillance   In our new building, the pedagogical machine of time and space intervals is fitted with a network of viewing windows for continuous surveillance. Spatially, classes are currently arrayed along long corridors like a series of small cells with administrative offices placed at regular intervals. Most cells keep their doors open to subject themselves to the gaze. The gaze is calculated in its distributed multiplicity of surveillance. The pyramid is the perfect gaze apparatus. Because you cannot see into all the cells simultaneously, the gaze is subdivided and networked at relay points and levels.

Instructional Surveillance   Pedagogy requires a disciplining gaze. Teachers do roll calls, mark down absences and lateness, and note down who did and did not do their exercises. The gaze is defined, regulated and inscribed at the heart of teaching practice (Foucault, 1977: 176). Once more, a story can explicate what analysis dictates.

Gazing Professor's Story   I collected an instructional surveillance story from a Pennsylvania Business School Professor:

> *Rob*: We are observed by two colleagues for every semester till we are tenured and once a year by our Chairman. The current head of the tenure committee does not believe in that kind of evaluation. He spends two minutes in the room and writes up the report. He recruits others who think the same way.
>
> *Dave*: Do you do this?
>
> *Rob*: I spend 20 minutes and I spend the 20 minutes because I had to at least go through the motions. Unlike the senior colleagues that walk in and walk out. We already knew what we were going to write, but being untenured, we were coerced into sitting for at least that long.
>
> *Rob*: [continues] We are unionized. The Dean is not allowed in our classroom. But, in the last faculty meeting he let us know he expected to be invited to our classes.
>
> *Dave*: So do you have surveillance there? Do you mean there is a whole system for professors observing each other and reporting on what they see? That seems like the gaze to me.
>
> *Rob*: It is. Particularly for new faculty, then they sit in for the entire class.

Recording Mechanisms

Management by objectives (MBO) is supposed to align individual and organizational goals so that expectations are clear and performance standards are realized. However, MBO is also the gaze:

> *Dave*: At my university, we write MBO service reports. At the beginning of the year we submit our plans for teaching, research, travel, university service, consulting and the like to our department head. He reviews the objectives, writes some feedback, and then discusses the MBO document with the dean. The dean gives his input, and if needed, the document is revised. I then have to write an end of the year report, justifying my behavior over the year to show how I did or did not accomplish my goals.

What is interesting to me is that I deny the validity and impact of the MBO process. It does not help me perform better, because I cannot plan out a year in advance what I will be doing at a micro level in all these areas. It is not helpful to me professionally. What it does do is document me and inscribe me such that my academic zone of freedom is reviewed and re-reviewed at two levels. MBO is pure gaze.

Penal Mechanisms

Faculty and students learn a discourse of management written by the university. The university has adopted some of the prison models and at the heart of every discipline system is a penal mechanism (Foucault, 1977: 177). The university, in fact, is an arrayed network of minor penal mechanisms enabling disciplinary power to be both subtle, discrete and omnipresent. The objectives of the penal mechanisms are to control stealing, cheating, abuse, but also grander things like quality, teaching discipline, perfecting the soul, learning limits, intelligence, adulthood; not to forget the docilization of the generation. In fact, straying from the norms of correct behaviour transmitted in handbooks, memos, orientations and stories is to be dealt with sternly by penal mechanisms. Students in universities are caught in a universality of punishment and penitence that is drawn from the fabric of prisons, armies and monasteries.

Micro-penalty mechanisms intensify instructional training by repetitive exercises and lessons. Reduce in rank anyone who does not keep up with the pace of the university machine. In some provinces in Canada, two semesters of below-average teaching reviews mean dismissal of a tenured professor. I know a management professor who is an excellent teacher, an overachieving writer, but who taught his course with some new approaches, received below-average reviews, and is now being dismissed. We as management faculty correct defects in the student's speaking, writing, computation, calibration, and also attitudes, attention, gestures and deportment. This is done through at least five mechanisms.

Examinations   Teachers judge. As the Inquisition fell out of favour, the examination of everyone in every way became the unlimited providence of every institution and every petty bureaucrat, military inspector, including teachers. In the old university, the examination was more visible, more of a joust among pupils pitched against each other in verbal combat while the master controlled the battle. The PhD oral examination remains the most direct and ritualized carry-over from the Spanish Inquisition; a spectacular display of power potency; a manifest gaze of the sovereign; an inversion of visibility. Now the gaze is more individuated, segmented and less the visible spectacle. The power is invisible, but the subject's visibility is compulsory. Students are situated in a network of writings that capture, fix, classify, transcribe, average and norm them into a cumulative system of binary computer data.

There are interesting assumptions about exams. Exams combine an observing hierarchy with normalizing judgements. Exams discipline. Exams punish. Exams classify, select and exclude. Exams establish truth. Exams are ritual play of questions and answers (stages include the visit, question, diagnosis, deliberation, judgement, sentence). Exams mark the end of apprenticeship in the basic elements of a discipline. Exams are scientific appraisals of student performance. Exams segment, rank and differentiate students. Exams are part of the informational case reporting that tracks student progress through the transformations in the university machine. Exams extract and constitute a knowledge of student as a case file, computer file, an accumulation of information on the student's body. It is part of the penal accountancy of merits and demerits, privileges and impositions, carrot and stick. Exams order good and bad students in relation to one another, distribute people by aptitude, conduct, quality, skill, order penalty in terms of grades. Exams are one of the primary gaze mechanisms. The teacher views the work of the students, but it is a one-way mirror. In sum, the exam is a constantly repeated ritual of power; dominance and subordination, authenticating the movement of knowledge elements from master to pupil.

> *Rod*: At [a British university] I score the exams done at [an Asian university]. In the British system, you submit your exams to external reviewers who say, that is a stupid answer, sometimes they say that is a stupid question . . . Oh yes, they would look down their noses at a university system where professors just scored the final exams.

Normalization Mechanisms   The penal mechanism operates the normalization mechanism that holds the student and professor in a mechanism of objectification. Management pedagogy has turned to behavioural science to rationalize the discipline practices. Norms objectify human performance into categories. Human conduct is partitioned, dimensionalized, summarized, indexed and transmitted as digital scores. Normalization is coercion in management teaching in order to normalize class behaviour, supervise quality workmanship, and discriminate between bodies before graduation. The classification by hierarchy and distribution of object scores determines rank, and privilege distributions match the modern corporate environment. The subject is objectified into an array of binary computer scores scrupulously and meticulously maintained at the office of the registrar – and after graduation by the personnel department. The dominant power manifests its potency by arranging and transforming the subjects into objects and records of objects. Normalization depends on a rigid system of registration and documentation accumulation, classification and categorization, transcription, normalization. Exam scores are sacred and teachers are penalized should they entrust scores to assistants or secretaries. In my university final grades are to be hand carried by the instructor to the office of the registrar in the prescribed manner, during the prescribed time interval. Science is the means of the university to attain power over the student bodies through the normalization process (Foucault, 1977: 191).

> *Dave*: I work at a university that has unofficial grade quotas. We are expected to give higher grades to grad classes than we do to undergrad classes. If our grades are not 'normally-distributed' we get a letter in our file, or a message from the department head, and it can affect our merit pay. I think it is because our MBAs are funded by aerospace and other firms who will not reimburse any courses that are less than a B grade.

The Historical Account of a Person is their Resume   The scientific verbal and math scores of the GMAT (Graduate Management Aptitude Test) determine admission to MBA programmes. Real life is transformed into a single numerical score that determines one's admission rank into an MBA programme. The scientific exam fixes the individual in measurement space as a case, an object of power, an object of knowledge, an element of the hierarchical gaze and a normalized judgement. The transcript and the GMAT are apparatuses in the disciplinary function of distribution and classification in the university machine; the fabrication of cellular, organic, genetic and combinable individuality by the modality of these subtle power mechanisms to normalize individual differences. Before GMATs administrators had to be in the visible presence of the students being gazed at for possible admission. A scientific mechanism is not as painful an experience for the invisible gazers. If any hero of the Middle Ages, such as Sir Lancelot, applied to an MBA programme today, they would first be required to take a GMAT. Miller and Morgan (1993) have also looked at how the curriculum vitae is a disciplinary gaze on the professor.

Social science contributes greatly to the smooth transition from the Inquisition to the examination, from the combative exams of Harvard B-schools to the silent exams of the Jesuit classroom. Empirical measurement sciences help to classify, objectify and rank students by statistically reliable and valid norms. They offer normalization without end, analytic observation without end, investigation without end, examination without end, measurement without end, chronology without end, registration without end and the gaze without end.

Gratification–punishment Mechanisms   The more one possesses power or privilege, the more one is marked in the university as an individual (Foucault, 1977: 192). The disciplinary regime of individualization descends as power, becomes more anonymous and functional, exercised more by one-way gazes than by visible ceremony, by normative comparison, by interview. As students accumulate rewards, they can trade these rewards for privileges in the token economy: they become cadres in their own domination, trade credits to remove sanctions. Teachers make their rewards more frequent than their penalties if they want popularity. Teachers encourage the lazy to desire rewards. In each class there is a formal and informal penal accountancy of merits and demerits, a punitive balance sheet for each student, a micro-economy of privileges and impositions, a hierarchization of the good, the bad and the ugly and their relation to one another. Measurement precision is a prerequisite for the gratification–punishment mechanism. Grades are a reflection, not only of exams, but of one's performance in the penal accountancy. Good cogs get more rights and privileges.

The student reward system is inextricably linked to the reward system for teachers. Teachers administer the student reward system, students participate in teacher reward systems. The administrative rationale for external control of teachers is the implied acknowledgement of the inherent bias towards higher than normal distributions rooted in this reciprocity.

Panoptic Mechanisms   At the centre of the ideal panopticon is a great tower with a clock and windows from which one administrator can gaze on the workings of each of the classroom cells, each dorm room and each gathering place. The university as perfect panopticon would be a circle of cells on floors with windows opened to the gaze of the central tower and no windows to view (some still have no windows) the reality beyond the university circle of classroom cells and dorm rooms. Some universities do not have a central tower and instead order the classrooms and dorms along great corridors and quads in the shape of a star or cross. Some have both corridor and tower, 'Panopticism induces in the inmate a state of consciousness and permanent visibility that assures the automatic functioning of power' (Foucault, 1977: 201). The tower inside a circle is the perfect image of the perfect gaze. Even more perfect if the gazed cannot discern if anyone is now gazing or not. The power is perfect because the internalization of the panoptic consciousness renders its exercise unnecessary. Foucault refers to this as Bentham's principle: power should be visible and unverifiable.

At Loyola Marymount, that our tower is a symbol of panoptic power is manifest by the proliferation of this symbol on virtually every piece of university paper and souvenir. The students have become the principle of their own subjection (Foucault, 1977: 203). The university, like the prison, is a cruel and ingenious cage. The panopticon combines the best disciplines of prisons, monasteries, hospitals and armies into one overlaid, multilayered multifaceted system of panopticism.

Auxiliary Mechanisms A variety of auxiliary mechanisms gaze at the students, professors, and even those who are least subject to the normalizing gaze: the administrators.

Course Evaluation and Related Penal Mechanisms First is the inverted student penal mechanism (gazing at the professor). The gaze is inverted when the students gaze at and report the behaviour of the professor: time (lateness, absence, interrupted office hours); activity (inattention to detail, negligence in delivery, lack of teaching zeal); behaviour (impoliteness to students, disobeying university policy); speech (idle chatter, insolence, racist and sexist language); body (incorrect attitudes, irregular gestures, lack of cleanliness); sexuality (impurity, indecency, abuse). Students report these matters on course evaluations, visits to administrations, petitions for removal, and stories told along the university corridors. It is a power that is visible to the professor but mostly unverifiable. Everyone sees the professor, without being seen. Just as the student has a file, each professor is their objectified file and summarized by the numbers in their computer file. The origin of this inverted gaze is monastic. As in the novel *1984*, children are asked to gaze at their parents to ensure they follow moral codes, tithe their resources, and behave in a Christian fashion.

The 'bad' behaviour of a professor is a pretext for the administration to question his neighbours and interview his department head. 'What are his teaching habits?' The number of anonymous and temporary observers of a professor gives him an anxious awareness of being gazed at, categorized, ranked and subjected. He participates in his own self-gaze and self-reporting as he fills out university service, teaching and research reports. Do not forget travel reports, research reports and sabbatical reports. All very necessary mechanisms. There is more regimentation in the body life of the faculty than outsiders imagine. Academic freedom has been shrinking in direct proportion to the proliferation of panoptic mechanisms dispersed throughout the university production system.

The Registrar Penal Mechanism The registrar and its cousin, the controller, do the penal accounting for the institution. Their task is to code the continuous behaviour of students, staff and faculty. They are like the police, secret service, income tax office and vehicle registration office all rolled into one. The registrar is the most stern, multifaceted, and disciplined of all the disciplines of control. Their penal programmes involve monetary mechanisms such as: fines, late charges, processing fees, *and* strict conformity to regulations not even the most seasoned clerk knows in totality. Registrars register, record, key punch, code, recode, summarize, monitor and accumulate a centralized body of evaluative knowledge on every single person in the university.

The Admissions Penal Mechanism The first order of business is to classify the entrants. People need to be assigned to the right time patterns, sent to the right spaces, admitted to the right housing. Admission orients the mob, fragments, classifies and starts the recording system. The admission tests are done, the examination of the written application and the obligatory essay are completed. Cadres of students and faculty and administrators orient the parents and the students. Even siblings come to the events. It is a festive spectacle. There is public speaking, food sharing and idle chitchat is tolerated. The parents and the students view the polished side of the machine.

The Rank and Tenure Penal Mechanism Tenure is a system of graduated ranks, a disciplinary perfecting of the professor from visitor, to assistant, to associate, to full, and even to emeritus ranks. Tenure's primary function is to correct and perfect the professor's research, teaching and institutional service. The visibility of the gaze into the tenure progression is a trap. The professor is in a panoptic machine of discipline, a perfect cage. The professor submits all manner of reports, papers, travel information, teaching evaluations, speaking engagements, reporting every body movement, every articulation, every whereabouts. The professor does not know if anyone is reading all this documentary evidence, but since someone might be reading, the professor, like the student, learns to internalize the panoptic asymmetry of the gaze. Rank and tenure, as a committee, is an ideal panoptic mechanism. As in Zimbardo's famous prison experiment, the student subjects, in this case professor-subjects, adopt the role behaviour of the *actual* prison guards and prisoners. They mete out penalty and reward. They see but they are unseen.

Pupils fill out observations on each professor, writing them on the back of course evaluations. In this way each professor becomes a case, an array of comments and summary statistics, an object of knowledge that becomes part of the 'tenure case'. Rank and tenure can delay the case until professors document their own practices. The dean must comment on every single case and justify and rationalize the rank and tenure case. Tenure is an efficient technology of power disciplined to fabricate capital return to the institution in the form of research visibility, marketable teaching reputation and service to the disciplinary panopticon machinery. Rank and tenure form the most coercive and most artificial theatre used to catalogue, evaluate, examine and judge the life of the professor. It combines surveillance, inspection, interview, reporting and judicial penalty in one theatre, a theatre that is visible in its effects, yet invisible in the puppetry which produces them. Rank and tenure must rationalize and document the historical journey and formation and reformation of the professor through the progression of ranks and steps until one emerges as what one is documented and decided to be. Rank and tenure are the discourse of power in which dangerous professors are corrected and transformed by the rites of passage, and the ceremony of judicial discourse.

The Research Penal Mechanism This is one of many committees that reviews documents and makes decisions without speaking directly to candidates. The faculty record is examined, judgements are rendered, and correct faculty are rewarded; non-correct faculty are excluded from funding or offered more minimal funding. The applicants never get to read the letters of their deans and departments heads. In this sense the gaze is asymmetrical. The panoptic tower windows are one-way mirrors. Some faculty might be agitated if they did read the comments of their supervisors. The purpose of this penal mechanism is to define correct and incorrect research agendas. It is a mechanism of normalization; it is a mechanism of examination of the faculty track record; and it is a mechanism of correction. The faculty needs rehabilitation: he cannot write a decent proposal; she does not deliver a proper schedule of work; the project is not an important scientific endeavour; they are proposing something that is dangerously close to pedagogy improvement; the Academic Vice President will not approve this one.

AACSB (American Association of Colleges and Schools of Business) The recent AACSB-sponsored study has made recommendations which the AACSB Board of Directors adopted in its new accreditation standards in its Annual Meeting in April, 1991. The panoptic implications of AACSB are manifold:

1 What is the AACSB? It is an association of deans.
2 Who pays for their studies? AACSB collects member dues.
3 What do deans want to control? Faculty and students.

4   What do they control? Content, process, tenure, class size, what con-
    stitutes a professor, etc.
5   Who benefits? Colleges with accreditation derive a competitive advan-
    tage, in terms of attracting paying students away from colleges without
    accreditation.

Harvard, Yale and many other schools with PhD programmes have
avoided AACSB control. The new strategy of mission-specific accreditation
includes a plan to capture PhD-granting schools of business. AACSB also
has a plan to capture the 600 plus schools of business who have not been
remotely eligible for AACSB accreditation. The rhetoric is that AACSB is
getting away from its modernist command-and-control model which
normalizes all colleges into one mould, and into a 'flexible, adaptable, self-
defined, and mission-specific mode'. While this sounds 'empowering', I
think it is panoptic control in a more devious form. This strategic move, it
seems, would help counter a new and rival accrediting association that has
set out to take market share away from AACSB.

Why is it that administrators receive full copies of the AACSB documents, but faculty receive briefings, excerpts and interpretations? Could it
be that, as with the early distribution of the bible, the priests kept the book
to themselves so they could privilege their own interpretation of the
knowledge and ask for fees to get departed relatives into heaven?
Gutenberg's invention of the printing press was revolutionary because it
put bibles and other potentially revolutionary writings in the hands of the
common man. Early on this did not matter much, since only priests and
nobles could read anyway. But, even if the faculty possesses the old and
new versions of the AACSB 'testaments', the 'visiting team' of deans
interprets how a given college is to be scored. Since the team is made up of
deans this process privileges the 'dean's' voice and marginalizes the voices
of students, parents, faculty and corporations.

In all well-attended academy sessions on AACSB, few people are asking
one critical question: 'Why?' 'Why do we need to be controlled?' 'Why do
we need Big Brother looking over our shoulders?' 'Why are we more
interested in AACSB than in our academic freedom?' These two words,
'academic freedom', are as fundamental as 'freedom of speech' in our bill
of rights. If AACSB has its way, we are going to be seeing a tightening of
the external panoptic normalizing mechanisms which will also steadily
tighten the interior time, space, gaze and other panoptic mechanisms in
ways that will increasingly make universities resemble prisons.

A Summary of the Principles for Disciplining Professors

Principle One: Isolation

Isolate professors from the external world and monitor their trips into that
world. Isolate professors from one another and let them combine only in

ceremony, ritual, or under hierarchical surveillance. Isolate the professor population into homogeneous departmental groupings (an imprecise solution at best). Isolation is a precondition of submission derived from the monastic and prison models of administrative discipline. Isolate professors in a strict hierarchical framework with all lateral relations discouraged, and punish communications that do not follow the strict trails of the hierarchy. Rank by stages in the professorial transformation.

Principle Two: Regulation on the Treadmill

Professors are too dangerous to let them be idle. Before prisoners did productive labour as part of their rehabilitation, the earliest prisons had prisoners work in fixed time intervals on treadmills. Work is good for the soul as well as a punishing discipline. Workhouses are another model of organization that regulates away all idle time and all idle contracts. Regulation bends the time inclination of professors to rhythmic movements as they are controlled, assigned, distributed. The longer the period of regulation endured, the more docile the professor becomes. Regular exposure in a hierarchy of surveillance makes professors more docile still. Regulate professors according to the norms of a research and teaching and service society. Let the professors' movements in relation to other cogs in the productive machine be exactly and mechanically predictable. The tenure clock is ticking away. Sit in your cell and observe the time go by.

Principle Three: Transform the Professor during Tenure

Control the length of rank through the transformational value of each professor's teaching, research and service. Promote a professor who has demonstrated corrective perfection and send the professor to the rank and tenure committee for review. Actually it is worse, you send the record, not the body. At least criminals have the right to face their accusers and their jury. Rank and tenure will examine the professor's rigour by investigating his or her past, interviewing neighbours, and pouring over the accumulated case record. Put those who demonstrate improvement and docility in charge of departments and key committees. Select those who know professorial character traits and can influence mental attitudes most effectively, and reprimand professors who stray from the correct path. Give professors research grants and training in order that they might perfect themselves. Research work is an essential element in the transformative progression and in the socialization of the professor. Reform the evil-doer into a 'good' researcher. Professors enter a progressive system of ranks and steps whose pathway is illuminated by moral lectures from deans and department heads. Use punishment and rewards to give professors respect for university disciplinary mechanisms and the faculty handbook. Grant professors monetary rewards, research grants, better assignments, merit pay and reduced committee workloads once they demonstrate the requisite docility. The essential transformation function of the disciplinary mechanisms is to reform the professor and mould him or her through administration, supervision and normalization into the 'good' professor, a professor reformed by the encounter with the disciplines of scientific training, the life academic.

Principle Four: Co-opt the Professor through Cycles of Reform

Reform of the university reproduces exactly the same arrayed network of panoptic disciplinary mechanisms. Despite the idealism, the rhetoric, the documentation, the vision quests and the approving documents, the reform is isomorphic to the system it was before the reform was initiated. Let the professors form small groups, but keep them constantly stimulated by collective issues of curriculum redesign, book adoptions, fine-tuning policy minutiae, restating other people's statements of other people's visions and grade them on the manuscripts they fabricate. Do this while subjecting them to rigid hierarchical surveillance to ensure they reproduce and do not disturb any disciplinary mechanisms.

Principle Five: Practise Recidivism

Universities fabricate scholars who return as Masters students. Some recidivate to become doctoral students. A few are so addicted to university regimentation that they become permanent inmates; they become professors. Students are secretly recruited and programmed to commit recidivism. A life of high recidivism is rewarded with a life sentence to university life. Even those who are denied rank at a university are paroled to life beyond the ivory tower, only to recidivate into yet another university. We must certainly measure, diagnose, anlayse and record this recidivism process. Why are universities so addictive? We try to rehabilitate people so they will go into the real world and lead productive lives. Yet they keep coming back for more disciplinary life education. They cannot get enough academic discipline. Detention causes recidivism. Those leaving the university have more chance than before of going back to its halls. Professors and graduate students are former inmates of the university machine. Do they return for learning, for correcting deficit careers, or to sip the addiction of university life disciplines?

Conclusions

The university practises both a technology and a psychology of discipline. The university orders time and space rhythms into a grand machine. The cogs reconfigure only slightly with the signals of the bells, initiating the movements through time and space. The instruments of discipline are the gaze, endless recording and subtle penal mechanisms distributed in a network of devices throughout the productive corridor of the university machine. The penal mechanisms have been sanitized, rationalized and civilized from their barbaric and feudal university roots. Nevertheless, the penal councils and judgements utilize examinations, normalization, gratification–punishment, panoptic mechanisms and a supportive host of auxiliary disciplinary penal mechanisms to form the capillary subsystem of the university machine. Not just students are disciplined, the most disciplined of all are the professors. They are subjected through powerful isolation, regulation, transformation through rank and tenure, co-opted in cycles of reform, and they participate in recidivism. There are precious few academic freedoms within the university cage.

What are the results of the university panopticon for management education? Foucault gives us a framework for answering this question. We shall adopt his analysis of the carceral archipelago network to summarize the results, not for the prison, but for management education.

People are Disciplined for Norm and Rule Violations

Anomalies are not tolerated. Surveillance and penal mechanisms are networked to form a continuous gaze and hierarchical differentiation to judge and correct students and professors. Management education surveillance is discreet, the coercion vague, the divisions seem minor and the penalties are mild, but the total effect is severe. Punish the slightest indiscipline, gaze at the slightest irregularity in conduct, and maintain a framework and technology for reporting, monitoring, ranking and normalizing. AACSB and the Business Advisory Council want these courses. In the history of the ancient university, we find the sovereign chancellors discoursing directly with the deviant Galileo and Aristotle. Now the discipline takes a more circuitous route.

Management Education Recruits, Fabricates and Consumes its own Delinquents

Management education inculcates docility and by these same mechanisms fabricates non-conformity. At regional conferences, some of us wear T-shirts to manifest our rebellion visibly. Yet, management education, like the prison, takes care not to waste anything. Inassimilable persons are processed through the Academy as a special interest group. 'It is unwilling to waste even what it has decided to disqualify' (Foucault, 1977: 301). Delinquents are a continuous birth and death object of panopticism. Tenure is born at the centre of a system of insistent surveillance and cumulative disciplinary coercion. 'Do you dress this way at the university?' Someone once said, 'universities are places we send rebels to keep them off the streets, fighting for rank monies of no great account anyway'. However, I think 'rebels' have been systematically marginalized within management education.

The Power to Punish and Discipline is Natural and Legitimate

In feudal times, corporal punishment was a primary mechanism; the physical torture of the body has been gentlemanized and transformed into the scientific and technical and more anonymous tortures of the machine. Management education lowers the threshold of tolerance to penalty mechanisms. Management education is an extra-legal register of disciplinary mechanisms with legal sanction. Management departments yield verdicts, gaze through an imitative police work, discipline in imitation of the law, objectify and normalize in imitation of science, ritualize and solemnify in imitation of the church, and cure in imitation of medicine. Management education is relatively free of all excess and violence. The gradations of continuous and pervasive apparatus of discipline are less the violent form of corporal punishment, and more the taken-for-granted forms. There is nothing in disciplinary existence, except the graduation ceremony and the PhD exam, to recall the sovereign power of feudal times. The disciplinary mechanisms are sanctioned by scientific rationality. Technology makes discipline seem less arbitrary, less the spectacle, and teaches the graduates of its training to practise the mechanisms in the institutions that will employ them. A more precise conclusion is that the institutions of societies thrive on the consumption of university output: business, government and non-profit ventures need docile practitioners of the disciplinary sciences.

The Normalization of the Power to Judge

Judges assess, diagnose, classify the normal and abnormal, recommend rehabilitation, use many experts, decide the good of the subject's development. The judge has access to systems of inspection, insertion, distribution, surveillance and observation to perform and normalize function. Management education produces leaders who can operate the technologies of discipline. They discipline society.

The Body of the Human has been Captured in the Perpetual Gaze, Knowledge Accumulation and the Panoptic Cage

Management education is obsessed with methods to fix, decide, record, examine and ultimately objectify behaviour. These are often the subject of skill training exercises. After the age of 'inquisitorial' justice with its torture confessions, we entered the age of enlightened 'examination' for justice and the use of scientific instrumentation to make people docile and compliant through skill training. Management education is obsessed with examinations to qualify everything. They learn the technology and transport it to every niche in our social fabric. There is a seemingly uncritical usage of scientific analysis that is being applied to human domination. GMATs decide MBA entrance. Personality inventories decide management placements. Auxiliaries of bureaucrats and technocrats are accumulating an amazingly complete file and encompassing a mass of information on all aspects of the body human. The human being has been caged, not by the 'Rube Goldberg' machine, but by the hard drives of the computer, so many bubbles of binary memory. Memory, *the* collective human capacity, is being roboticized.

Management Education Meets any Force for Reform with Great Inertia

Management education is part of the university's network of disciplinary mechanisms and surveillance systems. Foucault sees only two ways in which the panoptic cage loses its grip on the body of the human.

First, the surveillance hierarchy will lose its usefulness when the utility for its continued operation makes the apparatus an ineffective way to make the workforce docile. Yet, at the present time, the call for networking with subcontractors, more temporary employees and wider spans of control makes training in the gaze highly valued by larger firms. Computers are everywhere; with their information-processing power, one executive can sit at his or her panoptic terminal and review, in spreadsheet form, the time and motion of a vast population of employees. The computer is replacing the panoptic tower as the ideal and perfect cage for human discipline. Like the panoptic tower, the human does not know what information is being seen, who is seeing it, and when the computer monitor is being turned on. The gaze is asymmetrical. (Some of us are not eager to link our PCs to the network.)

Secondly, as expert disciplines in science, psychology, psychiatry, educational psychology, engineering, sociology, accounting, management information systems and the like assume more of a direct supervision and judging role over the normalization process, there will be less need for an extensive network of direct hierarchical supervision. Although hierarchies in American corporations are quickly becoming flatter, and workers are more trained to supervise themselves, expert technicians control the panoptic mechanisms of discipline. The hierarchical pyramid thereby loses much of its utility. As standardized tests proliferate and you can sit at a terminal and analyse everyone's pattern, the psychologist is the expert who offers the promise, if not the fact, of controlling a vast array of panoptic mechanisms.

Foucault paints the disciplinary capillary, in a manner whose implications are profound for an 'Academy of Management'. For at the centre of the modern panopticon, there is no dominant boss, no sovereign monarch, no Theory X administrator, nor is there a dominant coalition, or a council of elders, or a board of directors. There is not a board of strategists distributing elements throughout the enterprise, at every level and region, linking the array of panoptic mechanisms to normalize the behaviour of all the humans. But there is a mechanism for calling out the strategist to enact small acts of cunning, petty cruelty and calculated technologies, and even to ignore insidious leniencies. In universities, the mechanism is us, with our internalized gaze and docile practices. The strategist, therefore, is not one person, nor a board of strategists.

Outside the Academy, the panoptic machine wakes up the strategist when the market and enterprise readings demand punitive mechanisms to 'do their thing'. One is reminded of the workings of the New York Stock Exchange where, when the averages dip or rise too far beyond the programmed norms, the computers whiz and putter and do their own trading. As if this image of the panoptic machine evolved to an Orwellian dimension is not scary enough, Foucault ends his history of the prison with this pronouncement:

> In this central and centralized humanity, the effect and instrument of complex power relations, bodies and forces subjected by multiple mechanisms of 'incarceration', objects for discourses that are in themselves elements for this strategy, we must hear the distant roar of battle. (1977: 308)

I hear the distant roar of science and technology battling to make humankind more docile.

Notes

I would like to thank Robert Winsor and Alan Cherry of Loyola Marymount, and Stewart Clegg, who visited LMU in 1992, for their helpful comments and critique.

1 Similarly, the fact that some total institutions, to use Goffman's term, have these physical constraints does not invalidate the application of the concept to other organizations, such as boarding schools, nunneries and campus universities, which do not.

References

Beale, H.K. (1936) *Are American Teachers Free? An Analysis of Restraints upon the Freedom of Teaching in American Schools*. Report of the Commission on the Social Studies, Part XII. New York: Charles Scribner and Sons.

Boje, D.M. (1991a) 'The storytelling organization: a study of story performance in an office-supply firm', *Administration Science Quarterly*, 36 (1): 106–26.

Boje, D.M. (1991b) 'Consulting and change in the storytelling organization', *Journal of Management Education*, 2 (August): 279–94.

Boje, D.M. and Dennehy, R.F. (1994) *America's Revolution Against Exploitation: the Story of Postmodern Management*, 2nd edn. Dubuque, Iowa: Kendall Hunt.

Boyne, R. (1990) *Foucault and Derrida*. London: Unwin Hyman.

Burrell, G. (1988) 'Modernism, post modernism and organizational analysis 2: the contribution of Michel Foucault', *Organization Studies* 9 (2): 221–35.

Califano, J.A.Jr. (1970) *The Student Revolution: a Global Confrontation*. New York: W.W. Norton.

Cantelon, J.E. (1969) *College Education and the Campus Revolution*. Philadelphia: Westminster Press.

Clegg, S. (1989a) 'Radical revisions: power, discipline and organizations', *Organization Studies*, 10 (1): 97–115.

Clegg, S. (1989b) *Frameworks of Power*. London: Sage.

Derrida, J. (1976) *Of Grammatology*. Baltimore: Johns Hopkins University Press.

Foucault, M. (1977) *Discipline and Punish: the Birth of the Prison*. New York: Pantheon Books.

Hetrick, W.P. and Boje, D.M. (1992) 'Organization and the body: post-fordist dimensions', *Journal of Organizational Change Management*, 5 (1): 48–57.

Hofstadter, R. and Metzger, W.P. (1955) *The Development of Academic Freedom in the United States*. New York: Columbia University Press.

Kibre, P. (1962) *Scholarly Privileges in the Middle Ages: the Rights, Privileges, and Immunities, of Scholars and Universities at Bologna, Padua, Paris, and Oxford*. Cambridge, MA: Medieval Academy of America.

MacIver, R.M. (1955) *Academic Freedom in our Time*. New York: Columbia University Press.

Mayer, J.P. (1956) *Max Weber and German Politics*. London: Faber and Faber.

Metzger, W.P. (1955) *Academic Freedom in the Age of the University*. New York: Columbia University Press.

Miller, N. and Morgan, D. (1993) 'Called to account: the CV as autobiographical practice', *Sociology* 27 (1): 133–43.

Rosenau, P. (1992) *Post-modernism and the Social Sciences: Insights, Inroads, and Intrusions*. Princeton, NJ: Princeton University Press.

Shumway, D.R. (1989) *Michel Foucault*. Boston: Twayne Publishers.

Summers, R.E. (1954) *Freedom and Loyalty in our Colleges*. New York: H.W. Wilson.

Name Index

Ackoff, R., 2
Adorno, T., 61, 83
Alderfer, C.P., 129
Aldrovandi, U., 41
Al-Maskati, H., 18
Althusser, L., 86
Alvesson, M., 6, 9, 72, 76, 88, 95, 97, 101,
    132, 133, 134, 136, 147, 149
Annas, J., 166, 167
Anthony, P., 4, 11, 17–33, 55, 57, 65–6, 69,
    95, 101, 106, 132, 168
Arendt, H., 42
Argyris, C., 64, 135
Aristotle, 17, 158
Ashton, D., 159
Astley, G.W., 46, 48, 88
Atkins, G.D., 78

Bacon, F., 85
Bakhtin, M.M., 147
Banham, J., 25
Baran, P.A., 76
Barnard, C.I., 87
Barnes, T.J., 85, 86
Barnett, C., 8
Bass, B., 64
Bateson, G., 66, 112, 118
Beale, H.K., 174
Beard, P.R.J., 132, 141
Beaty, L., 120
Benson, J.K., 76, 83
Bentham, J., 185
Berger, P., 61, 81, 105
Bernstein, R., 96
Bernstein, R.J., 78
Berry, A., 8
Best, S., 78, 80, 83
Bhavnani, K.-K., 148
Binsted, D.S., 136
Boje, D.M., 4, 7, 13, 106, 172–94
Boutall, J., 120
Boyne, R., 174
Braverman, H., 7, 62, 76, 133
Brown, R.H., 76
Buffon, G.-L., 41

Bullock, Lord, 30
Burawoy, M., 60, 76
Burgoyne, J., 4, 21, 162
Burnett, S., 143
Burrell, G., 2, 7, 79, 87, 175
Butler, D.W., 135, 147

Cain, W.E., 77, 78
Calas, M., 8
Caldwell, B., 78
Califano, J.A., 178
Cameron, S., 132
Cantelon, J.E., 178
Cavanaugh, J.M., 5, 7, 12, 76–89, 77, 89
Champy, J., 2
Checkland, P., 155
Child, J., 28, 134, 135
Churchman, C.W., 135
Cicero, 4
Clawson, D., 77
Claxton, G., 113, 121
Clegg, S., 1, 62, 77, 174, 175
Clifford, J., 86
Colletti, L., 81
Collin, A., 6, 9, 12, 25, 132–49
Collins, R.K., 26
Connolly, W.E., 85
Constable, J., 1, 19
Cooper, C.L., 119
Cooper, R., 2, 7, 42, 133
Craib, I., 61
Crosby, P., 1
Crossman, R.H.S., 163
Cumberpatch, Z., 143, 144

Daiches, D., 4
Daloz, L.A., 136, 147, 148
Dalton, M., 32
Daudi, P., 63
Dearden, R., 17, 18, 21, 22–3
de Castell, S., 95
Deetz, S., 73, 84
Deming, W.E., 155
Dennehy, R.F., 176
Derrida, J., 38, 39, 86, 173

Subject Index